TICKLERTON TALES

Shrewsbury
SY3 7TT

Also by Alan Dakers

FORDRITISHOPE

History of a Shropshire Parish
Hope Bowdler, Ragdon and Chelmick

TICKLERTON TALES

Life, folklore and people
from Medieval times in
Eaton-under-Heywood

ALAN DAKERS

ISBN 0 9512250 1 4

(c) Alan Dakers

Published 1991 by

A Dakers, Ragdon, Church Stretton SY6 7EY

Printed by

Hillman Printers Frome

for Sarah

ACKNOWLEDGEMENTS

The Shorter Oxford English Dictionary gives as one of its definitions of "compile" - *to construct a written or printed work out of materials collected from various sources.*

So it is quite natural that, in this book, I have gathered material and historical facts from many different sources and the principal works are listed below. However, much of what is included comes from people in the Parish to whom I am indebted and offer my sincere thanks. In particular, the notes, journals, scrapbooks, diaries and photographs of Mrs Lilian Hayward and the records kindly loaned by Jennifer, Lady Brown (née Buddicom).

Extracts, where used, are verbatim and so reflect the language and spelling of the period.

There are some cases where assumptions have been made, and the reader is asked to remember that is what they are, and not necessarily fact, although every effort has been made to ensure that they are relevant and a reasonable interpretation of the facts.

A great many records that have been consulted were handwritten and often proved dificult to decipher so, for any inaccuracies, I apologise.

Permission to reproduce the photographs, on the pages listed, is much appreciated: T Attenborough - 67/8,151,156,159 and 178. Lady Brown - 100 and 116. Local Studies Library x, 65 and 110. Mrs D Madeley - 118/9.

Reference details

"The Homes of other days" - Thomas Wright M.A., F.S.A. "The Salopian and West Midland Illustrated Monthly Journal, June/July 1878". National Railway Museum, York. "The English Village". "Eric and Us" - Jacintha Buddicom. "The Castles and Mansions of Shropshire" - Mrs Gatehouse Acton, 1868. "Old Houses of Wenlock" - H E Forrest. "Wenlock in the Middle Ages" - W F Mumford. "The English" - Christopher Hibbert. "Domesday, A Search for the roots of England" - Michael Wood. "The Shropshire Landscape" - Trevor Rowley. "Shropshire Field Names" - H D G Foxall. "Domesday Book - Shropshire" - Phillimore. "Shropshire" - Samuel Bagshaw, 1851. Shropshire County Archives, Local Studies Library, Shrewsbury. R W Eyton - "Antiquities of Shropshire". Shropshire Archaelogical Society. Shropshire Churches - Cranage. Shropshire Hearth Tax Roll - 1672. "The Forester's Lodge" - M Moran.

CONTENTS

PART THREE

PART FOUR

INTRODUCTION

Stand on Ragleth Hill, look toward the South East, Brown Clee and Titterstone Clee dominate the skyline.

In the middle-distance, the Wenlock Edge stretches away to the East and in the valley between lies the Parish of Eaton-under-Heywood.

Apart from some sheep, one or two distant rooftops, Eaton Church tower and the Edge Wood covering most of the sloping ground, there is little else to see. It is typical South Shropshire country that has changed little in the last four or five hundred years.

On a still, quiet day, you can hear the silence yet, with a little imagination, you can hear the rumble of farm cart wheels in the rutted tracks, the 'squeak' of leather horse harness or the 'jingle' of trace chains as shire horses take the strain ploughing or pulling heavily loaded carts. In high summer there is the swish of scythes and sickles as the hay and corn harvests are mown. The rhythmic 'thwack' of the flail in winter time echoing from a nearby corn barn. The shrill laughter and chatter of children on their way to school, to pick wild berries or just to play in the meadows.

Thin columns of smoke rise from cottages hidden in the valleys or woods, many that have been lived in for centuries. Suddenly, the peace, the dream is shattered as a low flying jet plane races by a few hundred feet from the ground and disappears out of sight beyond the hills. Silence again, it is the same valley, but the nostalgic daydream has been rudely broken.

What life may have been like, where all the people lived, who they were and what they did is something we can never know for sure, but in this book I have tried to recapture and illustrate some of those past 500 years.

The Parish of Eaton-under-Heywood lies in South Shropshire, between the Wenlock Edge, Church Stretton and Craven Arms.

Thomas Goodman, agricultural labourer, in his smock frock, at the age of 84. He was born, in 1800, at Wistanstow, and lived at Yew Tree Cottage, Soudley until his death on April 26th 1884. He married Mary Williams, a widow. She died on December 13th 1873. They are both buried in Eaton churchyard.

SHROPSHIRE

A BRIEF EARLY HISTORY

The area that is now known as Shropshire was inhabited by men of the Stone and Bronze Ages and, by the early Bronze Age (1500 B.C.), trade routes to the South East of Britain ran through what is now South Shropshire, and as much of this land was easily cultivated, Bronze Age people inhabited the area. By the 7th century B.C., the Celts had moved into the Severn Valley and the many hill forts are evidence of their existence here, where defence was a primary consideration in their live style.

The Roman conquest of Britain brought about dramatic changes in the way of live as laws, trade routes, dwellings and towns were introduced. It is from this era that written documents historians can be traced to form some sort of picture of what live was like. Roman rule in the area lasted for about 350 years, until around 400 A.D. The building of roads, for which the Romans were renowned, had a significant effect with the road from Londinium (the provincial capital) meeting the important road which ran north to Chester at Wroxeter which was, by 90 A.D., the fourth largest town in the country and was also a legionary fortress.

By the early part of the 5th century the last of the Roman legions left Britain and the long decline of urban live began. There is little historical record of what happened during the next few hundred years. The hill forts were probably reoccupied as strongholds, the town of Wroxeter remained important as a defensive centre for the surrounding countryside, but its character changed as its importance for trade and manufacture decayed, and slowly but surely the town dwindled and shrank down to the small settlement where Wroxeter village now stands.

During the dark and un-chronicled period which followed, described by Trevor Rowley as *"The Dark Ages are nowhere darker than in Shropshire; the early history of Mercia is hazy"* this area probably formed the eastern part of the kingdom of Powys and the English settlement began - peacefully at first - with King Penda of Mercia and the men of Powys, but after his death in 654, war carried the English westward for the next 100 years. Around the year 680 St Milburga came to Wenlock Abbey and the extensive estates the monastery already possessed were confirmed to her by King Ethelred of Mercia (674-704). It is remarkable that 350 years later Domesday Book noted *"the lands which the Church of Milburga holds"* and that was done before Offa became King of Mercia, and after three centuries of Anglo-Saxon settlement, Danish attacks and Norman invasion. Finally, by the end of the 8th century, the frontier between the English and Welsh speaking (Cwmry) people was defined by the great dyke which still carries the same name as the King of Mercia who planned it - Offa's Dyke.

A little more than a century after the building of Offa's Dyke, around 900/925, the county of Shropshire was created and named after the fortified town of Shrewsbury, by the son or daughter of King Alfred the Great, as part of the defence of the English Mercia (the west midlands) against the Danes who had invaded and settled in Eastern England. Each West Midland shire was originally so organised as to provide enough men among its inhabitants to defend the country town from Danish attack and to launch operations against Danish held territory. Alfred's descendants, kings of Wessex, united England and the shire survived as the primary area of local government. Shropshire is the largest inland county in England.

The monastic settlement that had existed for more than two hundred years at Wenlock was destroyed in 874, and the surrounding area laid waste by the marauding Danes. It lay desolate for more than a century until about 1017, when Leofric, Earl of Mercia and husband of Lady Godiva, endowed a religious house again at Much Wenlock, with a ; monastery and college for secular clergy. The possessions included in this endowment comprised some 18,000 acres of land (stretching from Wenlock towards Leintwardine) with an annual income of £50. Leofric died on 1057 and soon afterwards Earl Roger of Montgomery came into possession of his vast estates.

Only 150 years after the creation of Shropshire, a new conqueror - the Normans - began to establish their control of the English shires. There was resistance in many areas, and in 1069 a Shropshire landowner, Edric the Wild, gathered a band of followers and marched on Shrewsbury to besiege the Norman garrison there. He was beaten off and King William the Conqueror devastated the county. Within a year or so the King added to Roger of Montgomery's possessions by handing 'Shropshire' over to him. He (Roger) was one of the King's closest friends and most powerful companions and, created Earl of Shrewsbury in 1074, was given an unusual amount of freedom by the King. Earl Roger died in 1094 and was succeeded by Hugh, who was killed in 1098 fighting the Welsh. The Earldom then passed to Robert, (Earl Roger's oldest son) who had been involved in Normandy with the family possessions. They had ruled Shropshire almost as they liked until Robert joined forces with Robert, Duke of Normandy, and rebelled against King Henry I in 1102, who chased them back to France and their power was destroyed and Earl Robert forfeited his Shropshire lands to the King. Shropshire's government then followed the pattern established in other counties. The great castles of Shrewsbury, Bridgnorth and Montgomery are all that remain as testimony to the thirty years of power and domination of the Roger family.

THE MEDIEVAL YEARS

1066 to 1536

DOMESDAY BOOK

In 1086, William the Conqueror ordered his great survey of every town, village and hamlet to be carried out - the Domesday Book being the result and the basis and starting point for so much of English history, particularly rural England.

The entry in Domesday Book, folio 258 book 2, for the PATTON Hundred (Patinvne) shows the following entry:

TICKLERTON/TICHELVORDE
"The church held it before 1066. 7 hides which pay tax and 3 other hides exempt from tax. In lordship 1 plough, 6 villagers, 6 smallholders and 1 rider with 5 ploughs, a further 6 ploughs would be possible there. 3 slaves. Woodland for fattening 60 pigs. Value before 1066, 100s; now 50s"

Note:HIDE - a variable unit of area of land, enough for a house-hold, of around 120 acres (some say only 80 acres in Shropshire) and represents a family holding.

HUNDRED - originated in 100 hides - 12,000 acres, but this is not always strictly the case.

PLOUGH - Generally assessed as 8 oxen per team.

RIDER - (Radman) - a sub-group of the 'liberi homines', free men, of higher status than a villager, originally as men who rode with messages or did escort duty for the King or their lord, they may have also had some military functions, if only the defence of the border. The smallholders, or other villagers, presumably worked the riders' land when they were absent on duty.

SLAVE - or serf, the property of the lord.

In the notes appended it states 'Now (Ticklerton) in Eaton-under-Heywood parish', Eaton having been one of its members in 1086. It was in the Patton Hundred, then no doubt in the Munslow

Hundred, then in the Liberty of Wenlock, remaining with the Priory until the Dissolution. The Priory also held Herton (Hatton), Eton (Eaton), Tycleworthen (Ticklerton), Longfeud (Longville-in-the-Dale) and Lussekote (Lushcote). It is quite possible that Hatton and Wolverton should also be included. The actual heads of families for Ticklerton number 13, and to include all men, women and children there is a difference of expert opinion as to whether the 13 should be multiplied by 3½ or 5 to obtain the total population.

The social history of life in and around the parish of Eaton-under-Heywood through the Middle Ages to the present day is the subject of the following chapters.

FORTIFIED HOUSES – LIFE STYLES

After Domesday, Wenlock Priory became the wealthiest and most powerful religious house in Shropshire. The ecclesiastical power of the Prior was great, but greater still were his civil powers as a feudal lord. He administered justice through the Manorial Courts and had the power to punish offenders, even to giving the death penalty, and the place of execution is said to have been on the top of Wenlock Edge – Gallows Tree leasow.

Standing high on the Edge, looking south west towards Leintwardine, the vast lands of the Prior stretched out as far as the eye could see. Even today, the landscape bears a strong similarity to what it would have been like in Medieval times. Then, there would have been a lot more woodland than exists today and many of the fields would not have been enclosed and there would have been much more heath and moorland. With a little imagination, it is not too difficult to picture a little of what life was like for the people, though few in number, who would have lived and worked in and around Hope Dale and Ape Dale. Buildings, such as there were, have changed in appearance but not in function, and the villages or townships are larger now, but not so much as to disturb the general picture.

It is easy to imagine wolves roaming the Long Forest, which stretched for miles in every direction, yet records of wolves in Medieval England seem, in general, to be confined to the Welsh border country and the north. According to William of Malmesbury, King Edgar of England arranged for King Idwal of Wales in 985 to render 300 wolfskins annually in lieu of a tribute which he owed. The Welsh ran out of wolves in three years. This may be a far fetched story (it was written 140 years later), but there are few other later records known apart from a mad wolf which killed 22 people in Camarthen in 1166 and, in 1281, when Edward 1 is said to have exterminated them. He employed Peter Corbet "*to take and destroy all the wolves he can find in Gloucestershire, Worcestershire, Herefordshire, Shropshire and Staffordshire*".

THE MEDIEVAL YEARS

There is a record of wolves at Langley (near Acton Burnell) in the Long Forest in the late 13th century. Otherwise, it was only in Scotland that wolves lasted up to the end of the 17th century.

To medieval people, a 'forest' was a place to keep deer, not just a place for trees, and was land on which the King had the right to keep his deer and hunt. Modern 'forestry' has nothing to do with being a successor to the medieval forest,

There would have been very few people living there, and one of the only buildings of any substance that a traveller would have come across as he travelled westward would have been the Forester's Lodge at Upper Millichope.

Forester's Lodge, Upper Millichope.

This remarkable old house, built in Norman times, is still standing today. It was almost certainly the Lodge of the Head Forester who had charge of the Long Forest. The bands of marauders who infested these solitary and thinly inhabited woodlands, were not averse to paying an unwelcome visit to their natural enemy, the Head Forester. The Rev W D G Fletcher is reported to have said that *"Opposite the Forester's Lodge lies the Pond Close in which tradition says, the old mill stood & the place where the stream was dammed is still visible (1895)"*. Local legend asserts that the last miller killed a deer as it was crossing the dam, for which offence he was hanged (probably in 1255), after which the mill was destroyed and never afterwards occupied.

The severity of the forest laws and the almost unlimited power wielded by the foresters caused them to be hated by the native English, and of all the laws that ever disgraced the English statute book, the forest laws were the worst.

This, undoubtedly, accounts for the fortress-like structure of the dwelling. The stone walls, six feet thick at the base, taper off to be thinner higher up. The only means of access was by a doorway in the wall at first floor level. The place was impregnable as far as any means of attack in those days could affect it. There was no doorway at all to the basement, when first built, which may have been used as a storeroom for venison and other provisions, and was entered from the first floor by a narrow stone spiral staircase and there would have been a trapdoor down from the first floor. (A full description is given in a later chapter - Dwellings). It has also been suggested that it was used as a lodging house for important travellers visiting the area to buy farm produce. As these men would have been carrying large sums of money to carry out their cash transactions for their purchases, they might have considered it unsafe to lodge for the night else-where.

Between the Forester's Lodge and Stokesay Castle there would not have been many dwellings of any substance, perhaps a Manor House, moated to keep animals out, but none have survived except for Wolverton Manor, built in the mid-13th century, and still standing. Many of the houses today are probably built on the sites of earlier dwellings and they and Wolverton are referred to in greater detail in a later chapter.

The land in this area was being fought over constantly at this time, being near the troubled Welsh border, where marauding bands roved the countryside causing havoc and destruction wherever they went. In "Castles and Old Mansions of Shropshire" the state of the County at this period is described as:

*"Shropshire is replenished with castles standing thicke
on every side, by reason it was a frontier Country in
regard of repelling the Welshmen in the marches bordering
thereupon; where our ancestors by an ancient word,
named the confines of this Shire towards Wales, the
Marches, and divers noblemen of this tract were called
Barons of the Marches, or Lords Marchers, who had
everyone in his owne territory a certaine jurisdiction
in their owne courts, ministered law unto the inhabitants,
with sundry priviledges and immunities."*

During the immediate post-Conquest period a considerable number of *motte and bailey* were constructed in the west Shropshire and Welsh border area. A great many villages have the remains of one of these small fortifications which were normally in the form of a small circular mound (motte) with an attached defended court-yard (bailey). Over 150 have been identified in Shropshire and many are still shown on Ordnance maps, the nearest to the Parish being at Millichope. The motte and bailey castle was extremely effective both for attack and defence as, rather like the Roman fort, it could be quickly built within enemy territory. By 1225 most of the small motte and bailey castles were redundant and those not rebuilt in stone fell into decay and became eroded, par-tly destroyed or tree covered and, in some cases, all trace has vanished with the ditches silted up or filled in, and some were even small enough to have been ploughed away.

THE MEDIEVAL YEARS

In 1164 King Henry 11 assembled a vast army in an attempt to avenge the ravages Owain Gwynedd had committed in his kingdom and in 1230 Llewellyn, Prince of Wales, devastated large tracts of Shropshire. These are but two examples of this troubled period. As events such as these were commonplace in these difficult times there were, apart from the big castles, many of the larger dwellings that were fortified Manor Houses of which Stokesay Castle is an excellent example. Although it is a few miles outside the parish, it is worthy of description here, being one of the finest examples in the country, and is still standing.

The Court, Stokesay Castle.

The Manor was held by the de Saye family, who had fought at the Battle of Hastings and from whom it derived its name - 'Stoke-Say'. It was sold to Lawrence of Ludlow in 1281; he was said to be the richest wool merchant in England. In 1290, Lawrence obtained a licence from the King "*to strengthen with a wall of stone, and crenelate (furnish with battlements) his mansion*". The shape of the court was irregular and was surrounded by a moat, 22 feet wide. From one side rose the house and on the other three sides were walls. The only entrance was by a gatehouse and opposite, on the west side, stood the tower, 39 feet in diameter, and the Great Hall which was 51 feet by 30 feet and, adjoining, was an irregular shaped building which is believed to be the oldest portion.

THE MEDIEVAL YEARS

In the Civil War it was made a garrison for the King, being on the road between Ludlow and Shrewsbury made it important for maintaining communications between the two towns. In June 1645, when most of the Shropshire garrisons fell into the hands of the Parliament, the Governor yielded without resistance and thus saved the building from the fate that made a ruin of so many other old manors.

Stokesay Castle in the winter of 1896, North side. The Gatehouse.

THE MEDIEVAL YEARS

NOBILITY AND PEASANT - THEIR LIFE STYLE

At this period in the Middle Ages most Norman halls were made of wood and builders were not able to roof a wide span, so they were built like a church with a nave and two side aisles.

The Norman Hall, Stokesay Castle.

Light came from small windows in the walls of the aisles and warmth from a fire burning in a central hearth.   Wall chimneys were virtually unknown until the 14th century. The smoke from the fire escaped through a hole in the roof, but pottery louvres were being fitted by the 13th century, with screens placed in front of the doors to prevent the smoke from swirling about. There was often a gallery built above the screens where minstrels used to perform. The lord (or owner) had his dinner on a raised platform at the other end of the hall, walls would be hung with paintings or tapestries. Members of the household would sit at trestle tables in the main hall, the floor was generally rammed earth, littered with rushes, straw and scraps of food.

Unlike the nobility or gentry, the homes of the cottager or peasant were grim. Cottages were squat and dark. They had no chimney, smoke from the fire being allowed to escape as best it could through a partially open door or small window apertures, these were closed in winter with strips of cloth or pieces of wood. The interiors were commonly divided into two parts, one for sleeping and one for eating, with animals rustling about in the straw on the earth floor. Light came from flickering rush lights, but only when needed for some special task. Furniture comprised only a few stools, trestle table, bench and a chest of drawers for 'best' clothes and frames for the bags of straw upon which they slept. One corner would have cooking pots, dishes and a tub for washing.

At this time, even though stone was readily found, most cottages were built on wooden frames, with rows of sticks making up a lattice work wall, filled in with mud and straw. The simplest structures had the side wall timbers stuck in the ground at an angle and fixed overhead by a ridge pole. Slightly better houses had wall timbers or crucks carved so that it was easier to stand up. Then came the more elaborate ones with side timbers standing up straight from the earth, their tops being fixed to rafters, which were in turn attached to a ridge pole and the roof being thatched with straw.

Buildings were the biggest single user of timber, and it was neither considered a poor man's substitute for stone nor did it depend upon there being a woodland nearby, it seems to have depended on local etiquette or fashion. Oak was used in over 90% of buildings, it was the most expensive, commonest and longest lasting. Most medieval buildings were made from large numbers of small oaks, the carpenter choosing the sizes required and then squaring them up. Big oaks were sawn down the middle to make two rafters or a pair of crucks, but lengthwise sawing was expensive and avoided where possible. British oaks were, generally, too knotty to split and most halved timbers bear saw marks. The typical farmhouse, towards the end of the Middle Ages, would have been made up of some 330 trees. It was not until the 17th century that the fashion was to cover up timbers, making them structural rather than architectural, and this reduced the amount of timbers needed to about one third of a medieval house.

As there was an enormous difference between the houses of the gentry and the peasant, so the contrast in the matter of food and general living was just as marked.

Dinner in the great man's hall was always a formal occasion, generally eaten before noon, supper being served at four o'clock. Two meals a days were considered sufficient for the gentry, though a labourer would eat three times a day.

The food from the kitchens, where cooks sweated by the heat of roaring fires, scullions - near naked - had turned the spits, washed the pots and pans. The procession of servants bearing the food was led by the Marshal of the hall. Food was first served to the lord's table and his family, then to the gentlemen of the household and finally to the lesser servants.

Table manners were far from meticulous, the noise was tremendous, dogs barking amid the general hubbub of the meal. In the 12th century, and even up to the 15th, there were books on etiquette saying that wine must not be drunk when the mouth was full, the upper part of the body must not lean forward over the table with the head hanging into the dish, neither nose nor nails should be picked at meal times and the knife should not be used to carry food to the mouth.

The food served was various and plentiful; the provision of good fare was essential to a lord's standing and supplies would be purchased from Whitchurch, Nantwich, Shrewsbury, Chester, Worcester, Gloucester and even London to ensure the best and as wide a variety as possible.

Bread, baked by the household's own baker, was eaten at every meal. Meat was served in large quantities, beef and mutton regularly, then pork and veal, but venison was rare. Poultry was common. Gallons of milk, pounds of butter, large quantities of cheese and masses of eggs were supplied to the kitchens. Fish was also served, caught in local fishponds, or salted herrings, dried cod and smoked mackerel. Vegetables included dried peas and beans, onions, leeks and garlic plus a wide variety of herbs. Honey was used for sweetening and sugar, though expensive at 2s a pound, was used in wealthy households.

The following 14th century recipe lists three courses:-

1st course.   Larded boars head. A potage of boiled pork, liver and kidneys. Whites of leeks, minced onions and bread. Also beef, mutton, pork, swan and roasted rabbit.

2nd course.   Duck, pheasant and chicken stuffed with yolks of egg, dried currants, cinnamon and mace, cubebs and cloves plus two other pottages, one made of ground almonds seethed with good meat broth, minced onions and small parboiled birds - sparrow, thrush, starling, linnet, magpie, rook and jackdaw plus cinnamon and cloves. The other pottage contained powdered rice boiled in almond milk, brawn of capons and hens.

3rd and last course. This included rabbit, hare, teal, woodcock and snipe.

THE MEDIEVAL YEARS

This was considered a relatively modest dinner. Gallons of wine were drunk, most being imported from the continent. It had a short life and within a few months was very often undrinkable, *'turning sour and mouldy, thick, greasy, stale and flat'*. It was rare for anyone to refuse wine, 'teetotalism' was extremely rare and it is interesting to note that the word 'teetotal' was unknown then and did not form part of the language until 1834.

By the beginning of the 16th century, three meals a day had become more common than two.

The peasant's daily fare was pathetic by comparison. Each cottager would grow a few onions, cabbages, peas or beans, leeks and garlic, perhaps some herbs. A bowl of milk was not as often seen on a peasant's table as an earthenware jug of ale, nor was a piece of meat to be found in the metal pot that hung over the fire as a mess of vegetables and oatmeal potage which, with a hunk of dark coloured bread, had generally to serve for the evening meal. Sometimes there would be curds and cheese and, on special occasions, a chicken. Beef and other meat was seldom eaten although some might have a pig, living on nothing but waste and what it could forage, which they would slaughter.

It may seem surprising that there is no mention of potatoes, but they were not brought to this country until the end of the 16th century by Sir Francis Drake, and did not become part of the staple diet until very much later. The rabbit too, although eaten by the rich, was not available to the peasant at this time. The rabbit was not a native species in England and was only introduced in the 12th century, and was then an expensive delicacy. The medieval rabbit was not like ours today, it was delicate and needed cherishing in this climate. The word 'warren' that had for centuries referred to hunting rights in general, soon came to imply 'rabbits' as artificial enclosures were made for them. These early rabbits could not, at first, dig their own burrows, earthworks were put up to encourage them. Sheail records that among the tools used in Henry V111's warren was a great auger *"to make and bore cony holes"*. Cony was the old name for rabbit. However, as time passed and their numbers increased, it became impossible to keep them confined and there was conflict between the rabbit keepers and farmers who complained of damage to their crops, particularly those starting to plough up the heathland as arable farming developed.

As the rabbit adapted to the English countryside and became more abundant, so their popularity descended the human consumption scale. In the 13th century the market price averaged 3½d plus 1d for the skin. It was therefore still a luxury, being rather more than a craftsman's daily wage. By the 15th century it was 2½d and a possible Sunday dinner, as a craftsman need only work half a day to earn this. The price of rabbit continued to fall and by 1750 was 5d, about a fifth of a daily wage. In the

19th century they were cheaper still and became a regular part of the staple diet of the relatively poor. World War 2 found them becoming a pest, doing enormous damage to crops and, even with food-stuffs in short supply, efforts were made to exterminate them, though they were still appreciated as food. In 1953 myxomatosis was introduced via France from South America and promptly wiped out 99% of them. Their virtual disappearance has had disastrous effects on the grassland and heathland they used to maintain.

RIGHTS, TAXES AND MANORIAL COURTS

Work in the villages began as soon as it was light, shirts tucked into breeches, many went bare legged. They made their way to work the strips into which their land was divided or, towork in the fields of the Lord of the Manor. In the days of strip farming or cultivation, each strip would be about ⌐ an acre, often a man would have several strips scattered about the village rather than in a single block, so it was in each man's interest to work in collaboration with his neighbour, as they had to do when yoking their animals together to plough the lord's demesne.

The lord usually maintained that all manure found on his demesne and in the village streets was his, so it was a concern of the peasant to procure enough manure for his own land and often they had to resort to using straw that had been used in the cowsheds, mixing it with earth, before ploughing it in to his own land. The peasant ploughed his own land, sowed seed, mowed the grown crop with a scythe, cutting about an acre a day, and threshed the corn with flails. He also had hedges to cut, ditches to clear, his garden to tend and wood to cut. Finding time was always a problem since most serfs were bound to work for their lords on many days a year.

Hard though their lives were, they did have customary rights like the use of common meadows for grazing any animals they might have, gathering timber for fuel off waste lands, and were usually allowed to gather not only fallen wood but also as much as they could pull down "by hook or by crook". They might also be allowed to cut turf, dig out gravel and gather bracken for animal litter.

The ordinary man depended on the woods for building materials, brushwood for hedges and wood for fires. These demands were persistent and in 1235 the Prior's part of Shirlett Forest (which joins the Wyre Forest) was described as "*much wasted of old time and of late, affording no refuge for beasts etc.*" In Wrekin Forest the wood of Little Dawley was "denuded of oak trees of old and of late". So it was not merely for selfish reasons that the Prior sought to restrict the destruction of the woods, and it is interesting that, today, the continued cutting down of the world's forests is of great concern to all. The excessive use of the customary rights of haybote (wood and thorn for the repair of fences), *husbote and firebote* (right of the tenant to take firewood) were offences that carried monetary fines.

Details of trespass were often specified in the court rolls; cutting down trees, cutting green wood for fencing and roofing, cutting turves for roofing, peat for fuel and taking underwood. The penalties listed in the court rolls for Eaton in 1431/2 were:

"Attached by the bailiff: John Pygen junior for underwood 4d, William Pygen for 1 oak 4d, Thomas Alkokes for the same 4d, John Pygen senior for the same 4d."

The villagers rights seldom included trapping animals in the forest but poaching was, nevertheless, widely practised. What he got by poaching was felt to be compensation for what his landlord imposed on him for, in addition to the work he had to do, he might be asked to pay a 'wood-penny' tax for the wood he gathered, to take a basket of eggs to the manor house for the right to keep a few hens, to pay the lord a portion of the proceeds of selling a cow and, when he died, would probably be liable to *heriot* which entailed giving up his best beast or most valuable chattel, and even be liable for tallage – a tax of a fixed amount calculated on the basis of what a man could afford to pay – all this because serfs, and their possessions, were the property of their master, and it was sometimes said that serfs 'owned nothing but their own bellies'.

The free tenants of Hatton figure in a document which demonstrates the exceptionally harsh terms imposed by the priors on their tenants, the *terciary* payment on death (which appears to be peculiar to Wenlock Priory). A terciar was the third part of a person's movable property which the priory claimed on death. For example, when Richard de Weston died in February 1379, the priory claimed one ox for *heriot* (due by legal system to the lord) and, in addition, a third part of the value of the following articles; a pot 6s 8d, a pan and another article 4s, kitchen utensils 15d, a chest 2s 6d, a cupboard 2s, two tables 2s. In the margin the clerk noted the sum to be claimed – 6s 3½d. This was not all, a brown bullock, a hogget, a goose and a duck were to be delivered to the bailiff at Oxenbold, and in addition the priory claimed a little mare with foal 3s (terciar 12d) and ½ bushel of oats, a bushel of vetches in the granary and a third part of the corn in the barn and in the ground.

Other terciar entries tell of livestock, a worn out harrow, pans and axes, a cask for keeping bread, the meat in the larder, a bill hook and a ewer. Taken as a whole, these rolls suggest there was very little in the way of furniture.

THE MEDIEVAL YEARS

Everybody, rich or poor, bond and free, was subject to the terciary imposition.

There were many limitations to serf's freedom. He could not leave the manor without permission, nor give his daughter in marriage without payment, send his son to school without leave. He was not allowed to bake his own bread (because of the fear of burning down his cottage?), as all breadmaking was generally carried out by one villager in an oven or bakery belonging to the lord or the miller, the lord's tenant.

The following records from the court rolls of 1344/5 are relevant to the two examples above.

> EATON. Margery was the wife of Adam Hichesone, after the death of the
> same Adam with foresight sold one cow 7s. The same Margery hid ten
> bushels of first grade malt at the lord's loss.
> EATON. John le Hope de Eton married without the lord's permissionand is
> amerced (fined) 12d. Alice Balle married without the lord's permission and
> is amerced 6d. Sibyl Wilkyns has permission to be married and gives the lord 2s.

Mills for grinding the corn were generally water powered and were introduced at the end of the 12th century. In the late Middle Ages, windmills were quite common, particularly in North Shropshire. Few, if any, remain today. They were a hated feature of the countryside and the miller was often blamed for cheating, dealing out ill-ground meal and for rigorously collecting the proportion that had to be contributed either to the lord or to himself. In the 17th century a miller was paid a 20th or 24th part of the corn brought to him to grind, measured in a toll dish.

The lot of the medieval peasant has sometimes been exaggerated, starvation and famine were not common, but there were certainly a lot of peasants who struggled piteously to survive.

The role of women was important. The wife and daughters working in the fields was a common sight. Women, as well as cooking and gardening, brewed the ale, milked the cows, looked after poultry and winnowed the grain. When doing heavy work, driving the plough oxen, breaking stones and mending roads, they were generally rewarded at the same rate as men. Compared with the ladies of the manor, it could be said that they enjoyed a certain independence, and while they were not considered for any supervisory work, were regarded as fully capable of taking over the husband's holding in the event of his death or illness. There were prejudices against women and the English manorial system preferred succession to be to the male, yet daughters and widows did inherit, but pressure was put on them to marry or remarry as soon as possible, but many continued to hold their land, even though no marriage took place. Between 1350 and 1450 in the West Midlands, an analysis of family holdings showed that 60% that did not fall into the hands of the lord, went to female heiresses, mostly widows.

THE MEDIEVAL YEARS

MANOR COURTS

The number of courts held in the Manor of Eaton were not very numerous and appear to have diminished as time went on:

1344/5 – 3	1379/80 – 2	1411/2 – 1	1420/1 – 2
1431/2 – 2	1449/50 – 0		

The records of the proceedings of these courts were wrtten on long narrow strips of parchment and rolled up for storage – hence their name – court rolls.

This lack of courts could be because the records of each manor are not complete, the clerk failed to copy them on to the roll or the bailiff managed the affairs on his manor and accounted direct to the Priory. In some cases, perhaps, the manor court played an insignificant part in the life of the community, with the steward visiting the area once a year to take note of the buildings, fields etc., and using the ceremonial dignity of the event to emphasise the subserviance of the tenants to the will of the lord.

The matters which might come before the court covered the social life of the people, a jury (formed by two or three free-holders or burgesses) presented the evidence and the steward drew his conclusions; the penalty was decided by two affeeorors (who assessed the amercements or fines). Matrimonial, moral and probate matters were dealt with in Church courts.

The bailiff was the Prior's representative – the Prior rarely concerning himself directly with the management of a manor. A bailiff's name that has come down to us is William of Hereford, bailiff of Hatton, who arranged a lease with Robert de Hatton which was later found to be unsatisfactory..

At the time of the Dissolution it is probable that most of the documents that had been accumulated for more than 300 years by the Priory of their manors and other estates were destroyed. A few for the manor of Eaton have survived and, apart from those printed elsewhere in the text, are printed here, as they give an interesting insight into conditions there over 500 years ago.

EATON 1379/80. John Bencheweye surrendered the tenement and land which he held and gives the lord 2s by the custom which is called wainage....
John Berome surrendered the tenement and land which he held and gives the lord 2s by the custom which is called wainage.

EATON 1344/5. The whole township of Chelmondewyk de Hope (Chelmick) overburdened the pasture of the tenants of Ticklewardine (Ticklerton) and other tenants, and therefore they are distrained. Also various small utensils are seized for the lord and sold to John the reeve for 3d.

EATON 1379/80. The jury present that John Watkyns went outside the demesne during harvest...therefore he is amerced 6d. And that...(did not?) make hay for one day as was his duty. And that Richard Pickyns did not close his hedges.

EATON 1379/80. John Cok acknowledges that he has done damage to the oats of Richard Pickyns but he does not know the value and he places himself on the homage to answer at the next court. William son of Richard wages the law that he did not with his farm animals cause damage in the oats of Richard Pickyns of 1 quarter of oats valued at 4d a bushel as the same Richard Pickyns pleads.

EATON 1411/2. Roger de Welinton occupies the common pasture with more animals than he ought, to the great harm of his neighbours our tenants, therefore he is amerced 2d. And John Attekyn occupies the common pasture as does Roger Welinton therefore he is amerced 2d.

EATON 1431/2. All tenants have the prohibition by common consent that none of them may keep a mare on the common pasture unless it is worth 5s, and that no one shall keep a horse on the common pasture unless it is worth 6s 8d at 4 years of age, unless it has been castrated, under a penalty of 6s 8d forfeited to the lord.

EATON 1411/2. John Smyth has not repaired his tenement by the day fixed and incurs the penalty 6s 8d, and he must repair by August 1 under the penalty of 6s 8d. And ...Blyton does not maintain a sheepfold in his tenement and he must repair the sheepfold by May 3 under penalty of 40d. And Richard Jenkyns and John Wilkes have not repaired their tenements and must repair them by May 3 under penalty of 10s each.

EATON 1344/5. Roger son of Richard the son of Hugh, Richard Hichesone and Thomas Adies acknowledged thay they are bound as guardians of the Light of the Blessed Mary in 4 quarters of wheat and oats.

EATON 1344. John son of Enine de Plesh took a hive of bees in Longesetelke and carried it outside the demesne against the peace, therefore he is distrained to answer for the trespass.

EATON 1344/5. Hamon le Vyntener broke the neighbours' hedges and is an habitual evildoer.

EATON 1344/5. Agnes le Tynkeres is a common evildoer in the meadows of her neighbours therefore is amerced 3d. And Margery Tynkeres is amerced 2d for the same.

EATON November 4 1344. William son of Roger pleads and appears in a plea of trespass against Dominus Adam de Eton chaplain saying that he, Adam, broke his hedge causing damage of 2s., and Adam argues the law that he

did not cause any damage as is alleged against him, pledge of law Thomas
Tickleward. Roger son of Lucie acknowledges that he is indebted to friar
Walter de Eton in 2 bushels of wheat and 2d of money to his damage of 12d.

EATON February 18 1345. Adam de Eton chaplain failed in the law which he
argued against William son of Roger in a plea of trespass, therefore the
said Adam is condemned in the damages which the said William claimed from
him, nevertheless he is still amerced 6d.

EATON 1379/80. William vicar of Eton acknowledges that he is bound to
Richard Jenkyns in 1d of money and argues the law that he does not owe him
1 quarter of wheat price 4s 4d nor 2 bushels of wheat price 12d nor 2
quarters of oats price 6s 8d nor 3s 7-d for victuals bought by the wife
of the said Richard for the use of the vicar as Richard pleads against him
pledge of law...
Richard Jenkyns and his wife Alice argue the law that they did not remove
2 sacks price 3s from the house of William vicar of Eton nor has he kept
them, as he complains; pledge of law John Adkyns.   The same Richard and
Alice argue the law that they have not dispossessed him of a parcel of
land nor kept it for 3 years nor laid it waste as he pleads to his loss
of 40d. Also that they do not retain 1 trivet (a stand for pot or
kettle placed over a fire for heating) price 14d as the said William pleads;
pledge of law the aforesaid John Adkyns.
(Note: *the wife of Richard Jenkyns or Jenkes was Alice, daughter of Sir
Stephen Bowdler,Knt., of Hope Bowdler. The Jenkyns were living at
Wolverton/Wollarton*)

CHURCH AND CLERGY

At this time, there were perhaps 40,000 ordained men in
England. The priests were in what was known as Major Orders, and
these were then divided into two classes, those like monks living
in seclusion and subject to a religious order and known as regular
clergy.   And then there were those living in the outside world
and known as secular clergy. These ordained men represented one to
every twenty five/thirty of the population. There were also thou-
sands of men in Minor Orders, clerks, accountants, doctors and
lawyers. These were classed as clerics, having enough education in
Latin to be able to read verses from the Bible.
     The standing and behaviour of these clergy at this period of
time left much to be desired, and it is possible that because of
the close link with the Priory at Wenlock, those in this area
could not be 'tarred with the same brush'. A survey of the diocese
of Hereford in 1307 revealed that only 44 out of 281 parishes were
well administered. In an ecclesiastical document of the Hereford

diocese is to be found the story of the apalling Sir Edward, curate of Clunbury, who neglected his people, stirred up strife, refused to administer extreme unction (divine or sanctifying grace), was absent from divine service, kept a woman for a long time and baptized their son etc. Elsewhere, priests were accused of fornication with their maidservants or parishioner's wives, also for allowing their churches to fall into disuse or even ruin. One rector was charged with threshing corn in his churchyard, another with drunkenness, yet others as setting themselves up as tradesmen, lending money at exorbitant rates, refusing to conduct funerals and baptisms, forging wills and even disclosing confessions made under the Sacrement of Penance, with seducing women in church and even with practising Black Magic. However it is recorded that Hereford was exceptional!

In the next century there are more records of parsons being arrested for coining, poaching and even highway robbery.

It has to be said that chaplains were hard put to make a living after the rector (or prior) had taken the great tithe. They have been described as "*peasant priests, often obliged to engage in the open field system, fined, admonished and treated in many ways like their peasant flock to the detriment of their position*".

The peasants found the Ministers of the Church oppressive – tithes to pay, 10% of a parishoner's gross revenue, tithes on crops and cattle as well as all manner of other produce and possessions.

However, much as the clergy were distrusted and disliked, the Church was accepted as the natural centre of village life. Meetings were held in church, business and farming matters discussed in the nave, the bells rung to bring people's attention to the seasonal demands of the agricultural year. Plays performed and festivals celebrated with music and dancing.

Churches at this time would have had benches and pews for the clergy, the lord, his family and the parish clerk. There were no seats for the congregation and if the priest gave a sermon, the people in the nave would sit on the rush covered floor. Sermons were not all that common and pulpits were not installed in churches until the mid 14th century.

POPULATION AND PLAGUE

The population of England had increased quite rapidly up to the years 1250/1300, and some estimates give the total at 5 million or even 7 million. By the end of the 1300s there had been a dramatic and rapid decrease, brought about by famine and disease. Poor harvests were frequent and that of 1315 was calamitous, while the effects of the famine spread, cattle perished from a murrain or cattle plague which spread through the area. Agriculture had sunk into a very depressed state as a result of this and tenants were in the unusual position of pleading not to be saddled with any more land. The 'fines' for taking over land, either as heirs or for any other reason seem to have been high, considering the value of money and that these were ordinary common people. Most tenants found it difficult to pay their dues and it would have been impossible to pay for extra land. Here is seen a significant change with a money economy taking over from the payment in kind of feudal days.

From the court rolls of 1321 are some examples showing the court ruling that families should not take on more land.

TICKLERTON 1321/2. Richard son of Richard Keyne and Thomas son of Edmund and Adam son of the same Richard conceded to the lord ten shillings to have franchise and easement in the Manor of Eaton, and to be able to hold in peace the land which they now hold, and that they will not be distrained to take other land against their wish. Nor shall any of them be distrained to take land against his wish. For this agreement concerning easement each of them shall pay 12d a year.

1321. Isota, widow of Roger FitzHugh was fined forty shillings for the messuage and land held by her late husband with the crop already sown, to hold for life by performance of accustomed service.

5 November 1321. John FitzWilliam FitzThomas was fined ten shillings for easements and not to be distrained to take other land than the acre he now held till he was able to do so, and the Lord should approve.

13 December 1321. The Lord allowed Roger FitzFaber and another certain fixed days for gross arrears of their accounts. In 1322, 12d was paid for the licence to sell an acre of land at Lussecote and the purchaser was also fined 12d to buy and hold it for life.

In 1341 the Taxation of the Ninths was levied to enable King Edward 111 to continue the French wars. Because of poverty and distress, Eaton was assessed at £6-8-4 instead of £10 "*because the corn had suffered from tempest and there had been a general murrain among the sheep*". Yet, at about this time, Shropshire wool was fetching the highest price on the Flemish market. This prosperity must have missed this area because of the murrain.

Then in the summer of 1349 came a fearful pestilence – the Black Death. The bubonic plague was introduced and spread by rats from Southern India. They first affected the seaports, then spread rapidly along trade routes and, eventually, to practicaly every corner of the country. So many clergy died that the English language began to be used in places of learning and in documents instead of Norman French. The death roll in villages was up to half the population and even worse in urban areas. A description from "The English Village" reads:

THE MEDIEVAL YEARS

"What passed for villages were agglomerations of filthy hovels, whose inhabitants wore the same threadbare collection of rags for months on end, had bodies which crawled with vermin, who drank from the streams that served their cattle and pigs, and whose huts were havens for rats, fleas and lice. Nine-tenths of the population lived thus, and most of the remainder lived in towns which at their biggest and worst were congested stinking death traps in which any disease could spread quickly and disastrously. These people did not seek to live in filth, but they possessed neither the means to avoid it, nor the knowledge of its consequences. They believed that mice appeared spontaneously in bags of flour, that cheese and not the fly gave birth to maggots and that disease could be caught by speaking its name. For living in conditions of squalor and ignorance, they paid a steady contribution to the graveyard."

This decimation of the peasant workforce brought about a violent dislocation of the feudal work pattern and no event in British history has had a more catastrophic effect on the life of the people. There were further plagues in 1361, 1369, 1371 and 1375. After the Black Death labourers began to demand excessive wages and, to stop the peasants getting above themselves, a Statute was passed in 1351 that wages should remain as they were before the Plague.

One result of the Black Death was to improve the lot of the surviving peasants. There was plenty of land and an acute shortage of labour. There were, surprisingly, plentiful supplies of corn, cattle and sheep which had not been affected by the pestilence following the Black Death. Many peasants were able to increase their holdings by taking over strips of those who had perished. Many landlords, deprived of labour, chose to let their land, either for rent or payment in kind. Thus some peasants became sheep farmers and developed into quite well-to-do yeoman farmers.

However, such was the terrible effect of the Great Plague on the population that it was not until the 1700s that the population rose again to where it was just prior to the Black Death in the mid-1300s. By 1540 it was still only 2,500,000, by 1688 had risen to 5,500,000 of which 3,000,000 were reckoned to be poor labourers, the successors to the bonded peasantry of the Middle Ages. By 1801, 8,800,000 had been reached and in just the next 100 years the population quadrupled to 32,000,000. This huge rise was, surprisingly, not as a result of better health or lower mortality, but to a fall in the marriage age and larger families.

Literacy and education did not play a very important part in the Medieval life style. With the possible exception of Henry 1, Edward 111 (1327) was probably the first English king to have more than a few words of the English language and, until his reign, there is no evidence of a King writing. Few Norman and Plantagenent kings had a very firm grip on Latin. In most early Medieval noble households less emphasis was placed upon book learning than upon manners, etiquette and social graces, with daughters, in particular, receiving little education.

Until 15th century, villeins had to obtain a licence from the Lord of the Manor to send one of their children to school. For those who were to have any schooling at all, formal education began at 7 years old and lasted two or three years. Boys who were sent on to grammar schools usually went at 10 or 11 and expected to stay for five or six years. Very few children attained a high standard of literacy. Among the upper classes there was a common feeling that learning was for clerks, not for noblemen. It was not easy for sons of rustics to study letters, since the Lords of the Manor were aware that education might lead to taking Holy Orders, thus escaping from the servitude status of a potential labourer.

With the end of the Middle Ages, we move into a period when life in Hope Dale and Ape Dale, and the surrounding countryside, began to develop with the growth of farming, the increase in local population and the establishment of privately owned estates, many of which survived into the 20th century. It was always a sparsely populated area, lime and charcoal burning, farming and its associated trades being the occupation and source of income for nearly everybody living there. The fortunes of the wool trade in particular dictating the prosperity or otherwise until arable farming came to play a larger part in the overall picture, but it was never a rich area because of the nature of the land, with its many poor heath covered hills and woods. Medieval Shropshire had been one of the counties where the open field system of cultivation prevailed. Where the land had been held in crofts adjacent to houses, the tenants could do as they wished. Under Priory control there was an increase in the areas cleared of forest and the fields were enclosed. Thus Shropshire had moved earlier than many other counties towards enclosing the land into individual fields, well before the Enclosures Act of the early 1800s. The Priory manor cultivation was the three-field system, with two parts being sown each year and the third part left fallow.

TOWNSHIPS OF THE PARISH

Eaton, Hatton, Harton, Ticklerton and Wolverton

Around the middle of the 13th century, there are historical records beginning to appear for the Parish which help us to build up more of a picture of life there, how the various manors, houses and townships developed, up to the present day.

As has been recorded elsewhere, Wenlock Priory owned vast estates which included lands in the Parish. It was in September 1538 that Thomas Cromwell issued injunctions for a register of marriages, baptisms and burials to be kept in every parish. In 1540, Wenlock Priory surrendered and their treasures were all taken away, many of the buildings destroyed and the monks departed. The Priory estates were then all sold.

After the Dissolution, in 1544, Henry V111 granted to Sir John Packington, a judge in Wales who lived at Hampton Lovett in Worcestershire, the Manor of Eaton for the sum of £910-6-0. The grant included the rents of Thomas Jenkes (Wolverton Manor) and Richard Lakyn of Hatton, from Sir John Dudley, Lord Lisle and John Smyth of Mylychop (Millichope), lands in Longvelde (Longville) and Lushcott, also rents from John Philips and ten others in Tyklarden (Ticklerton) and Birtley, from John Ward and four others in Harton, from John Clarke and three others in Eaton, also Tycklarden Mill and a chief messuage and lands on either side of Strebeke brook with the Rectory and Advowson. Also woods called Eywood, Blackwood, Longvelde and Eton Edge. Not a bad deal for £910! These estates passed on to his daughters who disposed of them upon marriage.

At about the time the first census was taken in 1841, the tithe apportionment details were changed from 'kind' to money based upon the rateable value While it is difficult (if not impossible) to be precise about the ownership of land during the three hundred years following the Dissolution, there are interesting details of some of the families that came into possession of manors and lands and, through their descendants, lived in the area for a very long time.

The Parish of Eaton did not conform with the Domesday Manor, but was more extensive. For example, it included Upper Millichope which the Priory acquired after Domesday and extended to include East Wall, Longville and Lushcote. This very large Parish had, by the first half of the 19th Century, a population of around 550. Then, as outlying parts were absorbed into other parishes - Rushbury and Munslow - the population dropped, by 1951 it was 281 and today between 120 and 130. It is the present day Parish that is discussed here in detail, but the Forester's Lodge in Upper Milli-chope is included because of its particular historical interest.

EATON

The name Eaton means 'farm by a river' from the OE 'Ea' - stream. However, a place-name ending -ton was usually attached to a community rather than an isolated farm, and in view of the importance the Priory gave to it and the fact that a three day Fair and market were held there in the 13th century, leads one to believe it may have been a larger community than exists today. The extension to 'Eaton-under-Heywood or Haywood' came later. There are two likely definitions of the word 'Hey/Hay', from the OE 'Haefi' - meaning fence or enclosed piece of land, hence - enclosed wood. Or, as 'haie' - a small hunting park found in woodland areas and enclosed with a hedge to keep in red, fallow and roe deer, all of which were common in the Long Forest. Later, this referred to any enclosed woodland. In the 17th century Church register there are also entries spelt Aiewood and Eywood.

St Edith's church dates from the early 13th century, and is discussed in greater detail in a later chapter. The first incumbent to be listed in 1289 was Osbert or Godman, though the vicarage may have been served direct from the Priory at Wenlock because, in 1255, the Manor of Eaton was described as 'the Manor of the Lord Prior', held in demesne by the Priory.

In 1219 Henry 111 empowered the Prior to hold a Fair for three days on the Eve, Feast and Morrow of St John Baptist and a market on Thursdays. This was allowed on a quo-warranto (a writ calling upon one to show by what warrant he claims a franchise) in 1296.

In 1290 Bishop Swinfield visited Eaton, and the Prior gave forage for 36 horses in the Bishop's train. His Visitation lasted three days. His love of good living was well known and, in an account of his life, he seems to have had a lively recollection of the 'feed' the Prior had given him. His great retinue and numerous attendants must have come down on Eaton like a swarm of locusts. It is said that they ate up everything eatable, and they had to send to Church Stretton for further supplies of food.

In 1291 the rents were £12-9-4 and a century later £19-9-8.

In 1514 the Rent Roll for the Priory was £4-6-8 for Eaton which, with other rents from Lushcott, Longville, Ticklerton, East Wall, Harton and a charge of 6d on the Mill Pool at Hope Bowdler, made a total of £25-1-0. By 1541 they had risen to £30-9-4.

Sir John Packington, mentioned earlier, was the guardian of John Lyttleton of Frankley upon whom, after he married his daughter Bridget, he settled the Manor of Eaton. In 1551 John Packington and Richard Lakyn appear as Lords of the Manor, subject to a lease for 75 years made by Wenlock Priory to John Habberley, described as 'bailiff of the Haywood'.

John Lyttleton and his son Gilbert then, apparently, sold the Manor to Richard Lutley and his son John. John Lutley died in 1589 seised (in possession) of the Advowson (benefit of the living) of Eaton, of Knights fees and escheats (confiscated or forfeited lands) and lands in Wolverton, Harton and a mill at Harton. His heir was his only sister, Margaret, who married George Jenkes of Wolverton Manor, then aged 44 years.

In 1602, George and Margaret Jenkes settled the Manor of Eaton (and Wolverton) on their son Francis upon his marriage with Frances, daughter of Herbert Westfarling, Bishop of Worcester. The Manor remained in the Jenkes family until 1663 when Margaret Jenkes married Bartholomew Lutley of Lawton and Broncroft, and these lands are mentioned in their marriage settlement.Their son Philip Lutley, 'Lord of this manor of Eaton and Patron of this Church' married, in 1707, Penelope, daughter of Richard Barneby of Brockhampton (Herefordshire) and was father of Jenkes Lutley who succeeded as Lord of the Manor but died unmarried in 1745. He was followed by his brother Bartholomew Richard Lutley, who then assumed the name Barneby and died in 1783. Either he or his son John Barneby sold the Manor of Eaton to Sir Jacob Woolf of Milly-fant Abbey, near Wells who was 'of Eaton' in 1793. It was then sold to Robert Bent of Lincolns Inn Fields, London in 1801, from whom it was purchased by John Beck of Shrewsbury in 1806.In 1842 the Manor and farm of Eaton were owned by Maria Eaton of Shrews-bury, widow. In 1851 the Misses Eaton are named as landowners in Eaton, but before 1860 it was purchased by William Hanbury Sparrow..

HARTON

Harton may well have derived its name from 'hart' or 'stag' and, when considering its location, is a very probable explan-ation. This Manor was held under the Wenlock Priory and the Ward family were there for many generations..

John Ward is referred to, as is Richard Ward's daughter, Anne, who was heir to her Uncle Adam Ward of Harton. She married Col Thomas Smith of Birchen Hall (Herefordshire) and their daugh-ter Anne married Thomas Dunne of Gatley in 1814 who, as well as owning land in the locality, is reputed to have aquired Ragdon Farm from the Wildings by way of a bet struck at Bangor races. True or not, his family remained owners until 1947 when it came back into the Wilding family (of Ragdon) again. In 1842 the Harton Estate was owned by his (Ward's) executors and subsequently passed to Loxdale Warren. Then, after his death in 1913, the estate was auctioned.

TOWNSHIPS OF THE PARISH

TICKLERTON

Ticklerton was held under Wenlock Priory by copyholders (tenures of land of a Manor) as there was no specific Manor recorded, just a number of different farms.

After it was released by Wenlock Priory, several families were connnected with Ticklerton. At the Dissolution, John Phillips and ten others were tenants there. Thomas Edwards of Ticklerton appears in a deed of 1587. His grandson Vincent was 'of Ticklerton' in 1663.

In 1729 Lucretia, widow of Rev Henry Hibbins of Waddesden (Bucks) was buried at Eaton, no doubt having been living with her daughter, also Lucretia, who was married to Thomas Palmer of Ticklerton. Richard Palmer, who married Cecilia daughter of Thomas Edwards mentioned above, may have been of this family. They appear to have lived at Ticklerton Hall, where a stone dated 1635 seems to mark the date of the main building.

In 1842 Thomas Downes of Broome owned the Hall. In 1868, Elizabeth Massey and others (probably the trustees) sold it to W Hanbury Sparrow.

The Pinches family lived and farmed in the area for generations and Ticklerton Court was their home for many years. In 1572 Thomas Lewis of Ticklerton had a daughter and co-heir, Margaret, who married Fulk Pinches who was 'of Ticklerton' in 1607. His descendant, Elizabeth, daughter of William Pinches (d.1818) devised her estate to her husband the Rev Robert J Buddicom, whose family is discussed in detail in a later chapter.

An interesting piece of history relates that in January 1333 one 'William de Tykelwardyn' was appointed by the Abbot of Haughmond Abbey to be the first vicar of Ruyton X1 Towns in the North of the County. He, like the Vicar of Eaton, was only entitled to Vicarial tithes.

HATTON

Hatton derives its name from 'a heath farm or enclosure'.

It was held under the Prior of Wenlock by Robert de Hatton. As this was before surnames were in general use, we do not know who 'Robert' was, but as a Manor is referred to and because of the extent of the lands, it would probably have included the other farmhouses nearby, of which there are four today standing within a few hundred yards of each other.

The Prior and Robert de Hatton were in dispute concerning a hide in Hatton that had been demised (conveyed) to Robert by William de Hereford, Bailiff of the Prior between 1204 and 1215. This was probably the first *feoffment* (transfer of property) given by Wenlock Priory within the Manor of Eaton. This *feoffee* was later impleaded (raised an action against) by the Prior and Robert demanded a view (official examination) of the premises of the action. The dispute was heard in 1227, but there was no settlement and it was held in abeyance for ten years. Then, in 1237 on May 3rd, a final settlement was agreed by *Final Concord* at Salop. Robert had to pay Prior Imbert 20s per annum for the land and "provide ten men for one day in Autumn to carry the prior's hay at the said men's own cost" (J C Anderson). Why was it so late in the year? - perhaps due to bad weather at the traditional haymaking time. Also, Robert and his Tenants had to attend the Prior's *Halimot* (*Holy or Church Court*) of Eton three or four times a year, which customs Robert did not recognise.

There was still more argument between them. Robert had been accused of *attracting* 5 acres to his *fee* (property) because of the way the boundary line was drawn between his land and the Prior's land at Thikelwrthin.(Ticklerton) Finally, twelve Knights gave judgment that all the land to the east of a stated boundary was to remain to the Prior and all to the westward to Robert de Hatton. In 1255, the Inquisition of Wenlock Liberty states that "Robert de Hatton is Lord of the *Vill* of Hatton and pays the Prior 25s per annum and does suit to the Prior's Court by *afforciament* (strengthening the jury)".

Over the next few hundred years there were many changes of ownership. It was held under the Prior by the Lords of Harley then, in 1399, William St George, parson of Cleobury North granted to Roger de Willey, son of John de Harley, and his wife Katherine the Manors of Wilderhope and Hatton, to the use of Roger and Katherine with remainder to John and Joan Daras, remainder to Henry Grendon and his wife Elizabeth, daughter of Hamon de Peschale. Elizabeth Grendon brought these estates to her second husband, Richard Lakin.

In 1580 Rowland Lacon/Lakyn leased lands in Hatton to Thomas Edwards of Ticklerton. Hatton then passed from the Lacons/Lakyns to Edward Jones of Shrewsbury who, in 1635, sold for £400 an estate in Hatton to the Rev Richard Wredenhall of Rushbury. In 1681 a messuage in Hatton was sold to Bernard Hammond of Ludlow which had formerly belonged to William Acton. Previous to 1623 William Acton of Henley had married Jane Hammond of Hatton. The will of John Hammond (1681) shows he had three sons Vincent, John and Bernard and three daughters Susan, Jane and Mary. Vincent was buried in Eaton in 1718/9. His house, built of stone, was formerly the parish workhouse, and over the door is a stone inscribed with "H - V E 1679", evidently standing for Vincent and his wife, Eleanor. The farm was purchased by Thomas Powell of Bridgnorth (died 1805) and later by his descendant the Rector of Munslow.

In 1659 John Baldwyn of Munslow and Urian his son made a settlement of a capital messuage in Hatton, purchased from Richard Acton, and also a messuage purchased from John Botfield. Urian was 'of Hatton' in 1660, and several of his children were baptized at Eaton. His son, John Baldwyn sen. of Ludlow sold, for £700, in 1722 "that ancient messuage etc." in Hatton to Mary Lutley, spinster. In 1744, her heir Jenkes Lutley, sold this property to Bernard Holland of the Rea (Highley). This "ancient messuage" was the Upper Farm, dating from late Elizabethan times.

The Middle Farm was owned by the Exors of Charles Morrall in 1842, whose daughter and heir married M W Bellew Nugent.

WOLVERTON

Wolverton - could be derived from OE 'Wulfweardington' meaning Wulfweard's Farm. Wolverton Manor is almost certainly the oldest dwelling in the Parish. Built in the 13th or 14th century it was, without doubt, lived in by someone of importance by virtue of its size and construction (detailed later under Dwellings) and as far as it is possible to trace back through history, it would have been the Jenkes or Jenkyns family who probably built (or rebuilt) it and certainly lived there in an unbroken line for nearly 500 years.

Legend has it that the Jenkes/Jenkyns family originally came from Wales and were descended from Elyston Glodrydd (927 to 983), Lord of Ferlixland, Wales. A ninth generation descendant of Elyston Glodrydd was Jenkyn Cambray, who left Wales in 13th century and went to England where he lived at Wolverton, probably in an earlier dwelling with the Manor being built on the same site some hundred years later.

The following are the names of as many of the occupants and owners of Wolverton Manor as found in the family histories, Church records and early census returns. The Jenkes Family Genealogy comes, in the main, from a manuscript written by the Rev William Jenks, D.D.L.L.D. of Boston, U.S.A. in the period 1830-45.

Jenkyn Cambray - (the use of Cambray as a surname may be a misnomer as it is probable that this actually meant 'a Welshman' or 'from Wales', and was a misspelling of the word Cambrian, the latinization of Cymry, or 'son of John') - was the first family member who lived at Wolverton Manor, married Dorothy, 3rd daughter and co-heir of Sir Walter Collyng Knt. of Stretton. The undoubted high standing of the Jenkes family is clearly indicated in the marriage (around 1350) of Richard (presumably his son) to Alice, one of two daughters of Sir Stephen Bowdler Knt, of Hope Bowdler (a neighbouring parish). The other daughter, Cicely, married Edward Acton of Acton Scott. There is reference to a case in the Court Rolls of 1379/80 of Richard and Alice having a number of disagreements with William, vicar of Eton and again in 1411 with regard to maintenance of his tenement. (see page 18)

Thomas Jenkes of Wolverton (Richard's son) married a daughter of Thomas Middleton, and they had a son, John, who in due course also lived at the Manor and married, having a son Roland.

We know that in 1521 Roland Jenkes/Jenkys paid a rent of 17s 1d to the Prior at Wenlock for his lands at Wolverton. He married Mary, daughter and heir of Richard Moore. They had sons John, Thomas, Richard, William and Edward.

Once again it was the eldest son who inherited Wolverton, and John married Elizabeth Leyhton or Leighton of Cotes and Radnor, and they had two sons, Thomas and William.

Thomas Jenkes of Wolverton married Joyce Baldwin of Under Hayton and had four sons, George, Thomas, John and Angharat or Anghard.

We have now come to the end of the 16th century and the records read 'George Jenkes, gentleman, of Wolverton'. He married Margaret, the daughter and heir of Richard Lutley. Her brother, John Lutley, died in 1589 and left her the Advowson of Eaton, lands in Wolverton and Harton. Their sons were Francis, Adam, Jasper, Robert, Thomas and Arthur.

In 1602 George settled the manors of Eaton and Wolverton on his eldest son Francis, this also included appurtenances (minor properties) in Eaton, Millichope, Longville, Lushcott, Harton, Ticklerton and Wolverton.

Francis Jenkes, Gentleman of Wolverton, married Frances, youngest daughter of Rt Rev Herbert Westfarling, Bishop of Hereford – they had sons Herbert, John, Thomas and Benjamin. Francis Jenkes moved to New Hall (Eaton) where he died in 1627. Herbert, his son, was patron of the Church at Eaton in 1633

Herbert Jenkes of Wolverton, married Elizabeth, they had no sons but two daughters, and possessed Wolverton until 1640, when he too moved to New Hall. He made a lease for his two daughters, Margaret and Elizabeth, of certain lands in Eaton for 30 years from the day of his death. Elizabeth died unmarried, but Margaret married Bartholomew Lutley of Lawton in the parish of Diddlebury, who also had lands in Eaton. They were both buried at Eaton.

Rev John Jenkes, brother of Herbert, was the incumbent at Eaton in 1648, married Joyce Lutley, and died in 1695 aged 90. By 1696 Herbert, although still a patron, is recorded as being a lunatic, with Sarah Williams acting on his behalf.

An Elizabeth Jenkes married John Bradburne of Wolstaster, she may have been a daughter of Herbert Jenkes. Herbert Jenkes is supposed to have sold Wolverton to John Bradburne when he moved to New Hall in 1640.

The last references to the Jenkes family are for Francis, who was Patron of the Church from 1701 to 1740, and a Jenkes Lutley as Patron from 1740 to 1786. It then appears that the family must have moved away from the area.

In the next few years Wolverton Manor changed hands many times. In 1841, at the time of the tithe apportionment survey,

John Blockley was the owner. Then, in 1842, Hannah Beck, a widow from Shrewsbury, was owner, it soon passing to the executors of Peter Beck (her husband?) and then to J Loxdale Warren. He kept it, along with many other farms in the area until his death, when it was then sold by auction in June 1913 as "Lot 3" of The Alcaston Estate.

UPPER MILLICHOPE

Upper Millichope is named after the Millichope family who were 'hereditary foresters in the Long Forest' and is, of course, where the Forester's Lodge (referred to earlier and described later under Dwellings) is located to this day. The Domesday Manor was divided in early days with Lower Milllichope becoming a seperate tenure in the parish of Munslow.

Harton Road Bridge

ST EDITH'S CHURCH

Eaton-under-Heywood Church, c.1890

St Edith's Church at Eaton is not mentioned in the Domesday Book, and was probably not founded until the 12th century. If, as is generally accepted, the church is of Norman origin, it is surprising that it was dedicated to the Saxon saint Edith (Eadgyth of Wilton). She was the daughter of King Edgar and Wulfryth, born in 961. She was brought up as a novice but, as a King's daughter could have had an important position but refused such offers, remaining at Wilton with her mother, where she had been appointed Abbess. After her half brother Edward the Martyr had been murdered, she declined to become Queen. She built a small chapel for private worship in honour of Saint Denys and at its dedication Dunstan is supposed to have prophesised her death and the incorruption of her thumb (that it would never decay). She died aged 23 and miracles at her tomb helped establish her cult and her feast (September 16th) spread to many monasteries. Eaton is one of only three dedications known.

THE CHURCH

The Rectory was appropriated to the Priory at Wenlock between 1186 - 1189, but some dispute occurred at the time of Bishop Foliot (1219-1234) and the church was then devoted to the better provision of the Monk's Kitchen "saving the due maintenance of a vicar there", having a chaplain, who were unbeneficed priests, doing the work of a vicar. This was not uncommon in the Priory Manors. The chaplains were hard put to make a living after the Prior (or Rector) had taken the great tithe. They have been described as "*peasant priests, often obliged to engage in the open field system and fined, admonished and treated in many ways like their peasant flock to the detriment of their position*".

From 1831 to 1900 the living was held by the Rev Richard Sandford and his son Holland Sandford, first as a Vicar then, in 1868, it was restored to rectorial status, being again the benefice and residence appertaining to a Rector who was the incumbent of a parish whose tithes were not impropriate.

The Coats of Arms over the Chancel arch represent - Arthur Sparrow (Lord of Manor) - Joseph Loxdale Warren (Landowner) - Holland Sandford (Rector 1860-1900)

The Coats of Arms were restored in 1984 with money left to Eaton Church by Mrs M Lane-Clarke, widow of a former Rector of the Parish.

The Carolean Pulpit and Canopy,1670

The font and cover by William Carter

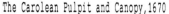

The church has a nave, of which the oldest portion is Norman, a chancel and embattled tower with three bells. The Carolean pulpit is richly carved with a canopy bearing the date 1670, this refers to the upper portion as the lower part has Medieval details and the linen pattern. The font is ancient, but the cover is modern and the work of a local artisan William Carter. It is four-square and some six feet in height. The north side represents an oak with acorns. The west side an elaborate *fleur de lys*, surmounted by the crest of the Sandford family. The south side has a beautifully worked wheatsheaf and the last panel displays a vine covered with grapes. Above all towers a cross with a vine trailing over it. There is a well carved monument to the memory of Philip Lutley (d.1731). An inscription states that the chancel was 'beautified' in 1743 by Jenkes Lutley.

In 1793 Mr Gwynne's account book shows that the church was replastered and repaired. The three-lancet window in the East end was given by Arthur Sparrow in 1868/9 when the church was extensively renovated. Prior to this, it was described as *"damp, dirty and bedaubed with plaster and yellow limewash, and had a most gloomy and depressing appearance. An ugly and useless gallery was removed."* The entire cost of the renovation exceeded £500, notwithstanding the magnificent gifts of the Lord of the Manor (three lancet windows) and Messrs Cox and Sons (a communion table). The old oak panelling was given by Mrs Hayward of Ticklerton in 1928 in memory of her late husband and parents, and came from the old Chelmick Manor farmhouse. There are monuments to the families of Lutley and Ward bearing coats of arms.

"There is a wooden effigy, 6' 2" long and supposed to represent the lord of the manor of earlier times. The head, which rests on two square cushions is covered with a close fitting hood, a long overcoat conceals the inner garments, the toes of the shoes are pointed. The hands, which are somewhat rake-like, are joined together in the attitude of prayer. There is also an aumbry (a recess for church vessels or a cupboard) and a mutilated floreated cross with the representation of a chalice - doubtless the tomb of a medieval vicar." *(Cranage - Shropshire Churches)* Life size figures such as this, in wood, from the 14th century are very rare and this is believed to be one of only two to be found in Shropshire.

The wooden effigy, c.14th Century

THE CHURCH

The Normans did no levelling when they built thus, as it was built on a natural slope, the floor of the Church slopes upward from West to East (possibly they did not wish to disturb the remains of those buried beneath the original Saxon church). The Churchyard is circular in shape and is probably the result of the fact that the three day Fair that was granted by Henry 111 in 1219 was held around the church, forming a circle. There was no burial ground until after the Reformation.

There are three bells, the first and third are by William Clibury, 1622 and 1615; the second is by Mears and Stainbank, 1869, given by the Rev Holland Sandford, replacing a medieval bell which was cracked.

In 1848, Rev Richard Sandford planted a young yew tree in the churchyard on the spot where an old hollow yew tree was discovered to have been "mailiciosly and wickedly" set on fire on November 5th 1793 at 2 a.m. Despite a 2 guinea reward offered, no one was ever found to be the culprit.

As recently as 1989 the Church was still in the private patronage of the Sandford family.

INCUMBENTS

There are several gaps in the following list as, before the Dissolution, the vicarage was served direct from the Priory from time to time, without formal institutions.

```
1289 Osbert or Godman
1309 Richard de Laverden
1313 Roger de Perston
1321 John de Orleton
1321 Richard de Estenor
     John Weyford
1441 William Hughes
1445 William Schery
1449 Maurice Taylor
1488 John Boteler alias Stretton
1515 John Upton   John Taylor
1541 John Upton (a monk at Wenlock Abbey)
1541 Thomas Haburley 1558 (Reg. T Boteler)
[1558?] Richard Clearke 1567 Patron John Lutley
1616 Ambrose Phillips M.A. Patron: Francis Jenkes
1633 Joseph Sond  Patron: Herbert Jenkes
     John Jenkes, 1648 buried at Eaton 1695 aged 90
     son of Francis Jenkes of Wolverton
     (James Logane 'minister' here in 1654,1658)
```

1696 John Ball Patrons: Jo Freke Esq. Jo William D.D.
      and Sarah, his wife, acting for Herbert
      Jenkes (lunatic)
1701 Thomas Hotchkiss M.A. Patron: Francis Jenkes
1703 John Taylor M.A. Patron: Francis Jenkes
1740 James Volant Vashon M.A. Patron: Jenkes Lutley
1742 William Oakeley M.A. Patron: Jenkes Lutley
1786 John Stanier M.A. Patron: Thomas Gwynne of Ludlow
1790 Thomas Gwynne jun.M.A. Patron: Thomas Gwynne
1799 Thomas Watkins B.A. Patron: Thomas Gwynne
1805 Thomas LLoyd Patrons: Henry & William LLoyd
      of Ludlow
1810 Thomas Alban Patrons: Henry & Wiiliam LLoyd
1831 Richard Sandford B.A. Patron: himself
1860 Holland Sandford M.A. Patron: Humphrey Sandford
      of the Isle
1900 Charles G N Friederichs AKC Patron H Sandford
1945 Reginald Howard Vincent AKC
1961 S C R Lane Clarke
1971 Edward Baty
1980 Michael Bromfield

THE REGISTERS

The earliest Register, dating form 1688 to 1758, consists of parchment leaves 14in by 6in, in a parchment cover, and contains baptisms, marriages and burials.

Volume 11, dating from 1759 to 1812 consists of 32 pages of parchment, 14in by 8in, bound in calf and contains baptisms and burials.

Later volumes contain - marriages 1754 to 1783, 1784 to 1813, 1813 to 1837. Baptisms - 1813 to 1880. Burials from 1813. Extracts exist from an earlier register, now lost, in Geo Morris' MS in Shrewsbury archives.

Study of the registers and the surveys of the Churchyard that have been carried out this century, produce some very interesting facts.

Date	Deaths recorded in the registers	Churchyard memorials etc
17th Century	230	3
18th Century	449	35
19th Century	545	111
20th Century	164	65

The details of memorials, tombstones etc. that have been found and recorded since 1915 are to be found in Appendix 2.

THE CHURCH

It is obvious that in earlier times there were no tombstones erected, certainly not of a permanent nature, for the majority. The "important people" were buried within the Church and as near the altar as possible, whereas the common folk were laid to rest outside in the churchyard. Even in death, the social distinction was maintained between the noble (or at least, the wealthy) and the commoners. An epitaph of 1793 in Kingsbridge, Devon, sums it up very well:

'Here I lie at the Chancel door
Here I lie because I'm poor
The further in the more you pay
Here I lie as warm as they'

There are many references in the records of 'Burying in Woollen'. This refers to an Act of Parliament of 1678 which stated
-No corpse of any person (except those who shall die of the Plague) shall be buried in any shirt, shift, sheet or shroud or anything whatever made or mingled with flax, hemp, silk, hair, gold or silver or in any stuff or thing other than what is made of sheep's wool only or be put in any coffin lined or faced with any material but sheep's wool only."

At the conclusion of the burial service the Clerk asked "who makes affidavit?" This had to be made within eight days of the funeral. Penalties of £5 (an enormous sum at that time) were made on the estates of persons not buried in woollen, on the house-holder in whose house he died, on the persons connected with the funeral, on ministers neglecting to certify non-receipt of the affidavit and on Overseers neglecting to levy the penalty. Half the £5 went to the Poor and half to the informer, so when anyone had decided to defy the Act, it was usual for a member of the family to act as informer and so reduce the penalty to £2.10.0. The Act was repealed in 1814.

There are many 'notations' in the registers connected with burials, such as:

"1680 Mar 13 Edward, illeg s of Margaret Child, being a vagrant person, and the Mother dead long before, buried."

"1695 Sept 11 A wandering woman dying in this Parish, buried."

"1739 Feb 3 Mary Hanley, a poor innocent woman, buried."

It appears that the 1790s must have been a very hard time in this area. There are many more references to paupers, both under baptisms and burials, than occur at other times. Also, although the baptism of base born children was not uncommon, this period again shows a greater frequency than normal.

THE CHURCH

N.W. view of the Church.(note absence of gravestones)

17th and 18th CENTURY

While the appearance of the landscape had remained virtually unchanged for centuries, the common field system was coming to an end. The large farms or manors that had been granted to a limited number of individuals, particularly under Norman rule, were being split up into smaller farms, the land being enclosed and fenced or hedged. In Medieval times, Shropshire was one of the counties where the open field system of cultivation had prevailed. Cultivation on the Priory manors was the three field system, with two parts sown each year and the third part left fallow. Where land was held in crofts adjacent to the cottages, the tenants could do as they wished and the average size each tenant held was about 20 acres.Wool and sheep were still predominant, but when prices fell, a move to arable farming took place.

Traces of the old 'ridge and furrow' cultivation were, until quite recently, to be found in fields at Hatton Grove, behind Greystones Cottage on the road from Ticklerton to Hatton and behind the old school.

Around the 17th century, most farm workers had to be content with low wages, perhaps as little as £3 a year where food and lodging were provided. At the end of the century, there were 750,000 farmers earning £42-10-0 a year, 280,000 'freeholders of the better sort' averaging £91+ and £55 a year by 660,000 'freeholders of lesser sort'. The following were the annual earnings of 'persons in law' - £154, artisans and handicrafts - £38, 'gentlemen' (of whom there were 96,000) - £280. Temporal lords - £3,200, Baronets (12,800 of them) - £880, and 30,000 Esquires - £450. There were 1,275,000 labouring people and outworkers with a yearly income of £15, and 1,300,000 cottagers and paupers with just £6.10.0. a year. *(according to Gregory King)*.

The Elizabethan age was a time of rising demand for fuel, some of which came from hedges. The 1590s and 1600s were terrible years of cold and poverty. Courts took an increasingly severe attitude to stealing hedge wood. For instance, in Essex in 1567 *"Any person breaking any hedge or stealing wood be put next Sunday or holy day in the stocks for two hours at the least, and the wood be placed before them, signifying the cause of punishment"*. In 1600, also in Essex, hedgebreakers were being whipped until 'they bleed well' and receivers of stolen wood were again spending all Sunday in the stocks. Although these are not particular references to Shropshire happenings, it can be assumed that these types of punishment would probably have been common throughout all the country at this period.

The time of the Great Enclosures was a time of transformation, when there was more new hedging being carried out than ever before or since. The hedges planted between 1750 and 1850, probably about 200,000 miles throughout the country, were at least equal to all those planted in the previous 500 years. The thousand million or more hedging plants needed to make 200,000 miles were big business and founded the fortunes of several Midlands nursery firms. *(The History of the Countryside - Oliver Rackham)*

According to Hooper's Rule, the age of a hedge can be determined by taking a 30 yard stretch and counting the different of trees and shrubs. The number of species counted is approximately equal to the age of the hedge in centuries. While this rule can only give an approximate age, it can distinguish between hedges of the Enclosures Act and those of Stuart and Tudor times. There are three hypotheses to account for the observation that older hedges have more species:

1. A hedge aquires further species as it gets older, with tree and shrub seeds constantly being brought by chance or birds, germinating and occasionally becoming established.

2. In earlier times it was the custom to plant hedges with a wide variety of species. Enclosure Act hedges were generally planted with one species only, usually hawthorn.

3. The older a hedge, the more likely it is to be natural rather than planted, and therefore to be mixed from the start.

The above refers to hedges in general, but it should be noted that in Shropshire there was a tradition, going back over several centuries, of always planting a number of different species when building a hedge.

Long before the 20th century farming practice brought about the ripping out of hedgerows in many parts of the country, to which Marion Shoard referred so forcibly in her book in 1980, the House of Commons Journal of 1792 (p.318) states *"The grubbing up of Hedge Rows is become general, and the growth of Timber in them is thereby totally destroyed, owing to the great Price given for Corn since the bounty took place for exporting Corn and Beer, which gives every farmer encouragement to grub Hedge Rows up, and convert them into Corn land."* Fortunately, this was not the case in this area of Shropshire, at least.

This small parish, made up of several townships, was very much under the influence of Wenlock Priory for a very long period and may not have been typical of the rest of the County, let alone England as a whole, but was nevertheless subjected to the same general conditions of population, famine, disease and the way of life, particularly of the country peasant.

DWELLINGS

14th to 19th Century

Farmhouses, houses, cottages, public houses and some of the people who lived in them.

The first real opportunity to locate all the dwellings in the Parish, their owners and occupations only came at the beginning of the 19th century when the Tithe apportionment manuscripts were prepared. These contained the name, size and type, rateable value, owner and tenant of every field, each with an individual field number for reference. Then, in 1841, the first full census was carried out which listed the names and ages of every occupant and, in most cases, the occupation of the adults.

Thus, from this time onwards it is possible to build up a fairly accurate picture of who lived where and what they did for a living.

It is also possible, though difficult and time consuming, to study copies of wills and old estate records to obtain details from earlier centuries, but even then you only find a small proportion of people and houses, generally the larger farms and seldom, if ever, cottages. There are other records that give a guide to the situation, Church and Poor rate accounts for example, but an account of the Hearth Tax for the year 1672 is very interesting as a guide to the size, age and number of houses at that time.

THE SHROPSHIRE HEARTH-TAX ROLL of 1672

The Hearth tax was *"Chimney-money or hearth money - express-ing that every fire-hearth or stove of every dwelling, except such as pay not to Church or Poor, shall be chargeable with 2 shillings per annum, payable at Michaelmas and Lady-Day to the King and his heirs."* This tax imposed by Statute..

This law or tax was very unpopular indeed and was declared to be an oppression and badge of slavery and was, accordingly, abolished by a further Statute in 1689 "and the window-tax was established in its room." One of the reasons for its abolishment was that it *"exposed every man's House to be Entered into and searched at Pleasure by Persons unknown to him."*

It was a profitable tax for the King while it lasted, for Shropshire in 1672 it produced £2,869-8-0 gross. There is no information, however, of the cost of administration, which must have been fairly high. The tax was payable by the occupier and not the landlord.

The only exemptions that were granted were on the score of poverty - those who did not pay Church or Poor rates, those who inhabited a house worth less than £1 a year or whose annual income was not more than £10 a year. They were recorded in the Rolls as 'paupers', but this did not mean they were destitute or in receipt of Poor Relief.

It is assumed that every hearth had its own flue and chimney *"for the joining of two flues in one common flue is apt to cause much inconvenience unless fires are burning in both fireplaces at the same time."*

From these Rolls of 1672 it shows that, in the Parish, there were 33 dwellings that qualified. (In 1841 census there were 64 listed). The identification of some of the larger houses has been possible, based upon the number of chimneys (firehearths) and the occupants that are referred to in other chapters. It is, perhaps, surprising that there were so many 'permanent' cottages paying Church and Poor taxes as early as 1672, and it makes one wonder how many of the cottages discussed in this chapter are actually more than 300 years old.

As the area gradually developed in the 17th to 19th centuries, there were two significant changes apparent. First, a new type of land owner came on the scene. Men like Moses Benson from Liverpool who had made money in shipping, in particular, in the 'black ivory' trade with Africa. He bought much of the Lutwyche Estate when it was sold in the late 1700s, and this included lands in Hope Bowdler and Eaton. The Sparrow family from Wolverhampton, solicitors, and the Buddicoms. Captain William Buddicom (1727-1802), a privateer in the time of George 111, who may well have accumulated personal monies as a result of his 'activities' and his great grandson, rector of Smethcote, came to Ticklerton with the inheritance of his wife, Elizabeth Pinches, of the Ticklerton estate.

The second, and more important change, was the prosperity that came about for farmers, with the boom in the wool trade in particular. Most of the farm houses that we see today were built, or re-built, during this period and many of them are illustrated and discussed later in this chapter.

As well as the sheep trade being very profitable, so there was a gradual move towards bringing more land into cultivation and enclosing open land into smaller fields. This resulted in a growth in the workforce and although it will be seen that in the 19th century census details, most large farms housed the men and women engaged each year at the May Hiring Fairs, there was a growing need for regular farm hands, estate workers and woodsmen and so the building of farm cottages began in earnest. These were fairly simple dwellings, more permanent in construction and a far cry from the hovels of branches, interwoven straw and bracken that had had to suffice for so many for such a long time. Local stone was used in nearly every case and there are the remains of small quarries on many farms, but it was from the Soudley quarry that the principal supplies came. The stonemasons who worked the quarries and helped build the houses came to live at Heywood, Soudley and Birtley to be near their work, and a large number of small cottages were built for their use, as well as for those working on the land.

A typical hovel at Ticklerton, c.1890.

It would be tedious to try and describe each and every one of the dwellings listed in the 1841 census and, in any case, little is known about many of them apart from their inhabitants, and even then it is not possible, in many instances, to be certain where everybody actually lived. There are, however, a great many that are interesting and worthy of description and these are discussed in this chapter. The occupants and location of all the houses can be found in Appendix 1. Earlier records appear in the chapter 'Townships of the Parish'.

In this chapter the field number on the tithe map (see over page) and the census reference number are given for each of the houses described. For example: Eaton, Manor Farm (412/4). The first number (412) being the field number in which the house stands and the second (4) where it appears in the census details in Appendix No.1. Each area or township has its own map and houses are shown by a small black square.

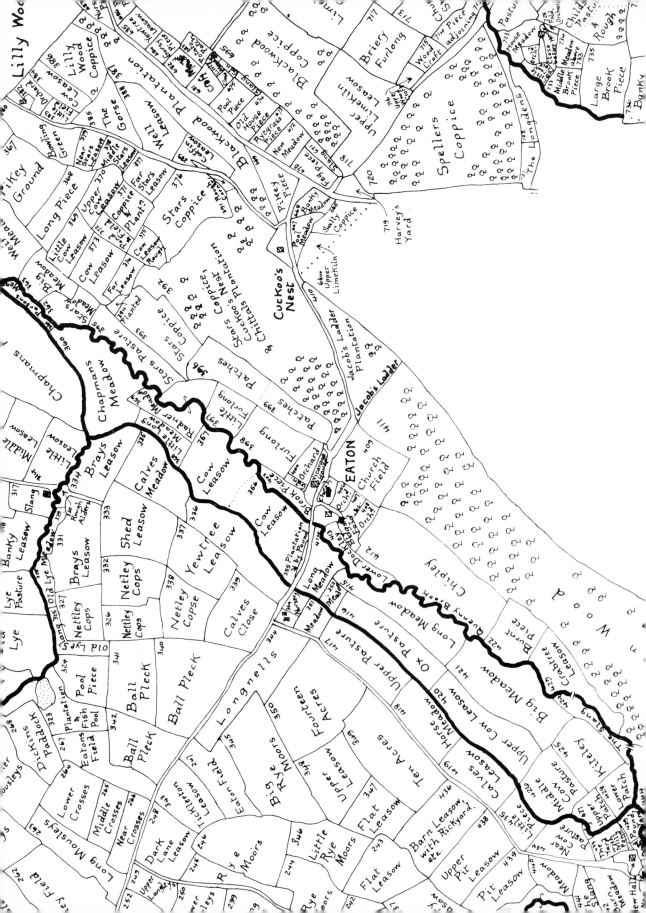

DWELLINGS

The following list is recorded under 'The Franchise of Wenlocke' for 1672 and as there are no separate headings for Harton and Wolverton, it is assumed that they were included here under Eaton.

EATON

	Firehearths	11(£)	s	(probable location etc.)
Mr Jencks	3	0	6	- Wolverton Manor
Edmund Blakeway	1	0	2	
Richard Hammond	2	0	4	- Ch Warden 1678
Richard Star	1	0	2	
George Corfield	1	0	2	
Mrs Jenckes	10	1	0	- New Hall
Edward Fewtrell	3	0	6	- Harton Manor
Edward Ruckley	4	0	8	- Eaton Manor
Widdowe Williams	1	0	2	
Richard Davies	3	0	6	- Harton Ch Warden 1666
	29	2	18	

In Eaton itself there were, in 1841, 12 houses (only 2 more than recorded above) and 77 inhabitants. The township extended to 1,649 acres with a rateable value of £1,026-3-0. There were two farms close to the Church, Manor Farm or Church Farm as it was sometimes called, and Eatonglebe or Whitefields.

Manor Farm (412/4) is no doubt the Manor referred to from time to time in the Priory records. The present house was built in the 17th Century on the site of an earlier dwelling. The farm was around 220 acres

Whitefields (317/6), originaly known as Eatonglebe, was part of the church property with some 60 acres, later being increased. There would always have been a dwelling on site, but not of any architectural significance, and the house today has been enlarged and modernised.

The Rectory (403/3), known as Bray House, was built by the Rev Sandford in 1835 for £140 and was described as "a large house of gentleman's residence type".

This was added to later by the Rev Friederichs. Reverend Sandford also paid £38 to have the trap bridge built, making access to the church easier. This bridge was made of iron and was not taken down all that long ago. What the vicarage was like in the preceding centuries is not known, but it is unlikely to have been of much consequence, bearing in mind the fairly low status it held under Wenlock Priory.

Artist's impression c.1900

The Rectory (now a private house) after rebuilding.

There is an old track that starts in a small gorge between the Rectory and the Church, after some 300 yards the track bears left, and a very steep path - Jacob's Ladder - runs straight up the hillside, emerging on the Edge with a magnificent view on one side towards the Clee Hills, the highest land in Shropshire (1,650 feet) having, at one time - on the top - the highest coalfield in England. On the other side are Caradoc and the Longmynd.

A small farmhouse, "Cuckoo's Nest" (390/1), used to stand in a slight hollow near the top, alongside the old track that runs down towards Upper Millichope. This was the main way of reaching villages on the other side of the Edge from Eaton and was once used by wagons carrying flour and grain to and from the New Hall mill.

Legend has it that when the Abbey at Wenlock was destroyed (which happened twice) the monks fled through the forest to the Church at Eaton by way of Jacob's Ladder, which enabled them to pass to safety, unseen. Today, it is a pleasant climb up to the summit.

There were three other cottages, one situated near the old railway bridge and is still standing today. (352/5 - illustrated below) Another has disappeared (405/2), only the foundations and remains of the old orchard are still visible and Lilywood (381/7) was demolished in the mid'80s.

Eaton Cottage. Originally it was semi-detached and is believed to have been a chapel or, at least, joined to one - note the evidence on the end wall.

Still in Eaton, along the road towards Harton, is the important New Hall Farm and the tiny miller's cottage.

New Hall (432/8), standing on its own, with only the Mill cottage (431/9) nearby, was built in the 1500s or earlier, and was probably rebuilt by Francis Jenkes of Wolverton Manor when he went to live there in the early 1600s. He died in 1627 and his eldest son Herbert came to New Hall from Wolverton in 1630.

Herbert Jenkes daughter Margaret married Bartholomew Lutley, and although Lutleys were lords of the manor and patrons of the living in the 17th and 18th centuries, they do not seem to have lived there.

By 1840 Maria Eaton was the owner, the farm being of 200 acres and from 1850 was farmed by the Hince family until 1881 when the Cleetons came and stayed there through to 1941.

DWELLINGS

It was originally an Elizabethan timber building to which brick additions were made a century later. The timber frame at the rear is a simple and very early type. There were two oak mullioned windows. The roof was formerly roofed with stone slabs, and these were later used for edging and paving in the garden. There is a fine ornamental chimney stack.

New Hall Farmhouse

The interior had many interesting features. The ceiling beams are massive and there were several open-hearthed fireplaces. Until around 1890 one of the upstairs rooms was lined with Elizabethan panelling. When this was removed it revealed a remarkable wall painting representing a hunting scene, hounds pulling down a deer with a huntsman spearing it in the neck.

Close study of the illustration shows that the house in the background has what looks like a small tower and even crenallated walls. As it is unlikely that the artist would have invented these features, considering the attention to detail in the rest of the painting, it is reasonable to presume that it was originally a fortified house (manor house). By the time the Jenkes moved there from Wolverton Hall, the need for fortifying one's house against maruders had long since passed, it may also have fallen into a poor state of repair so, rather than him building New Hall (as it is sometimes suggested), it is more likely that he rebuilt the old house, with new exterior walls etc. more or less as it stands today.

The 16th century wall painting. When New Hall farm was sold by auction in 1951, this painting was offered for sale on its own as Lot 3A! Fortunately, it was sold with the house, where it remains to this day.

This remarkably well preserved picture measures 6'3 " high by 7' wide, and Clive Rouse of Ludlow suggested that it was painted in 1560, by an apprentice of the artist who painted the picture of three ladies in Elizabethan costume, with musical instruments. (see over page) This painting was revealed when building work was being carried out in the late 1950s, but the heat and light was causing it to start peeling off, so it was immediately covered and the paneling replaced. There are traces of a similar painting on the mantelpiece, and it is probable that the whole room was orna- mented at one time.

New Hall was then purchased, in 1957, by Mrs Whitaker who, with Mr & Mrs Treasure (her daughter), came to live there and farm. They had been living at Spring Bank Farm in Church Stretton, but when land was sold to build Church Stretton school, thefarm became too small for their purposes. The house at New Hall was in need of a lot of renovation, there was no garden and only a few trees at that time. A roofed verandah was built on the garden side of the house, without in any way detracting from the -original design.

This sketch gives an impression of the Tudor painting. The woman on the left is holding what appears to be a Tudor rose, the musical instrument is probably a lute. (courtesy Shrewsbury Chronicle)

The water mill, photographed in.1890, was still in use in the 1930s.

DWELLINGS

The present gardens were entirely created by the Treasures and are opened to the public each year.

At the time the Hall was being restored (1950s), the old mill-house and water wheel were in a very delapidated condition and were demolished. Much of the old timber was re-used in the house to make the new staircase leading out of the main hall. The main hall ceiling was also taken out at this time, so that the main construction and the wall painting could be seen by visitors.

The water mill was very important to the Parish as this was used for grinding the local farmers' corn, as well as those from neighbouring parishes. It was in continual use up to the 1930s.

The big water wheel broke down in the early 1900s, the chocks that held it on to the spindle were found to be rotten. Phil Harley, the estate carpenter, felled a Hornbeam (a very hard wood) sawed it up and made the necessary chocks, jacked up the wheel and drove the new blocks into place. These lasted until the 1930s when it went out of use. It was replaced by a tractor driven pulley and belt. Today, all traces of it have disappeared.

Although the Eaton Brook ran close by, this was not used to drive the water wheel, instead a dam was built upstream at White-fields Farm and a huge plank cut from an immense oak in Harton Hollow in the 1600s 'was put to stop the weir'. The water from the sluice gate to the mill ran into what is known locally as the 'flem' (from the French 'flume' or Latin 'flumen')). This flem or ditch ran for about 1- miles across the fields, under the old

The miller's cottage (now derelict), the mill (now demolished) and New Hall. c.1890

railway line, crossing the road at Eaton just below the railway bridge, along Ox leasow to the mill. It was a constant problem to keep it cleared and free running. It is shown on the 1840 tithe map as a thick black line and early Ordnance maps as a Mill Race.

The Harton Hollow oak must have been an enormous tree, as two other planks from it were made into fine old oak refectory tables. One for New Hall and the other was part of the furniture in Wolverton Manor until it was sold in 1913, to Squire Buddicom at Ticklerton Court.

New Hall mill was the only one of which there is a definite record, but in earlier centuries there are many references to 'Ticklerton Mill' and 'Harton Mill'. Although nothing concrete can be found, there is believed to have been a windmill off the old Harton road, at the double gate where the Ticklerton brook is nearest the road. There are signs that it was forded at that point and a trail mark up through the field to the highest point, where old foundation stones are to be seen which are believed to be the old windmill. These are in field No.242, 'Little Cote Piece' on the 1841 Tithe map, alongside a double-hedged track which runs up to the Ticklerton/Eaton road. As far as 'Harton Mill' is concerned there are, near Harton, fields named 'Near Mill, Far Mill, Upper and Mill Fields' which give a definite indication of the one-time existence of a mill. This is not an unreasonable supposition, as in the late Middle Ages windmills were common in Shropshire, particularly in the North of the County.

DWELLINGS

HARTON and WOLVERTON

Harton was only ever a small township of two farms, there were no cottages at all at the time of the 1841 census, and it was only after the railway was built that Railway cottage (218/13) appears in 1871.

Harton farmhouse (480/10) is of stone, half timbered with brick chimney stack of the type prevailing in the district. The timber frame of the house appears to suggest it is early-Jacobean.

Harton Farmhouse

Harton Manor (460/11), a 17th century building has Jacobean star-pattern panels in the gable and an oak mullioned window with moulded base. In the kitchen is a big fireplace with a stone in the wall above it bearing the inscription '1615 - R.W. C.A.W.', doubtless the date of the house and the initials of Richard Ward

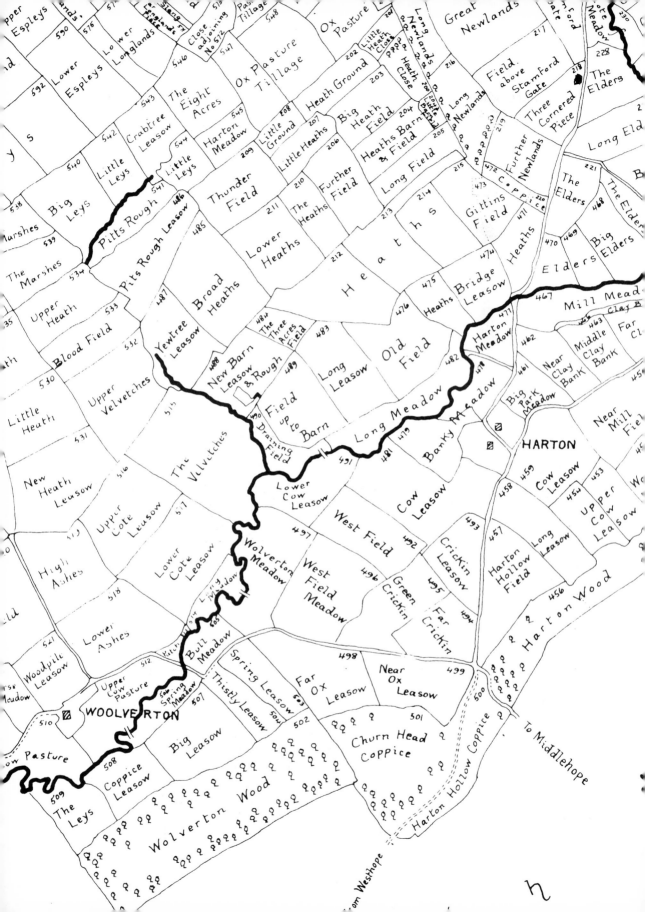

and his wife who had it built. There is also, in one of the bedrooms, another inscription in three lines – INANNO DO – MINI 1615 – RW CAW TH. The northern half of the house and staircase appear to have been added in the time of Charles 11 (1660). The Ward family owned Harton manor throughout the 17th and 18th centuries until, on the death of Anne Ward, it passed to the Dunne family. The verandah at the front has been removed in recent years.

Harton Manor Farmhouse

WOLVERTON

Wolverton Manor (511/12) is, without doubt, the oldest house in the parish that is still standing and lived in. In an earlier chapter there is refernce to the arrival of Jenkyns Cambray in the 13th century. Experts have endeavoured to put dates on the various phases of its construction and the house is, in my opinion, of such interest that it warrants a fairly detailed description.

It seems certain that when Jenkyns Cambray came to Wolverton there was already a dwelling of some description in existence, and in view of the importance it held under the Priory, was probably already of some standing. However, parts of the present building have been expertly dated as originating around the end of the 14th century and this is, to a certain extent, borne out by the fact that in 1411 a Richard Jenkyns was up before the Manorial court

DWELLINGS

"to repair his tenement by May 3rd next or pay a penalty of 10s".
This would not have been necessary if the house had only been
built in the previous century.

Wolverton Manor, as it appeared in 1913. (below) as it stands today.

The house today consists of a two-storied crosswing construction and a long low range at right angles which is mostly one
and a half storied, there are three dormer windows on the front
and one at the rear. Today the exterior is rendered and whitened,
covering the original timber framed medieval hall-house. The
interior is an excellent example of a late medieval three-part
plan of hall and passage, flanked by a lower service end and an
upper solar wing.

DWELLINGS

It was suggested in 'Old Houses of Wenlock' that it was at one time a monastery, but this is now generally discounted, following the exposure of the construction during recent extensive repairs and renovation. Some of the carvings could have been mistaken as being of a type found in churches, but nothing else supports any monastical link.

The hall is probably the best Shropshire example of a medieval box-framed hall with a hybrid cruck central truss. The feet of the principal rafters are curved, creating a type of two tier cruck truss. The spere-truss is of conventional aisled form and has the normal arrangement of 'nave' and two side 'aisles'. The entrance into the hall was through the central nave section.

On the back of the principal rafters of the spere-truss, near the apex, are mortices which originally related to the louvre opening through which smoke from the open hearth was extracted.

A ceiling was inserted in the hall around 1550. It has a main axial beam and transverse beam, with secondary intersecting beams dividing the area in rectangles into which are set joists in chequerboard fashion.

A view of the remarkable chequerboard ceiling.

The fireplace has a mantel beam and is of a different date from the ceiling. It may have come from the original dais at the end of the hall.

When the ceiling was inserted, there was still an open hearth fire and the lower bay was left open as a smoke bay. There is scorching at the ends of the ceiling beams. Around 1600 a smoke hood or 'fumbrell' was installed and, eventually, a brick chimney was built. At a later date a bake-oven was inserted and the cast iron door is inscribed "Smith of Ludlow - 20".

The Central Truss - a form of base-cruck and,
behind, the Spere-truss.

The Windbraces - double-cusped and chamfered.

The lower end of the bay is an addition, but two bays relate to the original building. There is a timber of 50 feet uninterrupted length from the upper end of the hall to the end of the second service bay.

The upper end has the usual layout of a great and small parlour. The 16th century panelling, depicting the 'four and twenty blackbirds' nursery rhyme (of Catherine of Aragon), remains on part of the wall, the rest having been used and ruined by an earlier farmer for stacking fertiliser sacks! Similarly, the ceiling bosses of carved lion heads have been mutilated or removed ,and only one has survived.

About 1660 a number of modifications appear to have been made to provide a lobby entry, improved staircase, and a new kitchen in place of the old screens passage and byre.

In 1913, when the Loxdale Warren estate was auctioned, Wolverton Manor was described as "Lot 3. 4 bedrooms, 2 servants' bedrooms and double attic with two staircases". The tenant at that time was Mr T Hamer, and there were 307 acres of land and 45 acres of wood, with a rental of £269-10-0".

In 1984 the present owners, Mr & Mrs R Orme, carried out major renovation, re-roofing etc. and revealed many of the interesting construction details that had been hitherto covered.

As with Harton, no other cottages were recorded in the area at the time of the 1841 census, but there are two entries in the Parish register - 1813 for John and Charlotte Blewit, a hoopshaver of Wolverton Coppy and, a year later - Thos and Elizabeth Smith, an agriculturist of Wolverton, which indicates the earlier existence of at least one cottage nearby. As well as being the home of a family of importance, working staff would also have lived in the house. Any other workers would have lived in hovels or travelled some distance to work from other parts of the parish.

Some of the massive timbers used in the construction.

DWELLINGS

TICKLERTON and BIRTLEY

At the time of Domesday, Ticklerton was the only township recorded in the parish, and over the years it has remained the largest township, although it has always come under the parish title of Eaton-under-Heywood.

TICKLERTON - Hearth tax for 1672

	Firehearths	ll(£)	s	(probable location etc)
John Phyfeild	2	0	4	- blacksmith
Samuel Whittley	2	0	4	- Upper House Farm Ch Ward 1681
Mr William Pynches	3	0	6	- Ticklerton Court
Richard Phyfield	1	0	2	
Edward Palmer	5	0	10	- Bank House Ch Ward 1713
Thomas Palmer	6	0	12	- Ticklerton Hall Ch Ward 1673
Roger Challoner	4	0	8	- Lower House Farm Ch Ward 1663
Thomas Oxenbold	1	0	2	
Jerench Lockier	1	0	2	
Francis Waynewright	1	0	2	
Richard Star	1	0	2	
John House	1	0	2	
Evan Thomas	1	0	2	
Joseph Lawley	1	0	2	
Widdowe Phillips	1	0	2	
Morrice Davies	1	0	2	
William Phyfeild	1	0	2	
Adam Oxenbold	1	0	2	
Thomas Martyn	1	0	2	
	35	3	10	

In the early 1800s there were 1,384 acres with a rateable value of £1,008-10-0. The three principal farms located there were:

Ticklerton Hall Farm (258/17). Ticklerton Hall is very interesting for a number of different reasons. This large and imposing structure is of more than one age and incorporates earlier work. The front is not symmetrical which probably indicates an adaptation when the main house, as it stands today, was finally constructed.

The floor levels are outlined by projecting courses; there are no stone quoins (cornerstones). As well as a number of pigeon holes in the upper walls, there was a large detached square dovecote, now in a poor state of repair. At the rear is a stone built malt house as well as extensive farm buildings set around a yard.

Ticklerton Hall

There are the initials 'P-R.L.' over a malt house window which probably indicates that the builder was Phillips or Palmer. A detached stone found inside the main house is dated 1635 which is doubtless the date of the actual building.

The fireplaces and staircases combine in a remarkable manner features of the Jacobean style (then going out of vogue) and the Queen Anne style (which had not yet come into fashion). Some of the timber partitions have the spaces filed with plaited lathes instead of wattles.

The rooms are large, downstairs the dining room and kitchen are 18' x 18', the lounge 16' x 10', breakfast room and the back kitchen 18' x 12'. Three of the bedrooms are 18' x 18', two are 18' x 12', the sixth 12' x 12' and there are four attic bedrooms.

In its hey day, it was the largest farm in the area with over 300 acres. The gardens and orchards were extensive. Cider making was carried on in a grand manner and there are extensive cellars. Today, while the house still stands, the majority of the land and has been sold, the main orchards have gone and some of the build-ings converted into houses.

Upper House Farm (152/15) or Court farm, as it was originally known, was some 250/270 acres. The stone farm house dated from the mid 1600s. There used to be an inscription on the gable 'J O M 1724' this has now worn away. The tenancy changed fairly regularly until the end of the 19th century, when John Cox came to live

DWELLINGS

Upper House Farm

there. For many years the 'big stone barn' (now converted to a house) was used for village entertainments, plays and dances. The Cox family continued to farm it until 1990.

Lower House Farm (189/16) was slightly smaller in acreage. The house has a wide ingle nook in the kitchen with a massive stone chimney breast surmounted by brick shafts. These, together with parts of the adjoining walls, are probably late Elizabethan. The rest ofthe building being built about a century later.

Lower House Farm

DWELLINGS

The history of The Bank House (174/22) has been one of the minor mysteries of Ticklerton for many years, but recent research and the discovery of an 1866 photograph have now solved it. As can be seen in the photograph taken across the pool, below Ticklerton Court, it was a large house with many outbuildings. In 1841, a sheep merchant, William Jones was living there and with 57 acres it was owned by John Griffith. By 1851 it had become "The Horseshoes" public house and was run by Benjamin Purslow. It remained a pub, now run by Edward Downes (also a farmer), until the mid-1860s when the house and some of the land was bought by Rev R J Buddicom and the rest of the land by the Rev Holland Sandford. The following is the Bill of Sale.

The Rev R J Buddicom

1868   *To: Saml. Smith Esquire*
Mar 25

Total purchase money		1600. 0. 0
Timber		146. 4. 7
		1746. 4. 7

Less
Amount to be paid by
Mr Sandford for land purchased 660. 0. 0
Do. for timber   13.17. 8

	673.17. 8
	1072. 6.11
1867 June 24 Deposit paid	160. 0. 0
	912. 6.11
Fee on Contract	2. 2. 0
	914. 8.11

"Public House, now Bank
House and ground"

The amount of over £1700 seems very high, even allowing for there being 57 acres of land included, as well as the house.

By 1870, George Garfitt - a farmer - was living there, and it was known as "The Bank". At around 1880 major rebuilding work was carried out, the name was changed to "The Laurels", and the house altered to look as it does today. By 1888 it had ceased to be a farmhouse. It was once again renamed and, as "The Bank House", was then let to members of the 'gentry'. W F Duncan Esq. is to be

"The Horseshoes" public house, 1866 (above). "The Bank House" (below) photographed in 1888
with W F Duncan Esq. at the door. Also known as 'The Bank' and 'The Laurels'.

seen in the doorway in the 1888 photograph. Further improvements and modernisation work was carried out and, in 1903, a bathroom was installed This was the first house in the Parish ever to have one and some of the original lead pipe work remains to this day. Occupiers in the succeeding years included the Misses Holt from Liverpool, Major Hornby, Brigadier General Leyland and H P Carver.

Ticklerton Court (155/18) is certainly better documented than the Bank House, having been in the hands of the Pinches and Buddicom families for hundreds of years. The original house was built about 1600, probably by the Pinches, and the cellar walls and portions of the interior support this date.

Ticklerton Court. (above) with the 19th century second storey and, (below) as it stands today, with the top floor removed.

DWELLINGS

Although it was generally known as 'Ticklerton Court', there was a time (around 1856), when the Rev R J Buddicom and his wife Elizabeth were still living at Smethcote Rectory, and they had let the house to William Darcy (late of Ticklerton Hall farm), that it was known as "The Mansion House". This name remained, certainly until 1863, when William Squire Buddicom first went to live there.

The greater part of this square stone mansion was rebuilt early in the 19th century, with a second storey added. It had about ten bedrooms, the staircase had unusually slender banisters and was probably late Georgian. In one of the bedrooms was a quaint old fire grate, designed after the pattern of the iron bridge at Coalbrookdale. On the top floor were two large square rooms and the servants quarters. Around 1917 a tiny room was discovered, the entrance to which had been covered over, and was only discovered when R A Buddicom was taking measurements of the house and some did not seem to tally. The room was found to be quite empty and no explanation for it being hidden has been found. At this time there was no bathroom, only an upstairs lavatory with a highly polished mahogany seat as big as a table, stretching from wall to wall, with a still brighter polished pull-up brass handle and a very elaborately patterned blue and white china pan. This lavatory was for the ladies only, the men only had a very primitive out-of-doors arrangement in the shrubbery.

In 1953, when the last of the Buddicom estate was sold, the Court was in a very poor state of repair and when Mr John Young bought it, the top floor was removed and the roof lowered.

Hill View, formerly 'The Masons Arms', photographed in the 1930s.

DWELLINGS

There were four other dwellings listed that are actually in Ticklerton. A house opposite Ticklerton Hall which was a public house called 'The Masons Arms' (255/20)

It probably opened when "The Horseshoes" was closed, as by 1871, Edwin Harley is recorded as a publican/labourer. Ten years later there was no mention of a publican or licensed victualler, and it reverted once again to being a private house. This was later the home of the Attenborough family who came to the village in 1918. Thomas Attenborough was the Eaton Estate overseer, forester and gamekeeper to Mr Hanbury Sparrow who, at that time, owned Ticklerton Hall, New Hall, Harton, Whitefields and the Edge Wood from Harton to Longville.

Thomas Attenborough. c.1922.

Two of the blacksmith's sons, Willy and Teddy Evans, c.1890.

DWELLINGS

There were also a pair of cottages at Hisbeach (253/19) on the road towards Eaton and the last of the four was, as far as can be found from the records, always the village blacksmith's house (257/21). It continued to operate as such for over 100 years. The Evans family were there in the latter part of the 19th and early 1900s. Today it is a private house, still looking much as it would have done 150 years ago.

The old Smithy, Ticklerton

Along the road from Ticklerton towards Eaton, the village School (263/14) was built in 1863. This is described in more detail in the later chapter on "Parish Life".

BIRTLEY

Taking the road from Ticklerton towards Hatton, the first cottage was the third of the public houses, the Pheasant Inn (162/23). The earliest record of there being a licensed victualler as tenant is in 1851 and this continued as such until sometime just prior to 1881. This, together with the other two, were no doubt much in use by the workmen building the railway from Craven Arms to Much Wenlock.

The final days of old Richard Davies, the last publican, tell a pretty gruesome tale. His wife had died and he was in his 70s, carrying on a bit of farming. The baker called on his weekly round, could not make anyone hear but, as the door was open, went in and found him lying dead on the bed. He had been there for a long time because, as the locals put it, "the rats had started on him"!

The pub had been thatched and where the garden is today, had been a cobbled yard where horses and carts drew up. After Richard

DWELLINGS

Davies' death, the Buddicoms bought it, removed the thatch and tiled the roof. Edward Hall, who had been living up on Heighwood Common with his father William, then moved in. He worked on the Buddicom Estate, as did his son Harold, who continued to live there until about 1960, when he moved to Hope Bowdler. The house was reputed to be haunted, and although the ghost noises were believed to be nothing more than wind under the floorboards, none of his family would ever go and spend the night there after his Mother died.

For a time it went under the fancy name of 'Birtley Villa'. Now owned by Dick Phillips, it has been considerably renovated and altered.

Pheasant Cottage, Birtley. One time known as 'The Pheasant Inn' and 'Birtley Villa'.

There were two other small cottages (170/24,662/26) on either side of the road before the Hatton Gate toll house and where the road doubles back towards Soudley. All traces of one have now completely disappeared. Behind 'Greystones'(163/25) there were traces of the old ridge and furrow cultivation. Further evidence is to be seen in a field behind the old School House which was ploughed for the first time in 1986, and the old ground formation could be clearly seen.

DWELLINGS

HATTON

HATTON- the Hearth Tax entry for 1672

	Firehearths	11(£)	s - (probable location etc)
Mr Urian Baldwyn	6	0	12 - Upper House farm Ch Ward 1669
Mr John Hammond	3	0	6 - Workhouse Ch Ward 1674
Thomas Bray	3	0	6 - Hatton Manor
John Davies	1	0	2 - Lower House Ch Ward 1682
	13	1	6

In 1841 Hatton included 644 acres with a rateable value of £407-5-0.

There are four farms located within a few hundred yards of each other. On the west side of the road lies a small farm, about 100 acres, that was known as Hatton Manor farm. (585/30)

It was a picturesque black and white house with fine old brick chimneys with spiral ornamentation. To this day some of the original exterior can be seen on the road side of the house. It has a small staircase with pierced balusters and a knobbed newel post of distinctly Jacobean character, which places its building in the early 1600s, or possibly even earlier.

Hatton Manor farm.

Upper Farm (654/28) is some 200 acres and the farmhouse is of stone, a building of late Elizabethan character. There are immense oak beams in the kitchen which instead of being chamfered, are moulded along the lower edges, resting on great posts with bracket heads all cut out of solid. The roof had, instead of tiles, thick stone slates. One of the outbuildings had a stone in the wall

inscribed "E.A.A.17." (Edward and Ann Acton), the lower part has weathered badly, but the date appears to have been 1761. There is a remarkably wide fireplace in the kitchen. The oak panelling from here is now in Acton Scott Hall.

Brian Baldwin of Hatton, who was bailiff in 1673, probably lived in this house.

Upper Farm, Hatton.

Of the other two farms nearby, Lower Farm (653/32) was 200 acres. Middle Farm (650/31), about 70 acres, is now farmed in with Upper Farm. A fifth farm, Hatton Grove (596/33), located near the Acton Scott parish boundary was another small holding. This is one of the few areas in the Parish where traces of ridge and furrow are to be found.

Once again we find there are no cottages for farm workers, other than a stone built house (652/29) which was at one time two cottages. It had timber filled gables and oak mullioned windows. The stone roof slabs which, until 1912, covered the roof were used to pave the footpaths. Over the door there is an old stone inscribed 'H - V.E. 1679'. The 'H' probably stands for Hammond, as a John Hammond of Hatton was bailiff of Wenlock in 1675.

This house was formerly the Parish workhouse until, in 1838, the Union Workhouse in Church Stretton was built to house 110 people. Thomas Benbow, agriculturist, and his wife Alice were living there from at least 1817 and, in 1833 the first reference appears to them as 'Innkeeper'. It then became known as the Blue Bell Inn and was run by Alice Benbow for the next twenty years or so. It is worth considering here for a moment as to whether her husband, who is not mentioned in the census details (although her eight children are), was related to the Benbow family who from 1823 to 1877 were landlords of the famous 'Admiral Benbow' at Ruyton X1 Towns.

By 1851 her eldest son Mathew is recorded as being a Farm Bailiff and from 1861 to 1881 her two sons William and Edward were tenants of Hatton Grove, but there is no mention of Alice who may well have died. In any case, the Blue Bell ceased to exist as a pub from about 1861.

'The Blue Bell Inn', formerly the Parish workhouse, now a private house.

The state and upkeep of roads, particularly in rural areas, was always a major problem and in 1556, under a Statute of Mary 1 (married to Philip 11 of Spain), the upkeep of road maintenance became the responsibility of Parishes, with two unpaid and unqualified people being appointed as road surveyors. They had to find people to do the work and raise the necessary monies.

By 1700 the roads, in general, were in an apalling state and demands of a developing road transport compelled the government and local people to look for a means of making travel not only better, but also possible. An Act of Parliament allowed for lengths of road to be let out to Trusts to care for them. Income was collected from tolls collected from the travelling public who were stopped at gates or 'pikes' - hence the name Turnpike.

The gate keepers occupied small houses adjoining the Gate and often the keeper would have a second job. The Toll House (557/27) at Hatton Gate is on the road between Hatton and Ticklerton. Although tolls were introduced in the county from about 1792, this Toll House does not appear in the 1841 census, but from 1851 to 1871 Sarah Hill is listed as Tollkeeper and grocer. It is also known that she used to make and sell mead.

With the opening of the railway, the toll roads would have ceased to operate

The non-turnpike roads were maintained by a levy on house-holders and landowners which was, in 1827, 6d in the £1 of the rateable value. In addition, farmers had to 'give' labour and carts for roadwork, varying from 2 to 18 days a year, according to the size of their holding.

There is an unusual inscription commenting upon the state of the roads in the late 18th century on the tombstone of Thomas Corfield of Ticklerton who died in 1793. "He is the author and sole cause of the mending of the roads in his (bad very very bad) neighbourhood".

The old Toll House, Hatton Gate.

DWELLINGS

SOUDLEY and HEIGHWOOD

The various officials who carried out the census every ten years from 1841 did not agree on the order in which to record the various houses, nor could they decide just where to place many of the properties in Soudley and Heighwood/Heywood/Haywood, all spellings being used from time to time. The early Parish registers also refer to Aiwood, Aiewood and Eywood. However, they all seem to have been included under Ticklerton, but the variation in the order in which they were recorded makes it impossible, today, to be certain who actually lived in some of the houses at different times.

While there were in the township of Ticklerton a few cottages for workers, in the rest of the parish the only lodgings for the majority of farm workers, for them to be close to their work, were in the main farmhouses.

There were two areas, however, that followed a totally different pattern of housing – Soudley and Heighwood. Here there were well over twenty small cottages, many semi-detached. A large number were built towards the end of the 18th century, with many dating from a lot earlier. Their construction was similar in nearly every case, being built of stone and with thatched roofs, later to be replaced with slates or tiles. There was only one pair of cottages, Wayside Cottage, built of red brick in the whole parish.

Just why this area should have had so many people living there can, to a certain extent, be explained by the growth and development of the quarry at Soudley. This provided work for a large number of men, with large quantities of stone being required for building and roads. No less than six cottages were occupied by stone masons during the 1800s. Fifteen were listed for agricultural labourers who, because there were no large farms there, would have had some way to go to work each day, but that would have been quite normal and is an explanation for a great many of the footpaths that criss-cross the fields to this day.

Looking first at Soudley. Apart from a few small holdings, nearly all the cottages were occupied by farm workers and owned by William Pinches, the principal landowner who lived in Ticklerton Court at the time of the tithe apportionment around 1840. Some of these are still standing, and although modernised, still look much as they would have done when first built.

Following the road from Hope Bowdler towards Birtley, the first house in the Parish was Stone House Farm, but when the boundaries were altered in 1988 it was included in Hope Bowdler parish. Stone House Farm (128/41) was never more than a small-holding and today operates as a market garden. Alongside was a cottage, long since demolished, that has a reference on the old Tithe map of "Court House" (126/44). It is possible,while no means certain, (why else was it so called?) that there may have been a much earlier building on this site that could have been used for the Manorial Court hearings, the details of which are referred to in an earlier chapter. Further along, on the left, is Soudley Cottage (124/35 & 36), originally semi-detached and sometime known as Pool Cottage and Ivydene. The Ticklerton side (Ivydene) was occupied in 1871 by Walter Lewis, a tailor who also ran a sub-post office in his front room. This continued to be Soudley Post office until after the Second World War and Mrs Eastment was the last postmistress there. The Post Office was then moved across the road to Wayside Cottage (138/37) and run, with a small shop, by Mrs Tom Miles until her death in 1982, when the Post Office was closed.

Soudley Cottage, originally semi-detached with Soudley Post Office in the right hand end.
(Also known as Pool Cottage and Ivydene)

Several of the Soudley cottages listed in the Appendix have been demolished and all traces of their existence have disappeared. Their original locations are marked on the map and the references are 133/42, 132/43, 140/40A. No new houses have been built there this century.

DWELLINGS

Up the Birtley road were three small stone cottages, Yew Tree Cottage (139/38) and another (140/39) that, although it appears on the Tithe map and in the census returns, was demolished before the end of the last century.

Wayside Cottage. Formerly semi-detached and the sub-Post Office and shop until 1982.

Yew Tree Cottage

The Alders, as it appeared in the mid 1980s, before alteration.

The third of the cottages was The Alders (142/40). William Hall moved there around 1883 from his cottage on Heighwood. He, like his son Edward and grandson Harold, worked for the Ticklerton Estate. By 1985 it had become derelict and was sold for £29,000, about the same amount as 747 acres (including nine cottages and seven farms) fetched when the Estate had been sold in 1953. The cottage has now been extensively modernised.

The area described as Heighwood needs to be looked at in two parts. The cottages alongside the old track or 'back lane' up beside the old Soudley quarry and on Common road were, in the main, all connected with quarrying. The area would have been a hive of industry with cart loads of stone being hauled from the quarry to all parts of the Parish, and much further afield, for building and road mending. The narrow track used to become badly rutted in bad weather and, in 1905, the road running from Soudley Post Office past the Common Farm towards Wall became choked up and fell into disuse. The only way for the Heighwood dwellers was up the steep, rocky lane past the quarry. It was very dangerous in winter, coal carts got stuck and there was at least one serious accident. Tradesmen refused to send delivery carts up there. The District Council refused to deal with the matter because they said it was only an occupational road. Eventually the work was carried out by the Buddicom Estate and subscriptions from local people.

DWELLINGS

Jones's Cottage c.1890. This is typical of the thatched, stone cottages of the area.

Just above the quarry, adjoining the first cottage, (97/45) was a tiny Methodist Chapel. There are many people who remember attending services there as children. Today it is now part of a modernised cottage/house on the site.

There were several cottages up this lane, some had a bit of land attached (or managed to rent some) and supplemented there everyday job with some cattle and crops. All but two of the cottages have been demolished.(100/46, 101/47, 105/48)

To the right of the quarry, above Soudley pools, is Quarry Cottage (95/49) and further on, a track leads to the Common Lane. Here is a most interesting old house.

It was, at times, referred to as 'The Barracks' (94/50 & 51). The reason for this name is not certain, but it is possible that during the period when the Royalists and Parliamentarians were fighting the Civil War in and around Shrewsbury, (as well as many other parts of Shropshire) between 1642-45, Royalist troops were garrisoned there. There is a reference in *Civil Strife in the Midlands by R E Sherwood* that refers to "King Charles continuance at Shrewsbury (1642) soon caused considerable inconvenience and hardship to the inhabitants of the town and surrounding district".

Another name it was given was "Sebastopol", (for which I can find no explanation) and in the census of 1861 as 'two chimneys'.Today, it is called "Woodside Cottage" and is, in fact. three cottages in one.

Quarry Cottage

Woodside Cottage, Sebastopol or The Barracks. The back view shows where a further building
was joined on - possibly stables - if, or when, troops were garrisoned there.

DWELLINGS

The other part of Heighwood is on the high ground and many of the houses and small farms probably date from around 1804 (but in some cases very much earlier) when 300 acres of Common land was enclosed to form the seperate farms and smallholdings that we have today. Claybrook, Common Farm, The Hollies, Mount Flirt, The Saplings, Whitefields, Greenfields etc.

This enclosure of the common deprived the cottagers and a great many poor people of much of their livelihood and must have been a bitter blow to them. None of the farms are notable for their architecture, but many families have occupied and farmed the land for generations. Some of the cottages have gone completely, and the stone from at least one was carted back to Ticklerton to be used in building the pseudo Tudor house, Meadowbrook, in 1934.

Whitefields Farm, known as Eatonglebe in earlier times

There are many references to Claybrook (288/60) In 1815/17 a Thos Wenlock, labourer, is registered as 'of Claybrook' and in 1821 John and Ann Hughes, a farmer, were there. Wenlock may have lived in the farmhouse, or in a cottage nearby that was demolished before 1841, when the tithe map was prepared. The farm was some 112 acres.

The field named 'Brick Kiln' confirms that brick making was a thriving business there until 1857 when the last kiln was finally demolished. The ponds that were formed from the clay excavations were stocked with fish - eel, perch, tench and carp - and small copses were planted to protect them. Today it is still possible to identify where they were but, sadly, they no longer contain fish.

Claybrook Farm, photographed c.1880.

Common Farm (1/59) was around 114 acres and Mount Flirt (15/52) 60 acres. There are many references in the registers to The Hollies (62/53) and, from 1816 was lived in by a succession of labourers, Thos Bennet, Thos Mawn, Martin Wallader and Wm Posturn. In 1841 it is shown to be a farm of some 60 acres.

Mount Flirt

DWELLINGS

On the opposite side of the road to Common Farm was a small cottage and croft (43/58), with a well. It is said that there was once a tiny Methodist Chapel built there too. However, both are now demolished.

Greenfields (28/57) was never more than a cottage and about 15 acres. The Saplings (306/61) was not built until 1857. It is obvious from the diary of Rev R J Buddicom that he and his wife, Elizabeth, used to visit The Saplings often and from a stone found in the end wall of the old house which reads - 'B R J x E 1857' - it shows that they had the house built and reallocated some of the Common Farm and Claybrook land to make up the 85 acres that went with the farm at the time of the 1861 census. The original house was built of the red brick, made at the nearby kilns, and it is likely that these were the last made there before the kiln was demolished early in 1857.

The affection that Elizabeth Buddicom had for the house is shown when on March 18th 1859, as a very sick woman, she went by carriage to The Saplings 'to bid it goodbye'. She was to die just two months later.

All these small farms were, nevertheless, large enough to accomodate workmen and servants living in, as well as the farmer's own family.

DWELLINGS

UPPER MILLICHOPE

Until fairly recent times all the farms and cottages in Upper Millichope were in Eaton Parish but, with no direct road connecting them with the rest of the parish, they naturally inclined towards Hungerford and Millichope and, eventually, joined up with them. There is, however, ample evidence of rights of way and old roadways to be found on the tithe maps, by way of Jacob's Ladder, Cuckoos Nest, Spellers Coppice and passing to the south west of Upper Millichope, towards Millichope Hall.

However, one house – Forester's Lodge – is more than worthy of description here. A remarkable old house dating back to Norman times (c.1280), when it was the house of the Head Forester charged with all the royal hunting grounds in the Long Forest and was also responsible for the supply of venison to the Priory at Much Wenlock.

Forester's Lodge.

In Medieval England a forester needed a strong, well protected house which he could easily defend against all-comers, such was his unpopularity with the people who bitterly resented what they saw as the King's greed and the denial of their own rights and liberties.

The impressive stone walls of the house, six feet thick in the lower part, and scarcity of windows clearly indicates the fortress-like defensive nature of the building. This made it impregnable from local attack in those days. It functioned much like a castle keep. The main living area was on the first floor and, originally, the only means of entrance was through a doorway at first floor level. The ground floor or 'undercroft' was only accessible from inside, either from the upper floor down a stone spiral staircase or through a trapdoor.

The Lodge was an oblong stone construction 42' x 29'. Today there is an entry at ground level, through a doorway with a semi-circular arch with a ball-flower ornamentation. These were re-used

The ground level doorway installed later.

The outline of the original doorway can be clearly seen at first floor level

ball flower stones, possibly coming from the 14th century Chapel at Upper Millichope. The original first floor doorway is now blocked, but its outline can be clearly seen by the quoin stones. There would have been an outside staircase of simple design that could easily have been retracted in times of attack.

The two small slit-lights for the spiral staircase can be seen in the western corner, where the wall bulges slightly. The third, wider, slit lights the first floor landing.

The framework of the gable end is not original and was probably installed when the Lodge was re-roofed in the 17th century.

The Hall window on the first floor, N.E. side, is a two light window with a roll moulded monolithic stone central mullion. There is another similar window on the S.E. side, this has a vertical timber in place of the central mullion.

The interior of the ground floor undercroft would have been used for storage and preparation of venison, its thick walls ensuring an even temperature at all times of the year. At a later date, when it was used as a farm kitchen, a chimney stack was added with a fire place and bread oven. The ceiling joists are massive, many being whole trees squared off.

The timber framed screen at the end of the living area. The central doorway leads to the attic.

The original stone spiral staircase has been blocked off and a later staircase built, which is used today.

The main living area in the Lodge was the Hall, on the first floor, but there is a mystery surrounding the fact that there are no signs of any heating or where any cooking was done, both of which would have been vital. There are suggestions that in the N.W. wall, which was destroyed at some time, there may have been a chimney stack and, if so, probably a lavatory chute too.

The west end of the hall is partitioned off by a timber-framed screen with three doorways, the central one giving access to the staircase leading to the attic roof space. This attic space was not usable until the re-roofing was carried out in the 17th century, at which time a small fireplace was built into the thickness of the S.E. wall, utilising the kitchen chimney stack.

The main window is of considerable interest. Defence is provided by the very narrow lights and the bar-hole positioned in the middle of the central mullion, with bolt holes in the window jambs. Yet, although defence would have been the first priority, it is elegantly designed and decorated, with window seats built into the embrasure. A similar 'sitting window', in a less complete form, is on the S.E. side.

The N.E. window. The narrowness of the lights was a defence feature.

A similar 'sitting window' on the S.E. side.

The remains of the original stone newel post of the spiral staircase can be seen in the N.W. corner. The doorway giving access from the landing to the hall, has a draw-bolt for security. The visible steps relate to the 17th century alterations. In the S.W. corner is the door jamb of the original inner door through which access to the hall from the external stairs was gained, again with a bar and bolt hole.

The timber framed partitions have a good quality wattle-and-daub infil.

The main part of the house is generally accepted as dating from about 1280 but, after about 450 years, it must have fallen into a ruinous state of repair. A major refurbishment was carried out with the addition of a chimney stack, re-roofing, the attic storey and the very early, cramped, stone spiral staircase enlarged.

Today, it is connected to the present farmhouse through a linking block cut through the six foot thick wall of the old house, and the undercroft ground floor serves as part of the overall farmhouse accomodation.

The wattle and daub infil

The attic fireplace, probably installed in the 17th century. The rush-light tapers have left marks on the wooden lintel.

DWELLINGS

OUTSIDE THE PARISH

Although being just outside the Eaton Parish boundary, reference is made to the following houses as they are not only of considerable interest, but also formed part of the estates owned by landlords of parish property already mentioned.
The 'firehearth' details refer to 1672.

ACTON SCOTT

	Firehearths	ll(£)	s	
Richard Pryce	10	1	0	Acton Scott Hall

ACTON SCOTT HALL

The Hall is a picturesque house of mellow brickwork with stone mullions and quoins. There was a house on the site as far back as Henry 111 (1216-72), but of this little remains except the massive stone masonry in the basement and part of the wall by the entrance. The existing structure is Elizabethan and dates from about 1580.

Acton Scott Hall

DWELLINGS

ALCASTON

	Firehearths	11(£)	s - (probable location etc)
Ness Hill	6	0	12 - Manor Farm
Edward Baugh	8	0	16 - Moat Farm
William Jones	4	0	8 - Pride Hill (demolished

in the 1930s)

ALCASTON MANOR

The Manor is a magnificent example of an Elizabethan house of 1570/80. The illustration shows it in all its glory before the right wing was demolished, possibly as the result of a fire.

The Moat Farm, opposite the Manor House, was built of brick on a stone basement in about 1650. However, recent re-roofing has revealed moulded timbers of a 15th or early 16th century date, indicating that the present house incorporated an earlier one

The moat is only filled in wet seasons. It can be argued that the Moat Farm was originally part of a Norman *motte and bailey* and was subsequently converted into a moated farmhouse. There are medieval fishponds below the house.

In the early 1950s a Royal Navy minesweeper was named "Alcaston". It was later sold to Australia and re-named "Snipe". There are details of this to be found in Acton Scott church.

The old Manor House at Alcaston, before the right wing was demolished.

PINCHES and BUDDICOM

The first part of this book has looked at what life may have been like between the time of the Domesday Book and the 19th century. Where possible this has been linked to this area and, in a great many instances, it has been possible to particularise it to families and houses in the Parish.

The end of the last century and the first part of this one was diligently catalogued by Lilian Buddicom (later Mrs Hayward) and it is with the benefit of her many journals, local records, plus the memories of present inhabitants that it is possible to paint a fairly accurate picture of life in and around the Parish.

It is divided up into sections, some overlapping with each other and some linking back to earlier chapters, this is unavoidable in endeavouring to recapture the way life was lived by the people of the parish.

We have seen how families like the Jenks, Palmers, Wards, Loxdale Warren and, much earlier, the Prior of Wenlock Priory, Earl Roger and his family played important roles as farmers and landlords. From the end of the 17th Century, and for nearly 300 years, two families in particular were to be closely involved and part of the Parish. They were the Pinches and Buddicoms. The Pinches were a Shropshire family and while little is recorded about them, there is a lot of the Buddicom history available.

However, it was not until 1845 that the two families came together, but much of the earlier Buddicom history has been included because of the interesting glimpses it gives of 16-18th Century life. Thus, it is with the Pinches and Buddicoms that this part of the book naturally begins.

THE PINCHES

The first reference to the Pinches family in Ticklerton comes at the beginning of the 17th century when Margaret. daughter of Thomas Lewis of Ticklerton, married Fulk Pinches. Margaret was the eldest daughter and one of three co-heiresses, and it seems probable that her marriage to Fulk, who came from Plaish in the Parish of Cardington, is how the Pinches came to be owners of so much land and property in and around Ticklerton. A glance at the family tree shows clearly how nearly all the family were either 'of Ticklerton' or 'of Harton', and most were baptised and buried in Eaton church. As well as living at Ticklerton, other members of the family lived and farmed at both Harton and Hatton, their names occurring frequently in the Church records and census returns.

PINCHES FAMILY

```
John Pinches        Thomas Lewis
of Plaish(1572)     of Ticklerton
     1                   1
Fulk(1607)      -   Margaret Lewis
of Ticklerton
                    1
Richard         -   Alice...
of Ticklerton
                    1
 ┌──────────┬─────────┬──────┐
William    John     Jane    Mary
of Tick.
  1
  ┌───────────────┐
       William  -  Anne....
                   1
 ┌─────────┬─────────┬──────┐
Richard    John    Elinor   Mary
of Tick.           b 1688   b 1689
d 1754
  1
  ┌──────────────┐
       Richard  -  Margaret Hotchkiss m.1676
                1
 ┌─────────┬─────────┬──────┐
William   John    Margaret  Anne
b 1678    b 1682  b 1691    b 1695
d 1752    d 1740
  1
  1
  ┌──────────────┐
       William  -  Mary Bright
       of Tick. 1  d 1724 aged 39
                1  m Esther Hallegrove
                1
 ┌─────────┬─────────┐
Richard   William  Humphrey
b 1719    b 1721   b 1722   4
d 1761             d 1805
  1
  ┌──────────────┐
       Richard  -  Mary Oxenbold
       of Harton   b 1718
                1  m 1747
                   d 1811 at Harton aged 93
                1
 ┌─────────┬─────────┬──────┐
Elizabeth William  Richard
b 1750    b 1751   b 1753
d 1822    d 1815   d 1789 at Harton
at Harton at Ticklerton
                   1
       William  -  Mary Bird m 1800
       of Tick.    d 1844
                1
 ┌─────────┬─────────┐
William   Mary    Elizabeth
b 1802    b 1806  b 1809
d 1849    d 1846  m 1845 Rev R J Buddicom
                  d 1859
```

PINCHES AND BUDDICOM

William Pinches c.1800   Mary Pinches c.1800

Thus, for nearly three centuries, there would have been a Pinches presence and influence in the Parish. The archives hold copies of William Pinches' meticulously kept, and beautifully written, account books of the estate, details of rates and the statute number of days required to be worked by each farmer and landowner in estate duty, road mending and the like.

The last generation of the Ticklerton branch of the Pinches family were the three children of William and Mary born in the early 1800s.

William, the eldest, never married. He was a fine big man with a florid complexion and was very keen on all kinds of sport. He kept the greater part of the United Hounds pack in kennels at Ticklerton Court. He was also a great naturalist, fisherman and an expert fly fisher. He used to shoot 7 or 8 miles of the Edge Woods as well as outlying covers on the estate. In those days there were plenty of woodcocks to vary the bag. One day he killed two marten cats, an animal with a fine bushy tail and about as big as a fair sized cat. (these would have been Pine martens, now extinct in this area). Many a polecat also died the death from his gun, which he described as 'this savage animal has not one redeeming quality and, when chased, like the American skunk emits a perfume by no means suggestive of mignonette'. He, with the Rev Robert J Buddicom, got some red grouse from Yorkshire and turned them out on the Long Mynd, the first ever known there, although there were always some black game.

PINCHES AND BUDDICOM

His father was doubtless a farmer of some renown and there is an interesting note from The Globe of February 13th 1812 which reads *'On Friday was slaughtered by Mr J Griffith, a butcher of Sowdley, a noted, handsome fat ox which was bred and fed by William Pinches of Ticklerton. This animal weighed 21 score and 10lbs a quarter upon average had 225 lbs of rough fat and sold for £67-10-0'.* (This weighed 17- cwt.and J Griffith was living in the cottage now known as Lilac Cottage, Hope Bowdler.)

William died in 1849, intestate. His younger sister, Mary, never married and she also died intestate in 1846. This left Elizabeth. She married the Rev R J Buddicom in 1845, and as the heiress to the Pinches estate, this now passed to her husband, and any connection with the Pinches family and Ticklerton ceased after 250 years.

Elizabeth Pinches as a young girl.

PINCHES AND BUDDICOM

THE BUDDICOMS

When the Ticklerton Estate passed from the Pinches to the Buddicoms, through the marriage of Elizabeth to the Rev Robert Joseph Buddicom, there began a period lasting more than a hundred years during which generations of the Buddicom family were to have a major influence in the area through the land and property they owned, their involvement in Church affairs and village life in general. In their different ways they could be described as a 'colourful' family and, before the next chapter recording 'The Buddicom Years', a brief reference to some of the exploits and adventures of their antecedents is worth recalling.

The Buddicom family originally came from Somerset but, by the 17th century, they were living at Northam in Devonshire. In 1686 George Buddicom married Elizabeth Thorne. He was certainly a sea-faring man as, upon his death in 1715, he left a ship to his brother Robert.

Robert's son owned and commanded a privateer*, the 'Joanna'. In 1714 he was captured by the King of Morocco and held in slavery for 7 years in Algerine. The description of the treatment and conditions endured by him and hundreds of other Christian slaves was horrific. Finally, along with 26 other Masters of Ships and 290 other Englishmen he was *redeemed by George 1 in exchange for gifts of firearms, powder and other military stores*, and returned to England in November 1721. He married Martha Packer in the same year and, later, died at sea. He was worth £13,000. (This gives some idea of the sort of money that was made by privateers).

His eldest son, William (1727-1802) was, at the age of 51, Captain of the privateer 'Intrepid' and was granted permission by George 11 to *"apprehend, sieze and take ships etc belonging to the French King"*. The document granting him permission, taken from the Admiralty Court List 1V, Letter of Marque list Vol.36 dated 30 December 1778 reads:

DEED 18572

Source - Record Office (Chancery Lane).
30 December 1778

Appeared personally John Mitchell of Jaffries Square, St Mary Axe, merchant on behalf of Captain William Buddicom now at Liverpool and produced a warrant from the Right Honble the Lords Commissioners for executing the office of Lord High Admiral of Great

---

*Privateers were the successors to the buccaneers of the 17th century, and even with the official authorisation of "letters of marque", frequently degenerated into piracy. In 1856 all European countries (except Spain) renounced privateering)

Captain William Buddicom, 1727-1802.

Britain and Ireland for the granting of Letters of Marque and Reprizals to him the said William Buddicom for the Apprehending Siezing and Taking the Ships vessels and goods belonging to the French King, his vassals and subjects and others inhabiting within his countries territories or Dominions and in pursuance of His Majestys instructions made the following declaration to wit that his the said William Buddicom ship is called the INTREPID is belonging to the port of Liverpool is of the burthen of 150 tons is square sterned a Billet head and three masts. That the said William Buddicom goeth commander of her that she is mounted with 16 carriage guns carrying shot of 9 pounds weight and 16 Swivel guns, is navigated with 60 men, has 30 small arms 30 cutlases 30 barrels of powder 20 rounds of great shot and about 1 ton weight of small shot, that the said ship is victualled for 6 months, has two suits of sails, 4 anchors, 4 cables and about 1 ton weight of spare cordage. That John Burrows goes Mate or Lieutenant, John Brown gunner, William Harrison Boatswain, John Denton carpenter, John Banks cook and Thomas Lancet surgeon of the said ship that Thomas Hodgson, James Lowe, Greenwood and Crosbie, Edward Grayson, Richard Wilding, Thomas Manley, John Webster and John Copland of Liverpool Merchants of the said Captain William Buddicom are the Owners of Letters of the said ship.

A vessel of this size would carry her guns on Upper Deck. Swivel guns ($\frac{1}{2}$ pounders) mounted on bulwarks.

She was some 70 feet long on the gun deck, 57 feet on the keel, 22 foot beam, 9 foot depth.

The guns of 1778 were the long type. A 9 pounder averaged 8' long, 26 cwt and 4.22" calibre. Service charge 4lb 8oz of powder.

The cost - ready for sea - £1,750 (hull & spars) £1,000 (rigging & stores) - £2,750.

(The name of the surgeon - Thomas Lancet - may well have been a nom-de-plume, as it seems almost too apt to be true!)

On March 31st 1779 he was surprised and taken by 2 French ships of 64 guns each and 2 frigates and taken to Brest where he was kept prisoner for 7 months. Then in May 1780 he was again taken by the Count de Grasse's squadron consisting of 25 sail of the line, 3 frigates, 2 cutters and a schooner, 4 leagues off the coast of Tobago which was being blockaded by the French. He was kept prisoner on board for 37 days before being landed at Martinico where the French General, the Marquis de Boulie, with whom he had been acquainted, obtained leave for him to proceed to St Kitts in exchange for a French prisioner.

Earlier, in 1753/4 he had married Jane Langerwood and they had 22 or 23 children of whom all but 3 died in infancy. The eldest surviving child, Robert Joseph, born in 1756 spent his childhood in his grandfather Langerwood's house in Rotherhithe, London until in July 1866 the house was burnt down in the great Rotherhithe fire and they lost all their possessions. He moved to Liverpool with his Mother and became apprenticed to a surgeon, Mr H Shortecliffe. In due course he too became a surgeon and must have benefited from his father's privateering against the French, as "he had charge of Napoleonic prisoners of war" and was presented by the town, in recognition of his services, with a tea and coffee service in silver.

Dr Robert Joseph was described as one of the shrewdest and the cleverest men, as well as being one of the most unselfish and warmhearted, but he had a very rough edge to his tongue when annoyed. As a professional man he was held in high esteem. However, in 1780, it appears that the girl he wished to marry was about to wed another when he faced her with "If you do not come away with me now, you will never see me again". She, Frances, daughter of Robert Pedder (an attorney) and Jane Tarleton chose him and they ran away and got married. They must have made it up with their in-laws as their younger son was named Edward Tarleton and the elder one Robert Pedder, incorporating both surnames. Their son, Robert, was the first Buddicom to enter the Church and became Rector of Everton, Liverpool and Principal of St Bees Theological College. He married Ellin Barber and they had eight children, one of whom, William Barber was born in Liverpool in 1816.

PINCHES AND BUDDICOM

William Barber had an outstanding career connected with the railways. He was locomotive superintendent of the Grand Junction Railway in 1840/1 at a salary of ú500 a year, building the Glasgow, Paisley and Greenock railway. He then designed and built an improved version of the 'Crewe' type engine, widely used in this country and France. He went to work in France, formed a company and was closely involved with the opening of the Le Havre, Rouen, Caen and Cherbourg lines in 1843. By 1851 his factory employed 2,000 men building engines. The 'Buddicom' engine as it was called, was exhimited in the Mulhouse museum. In 1847 he was awarded the Cross of the Legion of Honour by King Louis Philippe of France. He later returned to this country and must have had a link, albeit brief, with the Parish as he was named in connection with the gift of land for Eaton school in 1863. In 1874, he was High Sheriff of Flintshire, where he died at Mold in 1887.

"Saint Pierre" No.33. William Barber Buddicom's engine.

BUDDICOM FAMILY

```
                    Captain William Buddicom
                           1727-1802
                              1
                              1
              Dr Robert Joseph - Frances Pedder
              b 1756            1-m1780
              d 1842            1
                       _____1_____
                      1                               1
              Rev Robert Pedder - Ellin Barber   Edward Tarleton
              b 1781             1-m 1814          b 1783
              d 1846             1 d 1858           d 1858
                              _____1_____
                             1                                      1
              Rev Robert Joseph - Sophia Rufford      William Barber &
              b 1815             1 b 1818             b 1816   other children
              d 1895             1 d 1842
                                 1 m (2) Elizabeth Pinches 1845
                                 1        d 1859 aged 51
                                 1 m (3) Ann Landars 20/5/1860
                                 1             d 1880
                                 1 m (4) Kate Clarke
                                 1        d 1914
                                 1
                  William Squire - Elizabeth Haughton Hornby
                   b 1840           b 1842
                   d 1922          1-m 1866
                                   1 d 1914
                           _____1_____
                          1                                   1
                  Robert Arthur - Laura Finlay  Lilian Holland - John Le Mesurier
                   b 1874         b 1877         b 1878          m 1918    Hayward
                   d 1951        1-m (1) 1900    d 1964          d 1922
                                 1 m (2) Hilda Lewis
          _____1_____
         1              1                                  1
  Jacintha Laura   Robert Prosper - Monica Wheeler   Guinever Laura Olivia
  b 1901   May     b 1904  Gedye   m (1) 1929        b 1907    Norsworthy
                   d 1968          1-m (2) 1936 Cynthia Arundel d 1989
                                   1 m (3) Anne Marie
                                   1 m (4) Mrs Pearson
                                   1
                            Jennifer - Simon Brown
                             b 1937
```

THE BUDDICOM YEARS

Rev Robert Joseph Buddicom, 1815-1895.

The first of the family to be associated with Shropshire was Robert Joseph, the eldest son of Robert and Ellin, who was at Shrewsbury School, under Dr Samuel Butler, where he gained a first or second in Greek and distinguished himself in classics.

His first marriage was to his cousin Sophia Rufford, a beautiful if somewhat self-willed lady, a talented musician. The marriage was opposed by his family and was not a happy one. He had entered the church and had the living at Smethcote, near Leebotwood. It was a tiny living and the church itself was in a very bad state of delapidation.

They had a son, William Squire, born on January 9th 1840. Sophia died two years later at the early age of 24.

However, he was not one of the number who remain faithful to the memory of the dead, always fond of feminine society, agreeable

Elizabeth at the time of her marriage.

in manner and witty in conversation and desirous of pleasing, he soon became engaged to Elizabeth Pinches, a plain woman 7 years his senior. She lived at Ticklerton Court with her Mother, her brother William and sister Mary. She was a 37 when she married on 7th August 1845 and went to live at Smethcote.

The occasion of their marriage and the rejoicings of the parishoners is recorded in Eddowe's Journal of August 27th 1845.

"on the return of the Rev R J Buddicom and his amiable bride to Smethcott, the happy event was early announced to the residents by the firing of cannon and the ringing of bells, followed by the celebrated Dorrington brass band in their uniform, visiting the adjoining places and playing in first rate style. At every approach to the rectory, triumphal arches decorated with flowers were erected.

A large pavilion was erected and at half past one 100 individuals sat down to a good dinner. Afterwards the order to form into a procession was given and at three o'clock it proceeded to meet their worthy vicar and his lovely bride. The horses were taken from the carriage and the happy pair were conveyed to the rectory in the following order - Large Flag, with 'Welcome home' inscribed, band of music, friends – upwards of 300, three a breast and then the carriage drawn by 24 villagers. On entering the vill- age, twelve rounds of cannon were discharged, amidst the hearty cheers of nearly 2,000 individuals. The procession then returned to the pavilion, when upwards of 300 sat down to a bountiful dinner. At six o'clock the pavilion was cleared for the enjoyment of man's greatest pleasure 'the fair sex', and much praise is due to the ladies making the arrangements. Nearly 500 partook of tea sweetened and enriched with the cream of the valley, with an abun- dance of plum cake. There then followed many speeches and toasts and the display of fireworks by Mr G H Nightingale of Shrewsbury was of a most magnificent description. Mr Everall then proposed the health of Mr Pinches and success to his Fox-hounds, which was received with loud and hearty cheering.

The enjoyments continued until a late hour, and the firing of cannon, the ringing of bells, the hearty cheering and hilarity of the villagers will long exist in the memory of all present."

They were devoted to one another. A poem he wrote on her birthday went as follows:-

> *Another year swiftly passed away*
> *And once again I hail thy natal day*
> *More and more certain that my happy life*
> *Springs from thy gentleness my darlin wife*
> *The life which but for thee would wear a gloom*
> *As dark as night as dreary as the tomb*
> *Death has been busy in the byegone year*
> *And changes many round us far and near*
> *But for each other we survive and yet*
> *We owe to each of love a growing debt*
> *A debt which neither can expect to pay*
> *No more desire before our dying day.*
> *(Smethcote 1st February 1847)*

On June 5th 1849, Elizabeth is recorded as laying the first stone of the rebuilding of the church at Smethcote.

In the same year her brother William died and although she now inherited the estate, she and her husband continued to live at Smethcote and Elizabeth never again lived at Ticklerton Court.

In the 1851 census the house at Ticklerton is shown to be empty. However, they were obviously renting it in their absence as, in 1856, Rev Buddicom's friend William Darcey (late of Ticklerton Hall) was living there and, in 1861, an Isabelle Latouche – a lady – is shown as being the tenant.

They lived happily together for the next fifteen years, rest- oring the church, building the rectory and, at the same time, looking after the estate at Ticklerton.

THE BUDDICOM YEARS

Some of the diaries of the Rev Robert Joseph Buddicom are in the Local Studies Library at Shrewsbury and, although they are not complete, throw some light on the life of a country parson, how he lived and involved himself in the Ticklerton Estate, while still being the Rector at Smethcote.

Naturally, the income from the various rents due for the farms and cottages was important enough to warrant an entry on January 9th 1857 *"To Stretton for rent day, which was a good one"*. The recently constructed railway was obviously a boon for saving time, and was no doubt something of a novelty as, after his day of rent collecting, he went *"Home by train at night"* making use of the new station at Leebotwood.

Journeys to the estate farms were by carriage or on horse-back, and these visits are frequently referred to.

January 19th 1857. *"Over in carriage to see threshing by steam. Lovely day. Barley threshed and, after, oats"*. This was a very early opportunity to see corn being threshed, other than by the then traditional flail, and probably attracted many other farmers too.

They seem to have visited Claybrook and the Saplings on many occasions, as well as Ticklerton. Brick making had been carried on near Claybrook for many years, but its demise is recorded on February 11th 1857 when *"Sheffield's first day beginning to pull down the Kiln"*. This was probably James Sheffield, or his son Thomas, who lived in one of the Soudley estate cottages.

February 24th 1857. *"In carriage to Claybrook and on to call at Lutwyche"*. On this occasion combining an estate visit with a social call on the Bensons, who were also very big landowners in the district.

March 10th 1857. *"With Elizabeth and Miss Bird in the carriage to Claybrook. Splendid day. 26 lambs from 22 ewes and all alive and well"*.
(as an example of how breeding has progressed, 35 lambs would be expected today).

April 6th. *"Rode to Claybrook on Chestnut mare to pay the men"*.

June 8th. *"Carriage to Ticklerton. She (Elizabeth) walked down to the Saplings and managed pretty well"*. The illness, from which she was to die 2 years later, was obviously already affecting her.

August 6th 1857. *"Old Howells to pay £123 for the Saplings and Upper Saplings now in Claybrook. Young Howells to pay £149 for Claybrook. Myself taking part of 294 (a field of rough pasture) and plant"*. This appears to indicate a reduction in the Claybrook acreage. The only Howells family in the Parish at this time are recorded as being at Blackwood.

Shooting parties must have been popular on Heighwood Common, Soudley and the lower ground at Ticklerton.

September 1st. *"Early shoot at Soudley. Bagging in all 16 brace - but lost many winged birds in rabbit holes"*.

September 2nd. *"Shot on Common ground - 13) brace of birds, 5 hares, 3 rabbits. Men cutting Spring wheat"*.

September 14th. *"Shooting on Mr Darcey's lower ground.*(at Ticklerton Hall farm) *Birds uncommonly wild. 9) brace and 5 hares"*.

September 22nd. *"A shoot at the Hollies. Saw a great many birds. Bagged 17) brace and 3 hares. Winged 2 or 3 brace. The keeper next day picked up 3 birds"*.

As well as shooting, there was also fishing available. The pools near Claybrook were well stocked with *"a great many perch and eels"* and the Upper Brick Kiln pool with *"Plenty of carp and tench"*. The old Tithe map shows field No 40 as 'Pool common piece'. Alas, the pools are no longer there.

The health of his wife, Elizabeth, was of continuing concern to him.

September 25th 1857. *"Mr Clement (a doctor) here by 12.15 to poor Elizabeth, who bore the operation as well as usual"*.

August 14th 1858. *"To lunch at Acton Scott. Elizabeth managed the journey very well"*.

August 16th. *"Started for Llandudno. Had great dificulty in getting accomodation, but at last had a room out of the Queen's"* August 23rd. *"Started for Pembroke - Elizabeth very poorly on the journey"*.

March 18th 1859. *"In carriage with Elizabeth to the Saplings to bid it goodbye, then to tea at Mr Darcey's. My darling's last visit to Ticklerton"*.

March 27th. *" Elizabeth poorly"*.

May 15th. *"A terrible day. Requiring..... .... every few minutes. I took my two duties with difficulty. My darling prayed for"*.

May 16th. *"Restless - at 10 she asked for the Communion, which Jane, Willy (his son), Mr Bird and I took with her. Soon after she began to fail. The last words she said were 'Jesus take me'. My dear, dear love, now you are gone, I am alone. She died at 1.20 p.m. Mr Clement over at 2 to draw off the fluid"*.

May 21st. *"Mr Edwards over to breakfast. Exactly at 12 we started (for Eaton). Fine day and a very quiet, peaceful laying of my darling by her Mother - Goodbye dearest"*.

After Elizabeth's death, it appears that there may have been some dispute over the ownership of the Ticklerton Estate, there is a reference for June 20th *"Cooke (claimant for T. Estate) drove up. I saw him in Ellin's prescence"*. (Randle Cooke was the grandson of Richard Pinches and Mary, née Oxenbold, but his claim was groundless and it remained in the Buddicom family).

The Rev Robert Joseph spent November and December in France and, on May 20th 1860, he married for the third time to Ann

Landars of Moreton House, near Gainsborough. He found that his new life here and her tastes were not thoroughly congenial to him. The flat Lincolnshire country was in great contrast to the hills of Shropshire. His church at Moreton and the duties of the parish occupied much of his time. Illness often overcame him and and he was much affected by the long and serious illness of his wife who passed away in 1880.

Rev Robert Joseph then returned to Shropshire and shared Ticklerton Court with his son and daughter-in-law for the next eightyears. At 70, he entered the marriage state for the fourth time. He is reputed to have said *"if I survive I'll make it five"*, but there was little chance of this as the object of his choice this time was much younger than himself, Kate Clarke, a very pretty lady living at Redlap, near Dartmouth. But beyond a year or two of travelling and visiting, she saw but little of life with him as he became a confirmed invalid and hardly left his bed after 1891. He passed peacefully away in the presence of his wife and son in his 81st year and was buried in Stoke Fleming churchyard, near Dartmouth. (he was later re-interred in Eaton). Kate lived in Cheltenham until she died in 1914 and was buried, at her own wish, beside her husband in Eaton churchyard. She left £29,820.

Rev Robert Joseph only had one child, William Squire, his son by his first marriage. He could not have been given a better second name, because it was *"as a country squire of modest calibre"* that he lived his life at Ticklerton Court. He was educated at Marlborough College and at Cirencester Agricultural College. He became a J.P. and a Commissioner of Income Tax. He set about running the Estate himself, and also began to entertain a lot, moving into the 'county' set. Upon his death in 1922, an obituary notice said of him *"fond of home and had the qualities and bearing*

William Squire Buddicom, 1840-1922, with his daughter Lilian.

of a 'fine old English gentleman'. A good landlord, he observed fairness and equity in dealing with his tenants and was charitably disposed. A keen sense of humour never seemed to fail him."

Unlike his father, William Squire only married once and had two children. His wife was Elizabeth Haughton Hornby, daughter of Rev R Hornby and Maria Feilden. Maria was 25 when she married, and by the time she died in 1836 had had 18 children in just 20 years. A descendant of the Feilden family was Clementine Ogilvy who married Winston Churchill in 1908. Elizabeth died in 1914, leaving an estate of £7,803.

Elizabeth Haughton Buddicom (nee Hornby 1842-1914) near Soudley Upper Pool.

William Squire's first born, was Robert Arthur, born on November 7th 1874. He became a Classical Scholar at Charterhouse, went to New College, Oxford and took a Biological Scholarship at Keble College. He was President of the Oxford University Scientific Club, an Oxford Scholar at Naples Zoological Station and studied under Professor Weismann of Freiberg University. He was a much travelled man on the continent, Sicily and North Africa. He was appointed Curator of the Plymouth Municipal Museum and Art Gallery. In 1906 he turned an enormous house at Henley, with a river frontage, into a country club which became the Phyllis Court Club. It is still one of 'the' places of the Henley Regatta.

Aunt Emily, Lilian, her Mother, Robert Arthur and 'Dash' by the fernery. (below) Lilian by the tennis hut.

THE BUDDICOM YEARS

Robert Arthur, or RAB as he was generally known, married Laura Lucie Finlay. Her ancestry can be traced back to one of the beautiful Miss Marsdens of Bath who escaped from the French revolution on a pass signed by Robespierre. RAB and Laura had three children, Jacintha and Guinever who were still living in Sussex in 1989 and never married. His son, Robert Prosper Gedye, went to Harrow and Brazenose College, Oxford. He was a very keen sportsman, an expert fly fisher and cricketer. He gained quite a reputation locally for his wild ways, and took after his great grandfather with no less than four wives. He died in 1968.

RAB was later divorced. He married again to Hilda Lewis with whom he emigrated to Australia, where he died at Kyancutta in 1951. His first wife also married again, to F W Norsworthy.

Lilian Holland was William Squire's second child, born in 1878. She lived nearly all her life in Ticklerton. She had a governess and was educated at home until she went to Eckington House, Cheltenham, then to 'finishing school' at Morges, in Switzerland. She was presented at one of the last of Queen Victoria's Court presentations on 7th May 1896. She was married in 1918 to John Le Mesurier Hayward from Quorn Place, Leicestershire. She was 39. He died just four years later, the same year as her father, from cardiac asthma in a Shrewsbury nursing home. He left £5,219.

As will be seen, she was at all times deeply involved in the church and parish. She also became a considerable landowner in her own right.

Lilian's wedding day September 18th 1918. l to r Lucy Hornby, John Le Mesurier Hayward, Lilian Holland Buddicom, Robert Prosper and Guinever.

Ticklerton Court from the Pool Dam. c.1890.

Ticklerton Court has also been known as Ticklerton House and the Mansion House in earlier times.

The Pinches family had lived at the Court over a period of several hundred years. In 1824-6, William Pinches made extensive alterations at a cost of £840, converting it from a rambling gabled farmhouse into its square form and slate roof. His son, William, was the last of the family to live there and, after he died in 1849, it was some 20 years before the Buddicom family took up residence and ran the estate themselves. This era, the 'Buddicom Years', saw the Court take on a new lease of life. The staff were all dressed in uniform, the parlour maids in black dress and white apron, the grooms in livery. There was a lot of entertaining of the County set, a visit to Berriew (midway between Montgomery and Welshpool), the home of William Corbett-Winder, Lord Lieutenant of Montgomeryshire and a relative by marriage, was nothing unusual, travelling there and back in the day. The grooms would feed and tend their horses, sitting around awaiting the return journey.

The Halls were a local family who served the Buddicoms in one way or another for five generations. Harold Hall was the last one of the family who worked for Mrs Lilian Hayward, right up to the

Davies on the box. "Maud" (1896-96) and "Charlie" (1886-).Nurse Edwards (1890) on the Stretton
Road with 'Bob'.

time of her death in 1964. On occasions he acted as her butler, dressed in a grey suit from Burtons of Shrewsbury. Mrs Hayward (the last of the Buddicoms to live at the Court) was very nervous of being there on her own with no living-in staff. She was also very worried about 'what the villagers would think' when she had friends to stay. For example, her close friend the Rev Sheriff, who was 84, was never able to stay there the night unless Harold slept there too.

William Hall, Harold's father, was a brilliant gardener, producing exotic fruits, flowers and vegetables for the house during the winter months when they would not normally be available. He and Squire Buddicom used to fall out a lot, often arguing over what should or should not be done, but such was the relationship, between master and servant, that they would go off and have a drink together when it was all over.

There are many stories of the house being haunted. When Harold's wife Gwen worked there, neither she nor any of the other servants would ever go up to one of the top rooms after dark on their own. They were scared to death, believing it to be haunted. Harold had no such fears but, one night, he went up and opened the door, entered the room and the candle went out. He put it down, lit it again, and again it went out. He then fetched a torch, it too went out! He took it on to the landing and it worked! Time after time it went out when he entered the room - or so he said!

There were other strange noises that were heard, and nobody could account for them. It was said to be to do with a Buddicom who was buried elsewhere, wanting to return. True or not, but after Rev Robert Joseph was brought back from Stoke Fleming and re-interred in Eaton churchyard, the noises ceased, never to be heard again. His lead coffin had arrived at Harton station and was so heavy that John Cox of Upper House Farm had great difficulty, even with the help of a horse and sledge, to drag it from the station to it's final burial place in the Churchyard.

In her book 'Eric and Us', Jacintha Buddicom recalls that the middle room, entered from the back stairs, was also believed to be haunted. Nobody actually ever heard or saw anything, but all those that slept there (only when all other rooms were full) had the same conviction of being woken up by somebody entering or leaving the room. Besides this room, there was something very peculiar about the back stairs. In the summer of 1934, Guinever was ill in bed for several weeks and her old English sheepdog, Bob, used to lie 'on guard' outside her door, but he would never go up or down the backstairs which were directly opposite her door, but always went the long way round, through the upstairs hall, down the front stairs, along the back corridor and out through the kitchen - did he too sense something?

Running water and a bathroom - today taken for granted - were unheard of until 1907. Before that there were hip-baths in each bedroom, those with high backs were most sought after, the others being just round and rather shallow. Cans of hot water had to be carried up from the scullery, polished brass ones for visitors and grown ups, and brown painted tin ones for the children.

The water came from two sources, a stream from Soudley and a well in the cellar with a hand pump. Each day, it was the job of one of the gardeners to do an hour's pumping to provide water for the house. There was also a laundry room, with lines running out through the windows for drying.

The first bathroom in the Parish was installed in the Bank House in 1903. The Rectory was next, in 1907, and in the same year a make-shift affair was installed in a small room above the library in the Court. Water was run into tanks and heated over a 'Perfection' cooking stove. In 1922 a proper water heating system was installed. Up to 1938 none of the farms or cottages in the Parish had a bathroom.

Water from the Holly Bush spring was laid on to the Court in 1937, and to Upper House Farm and Ticklerton Hall the following year.

There was a lavatory in the Court around 1900, a magnificent affair, like a throne on a pedestal, but it's use was strictly confined to the ladies, men had to go outside and use the earth closet.

Electricity arrived in 1937. Before then a row of silver candlesticks was set out on an oak chest in the hall. Each person would take one on their way to bed where, on either side of the dressing table, would be two more. You never had oil lamps in your bedroom, but lighting elsewhere was by oil, with candleabra on the dining table.

In 1937, Jacintha Buddicom designed a new Tudor style house and had it built within sight of the Court, it was called Meadowbrook. Three old estate cottages were demolished to provide some of the stonework, along with old ship's timbers and a lot of the best stone available from the local quarries. It cost £7,000 — a considerable sum in those days.

A year later, Lilian Hayward moved in to the new house and Ticklerton Court was let to various tenants until it was sold, in 1953, to Mr John Young. By then it was in a poor state of repair, and major renovation was undertaken, with the top floor being removed and the roof lowered.

At the time of the sale, much of the furniture was put up for auction. Some of it went for give-away prices, beautiful bureaux and mahogany tables fetching only £6/7 and the total bringing only about £400.

Another small cottage was built between Meadowbrook and Upper House Farm. This was lived in by Robert Prosper until he died in 1968, the last of the male line of the Buddicoms who had come to Ticklerton more than 100 years earlier.

THE BUDDICOM YEARS

Lilian Holland Hayward (née Buddicom) 1878-1964.

The personal diaries of Lilian Buddicom (recorded in the next chapter) are interesting in that while they give a general account of village life, there is not one word about her family and the social life they enjoyed. For example, her brother's young family used to come and spend their holidays at Ticklerton Court, they used to mix freely with many of the Church Stretton families, the Audens and Hornes often being mentioned.

By 1917, the three children Jacintha, Guinever and Robert Prosper were considered by their parents to be old enough to make the journey to Ticklerton unescorted, and they used to spend many weeks of their school holidays there. Eric Blair, who went to Eton, was a friend of Prosper and often used to come and stay with them. Together, they learnt to fish and shoot under the careful tuition of Ted Hall, who acted as gamekeeper on the estate. Eric Blair was, in later life, to become famous as the writer George Orwell. Jacintha Buddicom wrote a most interesting book in the 1970s - "Eric and Us", in which are many references to his early friendship with the family in those early years.

With more than a year still to go before the Armistice, a letter from Lilian Buddicom referring to the summer holiday visit of the children reads *"I think our sugar will allow us to have it on the table, as I have managed to get a little extra this week"*.

Shooting party at Chelmick, September 1917.
l to r Eric (Blair), Guinever, Ted Hall, Prosper.

Croquet at Ticklerton, September 1917. Prosper, Guinever and Eric.

Evidence that some shortages were being felt, although areas like Shropshire suffered no real food shortage. Farmers grew their own corn and baked their own bread - the rent of one of the farms was always partly paid for in a certain number of home-produced loaves every week. Fruit and vegetables were plentiful, so were ducks, hens, geese and turkeys. Cows had plenty of milk, cream and butter and somebody was always killing a pig. There were plenty of fish in the pools and rivers too.

Although Lilian's brother, RAB (Robert Arthur), spent a lot of time at Ticklerton when he was running the museum in Shrewsbury, it was William Squire Buddicom, his Father, who was very much the boss of the show. Even after his death in 1922, RAB did not himself take on the running of the estate, but engaged Burd and Evans of Shrewsbury to manage it for him. His son Prosper later joined Burd and Evans to learn estate management. He then ran the estate for about four years, but never had any real interest in it. He shared his time between Shiplake (his Father's home in Berkshire) and Ticklerton, spending more time at the latter because of the shooting and general sporting life he could lead. He was a very keen sportsman and used to demonstrate fly fishing. Eventually, like his great grandfather, he also had four wives, although he more or less married his last wife by accident or, rather, because of an accident. He fell downstairs and broke his ankle and was confined to a downstairs room. He rang up Salts (the ironmonger in Church Stretton) and asked a Mrs Pearson to put some firelighters by for him. When Harold Hall went to pick them up she said "I must go up and look after him". She duly did, he took her at her word and married her. As soon as he got better and was told he could go up and down stairs again, she left. He never actually lived with her. In the early morning of the day she left, she got Jack Edwards to take her, and all her belongings, back to Stretton. At this time Prosper was living at the cottage they had had built at Ticklerton.

RAB, his Father, died in 1951 in Australia and left the estate to Prosper. In January 1953 he sold everything, 737 acres of land, 7 farms and 9 cottages for £31,415. At the same time, Mrs Hayward sold most of the property that she had accumulated over the years, including Lower House Farm and some 400 acres of land for £13,584.

He continued to live in Ticklerton until he died in Shrewsbury hospital in 1968, the last of the male line of the Ticklerton Buddicoms.

Mrs Hayward's husband had died in 1922, just four years after their marriage. She had, as will be seen from her diaries, always been closely involved with the church and village. She acquired property in her own right, as well as helping to run the estate.

She was an inveterate collector and recorder of all matters to do with natural history, archaeology and botany, local folklore, dialects, superstitions and the 'happenings' in and around Shropshire. All this information she jotted down in numerous exercise books, note books and scrap books. (Many of these are lodged in the Local Studies Library at Shrewsbury). Although she contributed articles to magazines she did not, unfortunately, ever put them all together in a book. Carrying out research into her many journals is not easy because, unfortunately, her handwriting is very difficult to read, so much so that there are stories of her sending written requests to someone in the Parish who, unable to read it, took it back for her to tell them what it said, for her to be unable to read her own handwriting! This has made the deciphering and inclusion here of many of her records not only difficult, but also there may be instances where words have not been accurately or correctly interpreted.

Life to Lilian Hayward was a perpetual challenge. If she was not writing on country walks in the area or an article for a local magazine, she was producing a concert or play in the village hall, organising the Women's Institute or some church function or the other. This activity was well rewarded by the villagers who all participated - young and old alike.

"Masque of Empire" a mime play produced by Mrs Hayward c.1937.
l to r kneeling: Mildred Perkins, Gladys Madeley, Mrs Hughes.
standing: Miss N Hughes, Hilda Parry, Hilda Pennington (Mrs D Madeley),
Mrs J Hughes, Mrs R Attenborough (top), Mrs E Johnson.

THE BUDDICOM YEARS

Following a hunting accident in the late 1920s in which she injured her back (some say she broke it), she slowly became more and more bent double, so much so that those who only knew her in later years, found it hard to believe she had been a tall, upright woman as shown in early photographs.

When she was 60 she set out to walk from John O'Groats to Lands End for no other reason than to show that a woman of her age could do it. (At that time, as far as is known, the only other woman to have done it was a New Zealander). She had a number of different companions to walk with her on different parts of the journey, and had changes of clothing delivered to her en route. She wore, much padded, size 8 boots! These became notorious and resided in a Shrewsbury museum at one time.

Mrs L Hayward, with Tom Miles, planting a commemorative tree at Ticklerton Village Hall, Coronation Day 1953.

Shortly before her death in 1964, she addressed the National Federation of Women's Institutes at the Royal Albert Hall and her speech, though brief, showed her love of Shropshire and her sense of humour. The following, which was given in her distinctive, high pitched voice, is taken from a B.B.C. brodcast.

"Lady Albermarle, fellow members, I live in South Shropshire. South Shropshire is one of the very best walking districts in England, partly because it has so many footpaths, crossing beautiful country, and partly because it has such good natured farmers and

landowners who allow us to walk almost everywhere. But we suffer from bulls (laughter). Since there are about 40 counties in England where County Council bye-laws prohibit bulls being kept in fields crossed by public footpaths. Shropshire is not one of those 40 counties. In Shropshire it appears that a bull that has not hitherto been dangerous, is allowed to have his first toss (much laughter) also, no compensation can be obtained the first time for the person who has been tossed or for their next of kin. Therefore I wish to support this resolution, and particularly paragraph 83, that the prohibition against bulls being turned out in fields crossed by public footpaths should apply to every county."

The following list of some of her representative activities gives some indication of her involvment in local affairs. Parish representative on the Church Stretton Board of Guardians and Rural District Council for rating and housing. Lady Visitor to Poor Law Institution. Chairman Parish Council 1946-52. Member Parochial Church Council. President (and Vice-P.) of Eaton-under-Heywood Womens Institute for 20 years. In 1914-18 war was Lady Superintendent of local St John's Ambulance Division and V.A.D. Commandant. In the Second world war was billeting officer for the Parish and representative for S.S.& A.F. Governor Church Stretton Modern school. Chairman of local Conservative Association 1923-39. President Local History Council, C.P.R.E. Council member. Folklore Society. Commons, open spaces and footpaths Preservation Society.

With her death in 1964, followed by that of her nephew in 1968, ended more than 100 years of Buddicoms in Ticklerton. A period during which the village school had opened and closed, the railway had been built, thrived and then been closed down, two world wars had been fought, farming and travel moved from the horse-age to mechanisation, most of village entertainment had been replaced by the cinema and TV, and the old village lifestyle had more or less disappeared.

Among the papers, notes and journals that have survived and are kept in the Local Studies Library, are the Diaries she kept from the age of 21 to 38, and these are reprinted in full in the following chapter as they, perhaps better than anything else, give a feeling of the real life in the Parish at that time.

1898 to 1916 DIARIES

A RECORD OF THE PARISH OF EATON-UNDER-HEYWOOD
(From the diaries of Lilian Holland Buddicom)

1898/1899

The winter of 1898/9 was a particularly mild one, there being little snow or frost. February and March were remarkable for heavy rains which flooded the brooks to such an extent that many of the fords became impassable. The inconvenience was much felt at Harton ford, which being so swollen that no carts could pass through it, the farmers had to drive three miles round by Eaton and Ticklerton to reach Harton station.

The winter was marked by the founding of the Eaton-under-Heywood Amateur Dramatic and Musical Society. On January 14th they performed the tragedy of Pyranus and Thisbe, adapted from Shakespeare's Midsummer Nights Dream. Mr Robinson admirably performed the double parts of Quince and the Wall, for the latter character being arrayed in a striking costume of bricks & mortar. Mr Edwin Evans represented the Lion and Miss C Corfield the Prologue. The parts of the lovers Pyranus and Thisbe were admirably acted by Mr Henry Goode and Miss Jane Minton, Miss Buddicom and four little girls Ruth Webster, Dottie Stephens, Jesse Easthope and Nellie Goode in white dresses with garlands and wreaths of evergreen, represented the lovers, yew and woodland trees. The little girls sang an appropriate song. Miss Hill recited the introductory speech and Miss Margaret Cleeton as Moonshine shone for the occasion. The room was full to overflowing and the entertainment proved a complete success. Admission was free.

On February 26th United Hounds met at Ticklerton Court, after drawing the Mouseleys, Dayus Copp, Pieces etc. they found in the Ironmongers Coppice, and after a long exciting run by Chelmick, Ragleth Hill, Helmeth, Caradoc, Lawley etc, they killed the fox near Longnor.

On March 18th, the Dramatic and Musical Society gave an entertainment commencing with a concert and concluded with a spirited performance of 'Cox and Box' acted by Mr Harry Rogers — Box, Mr Edwin Hall — Cox, and Mr Edwin Evans as Mrs Bouncer. On this occasion a small charge was made for admission and 13/- was taken at the door. In the interval between the Concert and the Play, a presentation of a purse containing £18 was made to Mr Duncan, our worthy station master, who was leaving us after 28 years of service at Harton station, while being succeeded by Mr Thomas.

On April 1st, the Dramatic and Musical Society gave another entertainment commencing with a Concert etc in which the performers were Mr R A Buddicom - conjuring, Miss Jane Minton - recitation, Mr Roberts - reading, Miss Medlicott, Miss Minton, Mr and Miss Poston and Mr Harry Rogers - Glees and songs. Concluding with a repetition of 'Cox and Box' which had been specially asked for. A small charge was made for admission. The money taken at these two concerts was used for putting up curtains and beams at the school.

At the beginning of the year the Rev Holland Sandford, who has been our Rector for so many years, was taken seriously ill. The duty was first taken by Rev W E Thompson, and later in the year by Rev Prebendary Elliot.

On August 9th Mr and Mrs Buddicom invited the children and Friendly Girls of the Parish to the number of 80. After tea the children played games and ran races. The winners receiving prizes and money. Before leaving everyone was given a present.

Owing to the long continued heat we have experienced this summer, the corn ripened unusually early and at least two of the farmers, Mr Venables of Eaton and Mr Davies of Whitefields, got in their crops by August 17th, an unusually early date for these parts, while the harvest was entirely finished by the beginning of September.

On September 17th the Harvest Thanksgiving Service was held at Eaton church, which had been tastefully decorated with flowers, fruit and corn. The bread used for Communion was made from flour from this year's wheat grown, threshed and baked in the Parish, as first fruits of oven, mill and field.

During the year, three series of County Council Classes were held in Eaton school. In January lectures on farm animals, health and disease by Mr Blake. In May and June dressmaking classes by Miss Wyre. In November and December Ambulance classes for men by Dr Barnett. All these classes were well attended.

In October war broke out with the Transvaal, many of the resrvists were called out. A fund was got up in the County to supplement the small allowance given by the Government for their wives and children. £17-14-0 was raised in the Parish by means of house to house collection.

This December the weather was very reasonable, but extremely cold and there were several heavy falls of snow. Christmas morning was very bright and frosty, but at a quarter to eleven a sudden snowstorm much disconcerted the churchgoers. By the time the service was over the snow had fortunately ceased, so we had a dry walk home.

On December 28th the children were entertained by Mr and Mrs Buddicom to celebrate the 21st birthday of Lilian Buddicom. After tea a Christmas tree was lit, each child receiving from its boughs a present, a bag of sweets and an orange. Before leaving the children sang some songs nicely.

1898 to 1916 DIARIES

The Amateur Dramatic and Musical Society gave a concert in aid of the wives and children of the soldiers killed in the Transvaal war on December 29th. 12/6 was taken at the door. The sum was sent to the Daily Telegraph fund. There were various songs and Miss Buddicom and Mr Roberts danced the Cachucha (a lively Spanish dance). The great novelty of the evening was 'The Soldiers of the Queen' sung in a most spirited manner by Miss Medlicott dressed up as a soldier in red cap and coat, with flags pinned on her dress. She carried a gun loaded with a charge of powder. At the end of the last verse, Kruger, represented by Mr Edwin Hall, dressed up in a black coat, top hat, tow whiskers and beard appeared. The soldier fired off her gun and OOM PAUL fell dead at her feet. The school children entered bearing flags which they waved above the victor's head. Miss Medlicott placed her foot upon the body of her fallen foe, holding her gun aloft and everybody sang the chorus. The audience taking part in the triumphant words: "And when we say we've always won, and then they ask us how it's done, we proudly point to every one of Englands soldiers of the Queen".

1900

In January the weather was mild and warm, some days were so balmy and springlike we began to think winter was over, we therefore felt the cold weather in the succeeding months more severely than we might otherwise have done. During the first half of February there were frequent falls of snow and on the 14th the snow was deeper than it had been for many years. A very violent wind drifted the snow, and many of the roads, specially those on high ground, became impassable between Ticklerton and Eaton, and also between Birtley and Acton Scott, a succession of huge snow drifts between three and four feet high extending from hedge to hedge, completely blocked the road. No carts could get through and were obliged to make detours across the fields. The school was closed for several days, as it was quite impossible for the children to attend. The thaw, when it came, was so gradual that the snow took over a week to disappear. For days the roads were a mass of slush and had hardly become passable when a very severe frost covered them with ice and they became so slippery that the horses could not move on them. The frost finally broke in the beginning of March.

On March 1st the news of the relief of Ladysmith became known, Church Stretton was decorated with flags, it was Market Day, so the town was very full. The people went half mad and marched round the town shouting and singing war songs and waving flags, no business was done for over an hour. The church bells were rung in nearly all the villages around. In Ticklerton flags were hung out and Teddy Evans, the blacksmith, fired off charges of gunpowder on the anvil.

The early part of the year was marked by the sad death of old Mrs Rogers, widow of Richard Rogers who farmed at Soudley. Mrs Rogers had one son called Edwin Duckett, she had behaved very badly to him, leaving him in great poverty. After her husband's death she invited Duckett to work on her farm, he married and he and his wife soon began to get the upper hand, from a farm servant he became a member and the principal one of the household, he managed everything, he sold much of Mrs Rogers stock, keeping the money paid for it for himself. He drank deeply and after a time began to behave very badly to his Mother and bitterly revenging himself for the injustices of his childhood. Mrs Rogers decided to leave her farm, but apparently could not break off old ties and quit the house where she had lived so long, for she remained on. Then things went from bad to worse, we were told that Duckett tried to gain possession of her Savings Bank book, that he threatened her with a knife. She became crazy, took to her bed and on February 25th, a fortnight later, she died. The farm was relet to her son Edwin Duckett who had caused his Mother's death. N.B. Duckett turned out better than might have been expected, and he and his wife farmed quietly for many years.

Harry Rogers, eldest son of our coachman John Rogers and nephew by marriage of Mrs Rogers who had just died, had undertaken a situation as gamekeeper in 1899, and the frequent exposure and living in a wretched little hut in the midst of damp woods gave him a severe chill and in December he had come home very ill. The illness developed into consumption, but for some months he lingered on in great pain, gradually going weaker and more attenuated. On March 17th, at two in the morning, he passed away. Five days later he was buried in Hope Bowdler churchyard, numbers of people attended the funeral of the young man and many wreaths and crosses were sent. These signs of respect seemed to give some slight consolation to the parents.

On April 8th, Mrs Pearce who lived in a cottage in the hollow, near Ticklerton, died rather suddenly of a complaint from which she had long suffered. She was a great loss to the village, for being of a cheerful, kindhearted and genial disposition, the neighbours had often been of the habit of dropping in to her cottage for a chat or a gossip. Her death, therefore, left a great blank.

During February hunting was almost impossible owing to the inclement weather, but at the end of the month the frost broke and we had a month's good sport. On March 7th the United hounds met at Ticklerton Court, amongst those who sat down to the breakfast was old Mr Bache, aged 77, he was a real link of old times having hunted in the very early days of the United. The pack was then hunted by three joint masters, the greater part of the hounds being kept at Ticklerton Court, where the old kennels still remain. In those days the United were a very rough pack of hounds, and hunted hares and rabbits as well as foxes. In his youth Mr Bache had been such a reckless rider that he was given the nickname of 'Dick the Devil'. Having drawn Hargrove, Mouseleys Plantation etc blank, we went down the Harton road intending to draw the Ironmongers Coppice. On the way, Mr Hill, Marshbrook House, caught sight of a fox curled up in the boughs of the old oak. He was cracked out, but as he ran to the drain at Harton, we left him and drew the Ironmonger's Coppice and found the same old customer who had baffled us so often, he took his favourite line through Hatton and Chelmick, over Ragleth, but there he was headed and doubled back through Chelmick, Birtley and Ticklerton across the rough ground to Hargrove Farm, where he was pulled down in a field close to the house. The ground was very rough and with the hounds running very fast, it was almost impossible to keep up. Only Mr Thomas, MFH, the Whip and Mr McClintock were in at the death, though several turned up a few minutes later. The Master gave the brush to Mrs Green, the first lady in, and the mask to me. We then returned to Harton and dug out the fox we had left there in the morning, after a very short run he was lost.

In March our Rector, Mr Sandford, was removed to the asylum at Church Stretton, and on the 28th his furniture, books etc were sold by auction. During the greater part of the year the duty was taken by various clergy from Shrewsbury, Birmingham etc. but we had no regular incumbent.

On April 23rd, Robert Arthur Buddicom, only son of William Squire Buddicom of Ticklerton Court, was married at Christ Church, Lancaster Gate, London to Laura Lucy Finlay, eldest daughter of Reginald Finlay Esquire, late of Queensland, Australia.

On August 20th, the members of the Girls Friendly Society and the children of the Parish to the number of 80 were entertained at Ticklerton Court. After tea, which was taken outdoors, Mrs Robert Buddicom sang and played the violin, and the children then played games and scrambled for sweets, everyone was given a present before leaving.

In the autumn, with the Rev Hollland Sandford being too ill to continue his duties, it became known that the living of Eaton-under-Heywood had been promised by the Patron, Humphrey Sandford Esq., to the Rev Nevil Friederichs, brother of the Rector of Acton Scott. He was inducted on November 4th by his brother. After morning service the Rector read the Bishop's mandate while the church wardens, Mr Cleeton and Mr Davies, and the Parish Clerk stood in the aisle bearing staves, they then escorted the new Rector to the bottom of the church, arriving at the door, the Bishop's proxy inducted him in the real, actual and corporal possessions of the church. The new incumbent then tolled the bell to signify that he had taken possession. The procession then proceeded to the font, *the pulpit and the communion table, the usual prayers and exhortations were read, special hymns were sung. The sermon was preached by the Rev F D Friederichs who exhorted the congregation to trust and obey their new Rector and to attend church regularly, and the following Sunday the new Rector read the 39 articles instead of preaching. However, even after his induction the new Rector did not reside in the Parish for some time, difficulties having arisen as to the delapidations, but retained his post as Chaplain to the Marquess of Camperdown, coming to Eaton to take the services each Sunday.*

1901

The winter was cold, but not exceptionally so. We had frost at intervals but no severe one.

On March 22nd Ethel Mary Roberts, the daughter of our schoolmaster, married George Bandell. This year the prizes for attendance were won by Ruth, Mary and Richard Cleeton, Ruth making 419 attendances out of the possible 426. The prize for writing was won by John Cox.

The Coronation of King Edward V11 was celebrated by bonfires being lighted on the hills on June 30th, by a Parish tea and dance at Eaton rectory on July 2nd, by which date the King was declared out of danger. The King specially desired that all celebrations and rejoicing should take place as arranged, though the Coronation itself could not take place because of his serious illness.

The Girls Friendly Society Industrial exhibition was held at Stokesay Castle on July 24th. The Bishop of Hereford attended the exhibition and addressed those present. Although the day was wet, a great number of people came and our Parish did exceedingly well, Lucy Davies and Clara Corfield gained first prizes.

The early summer was fine and warm, from July onwards we had constant and depressing rain.

In July and August technical classes in butter making were held in Mr Cox's barn. Demonstrations given by the teacher, Miss Hunter, followed by ten practical lessons. At the end an examination was held, 18 girls attended and four scholarships were awarded to Lucy Davies, E Hill, myself and Miss Hartley of Hope Bowdler. These scholarships enabled us to learn butter and cheese making for eight weeks at the Technical School for girls at Radbrook, near Shrewsbury. After the final examination we were awarded certificates, Lucy Davies gained higher marks than any previous pupil at the Dairy school.

1902

There are no entries for this year, possibly Lilian Buddicom was away from Ticklerton.

1898 to 1916 DIARIES

1903

Early in January two old people passed away. Mrs Jones who lived next door to the Post Office and James Carter, the Parish pig killer. On the morning of the very day on which he died he had killed our pig and William Hall's and was on his way to perform the same office at the Hope Bowdler rectory when he fell down dead in the road.

On March 22nd old Edward Rogers of Soudley died, he was, I believe, the oldest man in the Parish and had many tales to relate of times that now seem very different, specially of Election riots in the old days. He was formerly our gardener, as his son-in-law William Hall is now.

In December of 1902 the Bank House, Ticklerton, was taken by two young ladies from Liverpool, Miss Elizabeth and Miss Mary Holt. Their solicitations were so urgent that a bathroom was added to the house at the back, the alterations and additions were planned by Mr Robert Buddicom and carried out under his superintendance in the Spring and early Summer of 1903. The reservoir etc. was made in the orchard at Ticklerton Court. I may mention that this was the first bathroom that had been put in the Parish.

The children of the Parish were fortunate this year in the matter of parties, one was given by the Rector and another by his friend Mrs Gatehouse, who was staying at the Upper Farm. Most of them were at the party given at Ticklerton Court.

Several balloons were sent up during the Shrewsbury Flower Show August 19th/20th and two descended in the immediate neighbourhood, one at Stone Acton and the other actually in the Parish between Eaton and Rushbury.

In September Mrs Gatehouse gave a dance to a great many people in the Parish, it was held in the big barn at Upper Farm, Mr Cox's. It was thoroughly enjoyed and dancing was kept up until a late hour.

Bad weather continued throughout the year, with very little intermission, and the harvest was the worst for many years. Nothing prospered, every crop did badly or failed entirely. There was a good crop of hay but many could not get it in, there was also a good crop of corn but much did not ripen, and what did was harvested in a very unsatisfactory state. The potatoes failed or were diseased and turnips scarcely a third their usual size. Fruit, specially apples, was very scarce. Even the wild fruit such as blackberries, sloes and bilberries, which are generally quite a source of income to the poor, were so scarce and so small as to be hardly worth gathering. It was disheartening for the farmers, and the Harvest Thanksgiving seemed a farce.

The Misses Holt gave a little party on Guy Fawkes Day, set off fireworks etc. On December 11th a very excellent concert got up by the Misses Holt took place in the school, they sent the pro-

*ceeds amounting to £3-10-0 to the Salop Infirmary. They arranged
everything very well, having a small stage put up and bringing in
their own piano. Two Miss Buckles, their cousins, played the
violin and 'cello. Mrs Buddicom played "The songbirds in the wood"
which I accompanied on a warbler. The school children sang glees
and six of them sang an action song, "Jingle Bells" for which they
wore bells which they jingled merrily. Miss Corfield recited, Mr
and Miss Melville and Mr Edward Evans sang. Six little girls
trained by me sang "Yen How and his six little wives", Miss Jane
Minton making a most effective mandarin, four others carried
Japanese lanterns and all wore Japanese costumes. It was a very
pretty song.*

*Jasper More who represented this Division of Shropshire for
many years, died very suddenly on November 25th. The election of
his successor was the great excitement of December. Two candidates
came forward, Mr Rowland Hunt of Boreatton was the Unionist candidate, while the Liberal interest was represented by Mr Fred
Horne, a farmer near Shifnal. Both these gentlemen and their sup-
porters held many meetings in the neighbourhood, but most of them
were quite orderly. The Misses Holt took the most interest in the
Election, being keen Liberals, they drove about canvassing for Mr
Horne and they attended many of the Liberal meetings. They hired
two brakes and took most of the men from Soudley, Ticklerton etc
to the Liberal meeting at Cardington. The Election took place on
December 22nd. Mr Hunt was returned with a majority of nearly one
thousand.*

*At Christmas the usual carol singers came round, beside var-
ious youths and children who sang more or less badly, we were visited by the Heywood Glee party, who sang their carols in parts exceedingly well. Another night the Hope Bowdler Bell ringers came,
they were eight in number, and brought with them 50 bells. They
played from music, each note having its corresponding bell, each
man had several bells in his charge. They first played "The Har-
monious Blacksmith", it was a beautiful moonlight evening and the
bells sounded so sweet in the clear frost air.*

*On New Year's Eve the Misses Holt gave a delightful enter-
tainment in Mr Cox's barn for many of the Parish and around. They
got two professionals, a conjurer and a comic singer whose perf-
ormances were very good.*

1904

*For many years Mr Buddicom has annually subscribed one guinea
to the Shrewsbury Infirmary, this subscription admitted one in-
patient or four out-patients from the Parish. Last year, however,
their funds being low and the subscription by no means covering
the benefits of the expense obtained, the Infirmary decided that
the one guinea subscription could in future only admit two out-*

patients. The recommendations, as they are so called, are so very valuable that we decided that the subscription must be increased. To raise the money a dance was held in the large barn at Mr Cox's farm on January 22nd. We held a committee meeting at Ticklerton Court, everybody very enthusiastic and ready to help. Ted Cox arranged to lay the carpet and Teddy Evans arranged about the band. These two acted as stewards and Willie Bebbington as M.C. A number of girls spent the day making long evergreen wreaths, we put them up round the walls, along the beams and stretched lengths of red material below a sort of frieze of trails of ivy. Curtains were hung over the doors and the barn looked very gay and cheerful when lit up with 8 lamps which we had borrowed. Mrs Buddicom and myself came in for a little while at the beginning and the Rector stayed until 2.30 a.m. The barn was soon filled and presented a gay and lively scene. We had three instruments, Mr Finch of Rushbury played the violin and two of his band the cornet and piccolo. There were 24 dances on the programme, but they had several extras. Being Leap Year, there were two leap year dances which caused great merriment. The other dances were the waltz, polka, mazurka, scottiche, barn dance, lancers, quadrilles, gallops, circassian circle and change polka - the principle of this is that when the music changes the partners seperate, each taking another from among the dancers. Mrs Cox, Mrs Robinson and Mrs Cleeton undertook the refreshments, which were nicely served in the kitchen all evening, they consisted of tea, coffee, lemonade and cakes and sandwiches of many kinds. The Misses Holt sent a great many. The price of the tickets, including refreshments was 1/6 for ladies and 2/- for gentlemen. We made £9-15-0, but the expenses, band, hire of carpet, Mrs Cox ample refreshments etc came to £5-2-5. Of the £4-12-7 that we cleared, £2-2-0 was sent to Shrewsbury Infirmary as an increased subscription, being added to Mr Buddicom's one guinea, the balance was brought forward for next year.

In April I held dressmaking classes for some of the girls. County Council dairy classes were held in the summer, attendance was very poor, because laundry classes had been wished for, two scholarships were gained.

On September 17th the Misses Holt got up sports which were held in the field at the Bank House, prizes being given and a tea tent provided. Admission was charged and it was expected that several pounds would be cleared, but expenses exceeded receipts.

Mr Friederichs gave a tea party to the school children that summer.

In December we were pleased by the appearance of an otter in our pool, though not uncommon in these parts, otters are shy and are seldom seen, this one was quite unconcerned by the many spectators who came to look at it and would lie on the bank sunning himself, he stayed some days.

1898 to 1916 DIARIES

On December 2nd we had a dance, of which the object was to provide money for the Infirmary tickets and was conducted on the same lines as the last, and two pounds was cleared. These dances give a great deal of trouble and we decided to hold no more.

Our late Rector, Rev Holland Sandford died at Church Stretton on December 24th and was buried at Eaton on the 26th. There was a large attendance and the next day Mr Friederichs preached a beautiful sermon.

On December 30th the Misses Holt gave a delightful entertainment in the barn, two professionals from Liverpool delivered, said various recitations, songs and sketches, which were all much appreciated. At the conclusion refreshments were handed round.

Mr Thomas, our Station master, being transferred to another station, a presentation was set on foot, £9-2-0 was collected. The presentation took place in the barn, where Mr Buddicom handed the money to the recipient after making an appropriate speech, Mr Thomas responded but became inextricably mixed in his speech. Mr Davies rescued him by proposing three cheers, we all cheered each other and sang "for he's a jolly good fellow" and went home in great spirits.

1905

On January 6th a concert got up by the Misses Holt took place in the barn, the proceeds were sent to the Infirmary.

In the Spring, Mrs Easthope died at Birtley.

The Industrial Exhibition took place in Hereford on July 25th A few exhibits were sent from our Parish, I won a first prize for dressmaking, Mrs Buddicom won a second prize for needlework, though her exhibit was far superior to that which gained the first prize.

The cottagers of Heywood had long suffered from their very bad road, the lane leading from Heywood to Parish wood, which runs from Soudley Post Office past the Common Farm out on to the high road between Hope Bowdler and Wall, was choked up and fallen into disuse. The only to-and-from Heywood was by a steep rocky lane, very dangerous in winter, leading past the quarry to Soudley. Several coal carts had stuck in the ruts and at least one serious accident occurred. After this the tradesmen declined to send provision carts up this dangerous road. The District Council declined to assist in the matter because the road was only an occupation one. Convinced by the earnest solicitations of those living in the hamlet, Mr & Mrs Buddicom decided to improve the old disused lane above mentioned, the hedges were cut and laid down, the ditches were dug out, the road drained, remade and pitched — 373 loads of stone being taken from Mr Buddicom's quarries for this purpose. This work gave employment to several men for many weeks, the total cost was £77-7-1. Mr Wray, who owned several of the cottages in

Heywood, subscribed 10/-, the cottagers in and near Heywood and several neighbouring farmers gave in all £1-8-9 and a few days labour. Our own friends gave £8-4-0. This comparitively small sum being quite inadequate, we decided to hold a sale of work. We worked very hard all through the winter making and collecting things to sell and we held the sale on May 31st. Very few of the farmers or cottagers helped, our own friends were most kind and we cleared £26-5-0, selling another £6 worth of articles afterwards. The remainder, £34-19-4, was given by Mr & Mrs Buddicom. Later on the District Council improved the steep road passing the quarry, Mr & Mrs Buddicom subscribing a further sum of £12.

In the autumn a drive was made at Ticklerton Court, it was planned by Mr R A Buddicom, and carried out by local men, even to the pillars and stone balls. On November 27th we gave a supper to the 8 men who had made the road to Heywood and our drive.

On November 24th our Rector gave a dance to his congregation in Cox's barn. The room was not too full and we all spent a most enjoyable evening. As the invitations were sent to members of the congregation only, many of those living near were excluded. Mr Bebbington and others begged Mrs Buddicom to get up another Infirmary dance and she unfortunately did so, it gave great offence to our rector who had given his dance to encourage those who attended church. Also we unfortunately held it in Advent and the following Sunday he preached against those who desecrated the solemn season of Advent. The dance was not a financial success because instead of having a subscription for the Infirmary, we were some shillings to the bad.

On December 20th the Misses Holt gave a meat tea to about 100 farmers and cottagers, next day they gave a children's party. We hoped these entertainments would not shake our people's politics. The Misses Holt spent a great time canvassing for the Liberal member and getting up meetings. Our member, Mr Hunt, was however returned by the large majority of 760, we felt very satisfied and very few Unionist members were returned in the election of 1905/6 and those by small majorities.

1906

The Misses Holt left the Bank House in May. They had done so many kind actions in the Parish but had been a great source of political agitation and unrest.

In August we gave an afternoon party at Ticklerton Court to our tenants, wives and children, the G.F.S. girls and schoolchildren. After the tea, Miss Fairfax-Brown, Bank House, drove about the lawn in a pony cariage which we had decorated for the Stretton Cake Fair a few days before, scattering sweets to the children.

1898 to 1916 DIARIES

The Stretton Pierrots then gave a most excellent and amusing performance.

In November old Mrs Morris of Eaton died in her sleep.

Mr Roberts, who plays the harmonium in church, had such rheumatism in his hands that for some months he was unable to play, his place was taken in turn by Mrs Buddicom, Mrs Fairfax-Brown, Miss Lucy Davies and myself.

Mrs Buddicom had for many years a clothing club, giving a 4/- bonus to each member, it had gradually dwindled so that by the close of 1906 she gave it up as it seemed to be no longer needed or desired.

1907

It is probable that Miss Buddicom was away from Ticklerton during this year.

1908

In 1908 young Mr Bebbington of Harton married Miss Preece of Church Stretton. Edwin Evans, the blacksmith, brought a bride home and Morris of Eaton married again. Heather Rogers had long been engaged to Miles whom she married in the Spring, she seems to have done so that her child might be born in wedlock, for a few weeks after her wedding, just before her baby was born, she went to live with her parents and absolutely refused to go back to her husband. Miles, of course, thought himself very ill used, he gave up the cottage he had taken and went to live with his brother's widow, Mrs Miles at Woodside cottages, quite near his wife's parents home.

In June the Fairfax-Browns left the Bank House, which has been taken by Major and Mrs Hornby.

In the autumn Miss Davies of Whitefields, the sister of our church warden, died after a long illness, she'd been much liked and respected. Old Mr Hill of Lower Farm, Ticklerton, died, just before his death numbers of owls were heard hooting in the village. Owls hooting is supposed to be a sign of death approaching, and it was rather curious that after Hill's death we did not hear any more owls for a very long time.

After Mr Roberts, the schoolmaster, left there was some difficulty in finding a successor to play the harmonium in church. Young Mrs Bebbington and Lucy Davies played for some time.

The Old Age Pensions Act was passed this autumn. By this Act men and women of good character of the age of 70 or over with small means are to receive a pension of 5/- a week, among those benefiting are Easthope of Birtley, Walter Lewis the postmaster and Evans of Heywood.

The weather was extraordinarily mild, there was one day's frost in November and not another frost until December 23rd.

1898 to 1916 DIARIES

In December a tea and Christmas tree was given at Ticklerton Court to the girls and children.

1909

Old Evans of Heywood did not long enjoy his pension, for he died in March during the bitter weather, he was 84 years of age.

The Rector took his usual holiday during February, March and April. During his absence, Mr McColl, was installed as locum tenens, we liked him very much, but his sermons were very long.

Extremely cold weather was experienced during the early part of the year, and in March the ice bore for several weeks. A curling match took place on Soudley Pools between Church Stretton and Plaish, the former won.

The Liberal promises of 1905/6 remained, as usual, unfulfilled, for provisions far from growing cheaper, increased in price, and this always seems to occur when Liberals are in power, and the rates rise also. Bread which stood in 1905 at 4½d the quartern rose to 6d by 1908.

1910/1911

The only entries during these two years are:

In 1911 Sarah Medlicott at the Pear Tree married William Kirkham, Claybrook and they took a farm near Wenlock. Mary Evans, Soudley, married a man named Bownes, who turned out such a drunken bad lot that she had to leave him. Emily Cox, Upper Farm, married Mr Cheetham of Leeds.

1912

During our Rector's usual holiday, the duty was taken by Mr Jardine. He lodged with Mr and Mrs George of Ticklerton. Penny Easthope of Birtley passed examinations and obtained the certificate that allowed her to take the post of District Nurse, she was obliged to live in Acton Scott Parish and her family accompanied her with the result that our Parish lost a very excellent ditcher in the person of her father.

In February the United Hounds met at Ticklerton Court.

There were deep snows in the winter, followed by a fine hot spring.

An unusually fine trout weighing 4½lb was caught at Soudley Upper Pool by Mr Payne of Church Stretton.

During 1911/12 B Sparrow Esq erected a Dutch Barn at New Hall Farm, and W S Buddicom a large building to hold 20 cows at the Lower Farm in Ticklerton. Mrs Buddicom added a study and bedrooms to the Bank House and the Rev G Powell of Munslow did extensive repairs to the farm and cottages at Hatton.

In Spring a national coal strike took place, our people suffered some inconvenience being obliged to burn wood, which many of them obtained from our plantations, fortunately the strike ended before there was any real suffering. This was followed by a great disorganisation on the railways caused by a shortness of coal, many of the main line trains were taken off, and the Wellington - Cravens Arms line, only one train a week was run for nearly a month, when the strike ended

In April Aubrey Price of the Saplings married Miss Marsh, The Post Office, Wall. Clement Venables of Eaton married Elizabeth Cox of Upper Farm, Ticklerton and they went to live at the cottage close to Eaton railway bridge. Later T Hughes of Heywood married Christiana Harley of Soudley, who was many years older than himself, he went to live with Christiana and a little boy in Christiana's cottage.

The summer was exceptionally wet, and few of the farmers were able to get in their fine crop of hay in good condition, fortunately they were favoured by such magnificent weather in September and October that even bad farmers got in the harvest satisfactorily.

Mrs Edwards having left the village, the School house was let to a family of the name of Hayward, Mrs and Miss Hayward playing the harmonium nicely in church on Sundays.

Major Hornby, Bank House, was proposed as Liberal candidate for South Shropshire at the next election.

Jasper and George, sons of G Whittingham Jones of Soudley won prizes at the Little Stretton pony show.

In August, Mr and Mrs Humphrey of Soudley, who had not prospered at home, went out to Canada with their children to join Mrs Humphrey's parents who had emigrated some years before.

About 23 years ago, Charles Roberts, now a smallholder near Burwood, was a labourer living at Birtley with his wife and daughter, his wife died at the birth of a son - George - and this child was adopted and brought up by Mr Duncan, our station master, and his wife. George was an exceptionally precocious, intelligent child. When his adopted parents left our Parish for Heswell, Cheshire, he attracted the notice of a lady who helped so materially with his education that he succeeded passing through a theological college in September 1912. George Roberts father did not long remain a widower, for within a year he married a hard working young woman with a little money by whom he has numerous family, besides his daughter by his first marriage, Elizabeth, who this year married Sandells, a small farmer near Wentnor. The Roberts come of good country stock, who once knew better days. They are an industrious, steady family that deserve to get on in life.

William Kirkham of Claybrook died. After his death his widow and sons continued to work the farm with the assistance of Richard, William's brother, who though quite blind was the mainstay of the farm. In November he cut his arm and blood poisoning set in, he seemed to get better but on November 11th, when Mrs Kirkham went to to call him, she found that he had died in the night. He was buried at Eaton.

The churchyard wall dividing the south side of the church from Venables land had yearly been growing more and more ruinous, until at last the cattle could pass through. The Rector, finding it quite impossible to raise funds to rebuild it was about to put up a railing when Mr and Mrs Buddicom interposed and had the wall rebuilt at their own cost. Mr Buddicom gave the sand and the extra stone required and the rebuilding was carried out by a mason named Evans and his son, who did the work at 6/6 the square yard, the total cost including the inscription stone, but excluding the sand and extra stone, was £50. The work was finshed just in time for Harvest Thanksgiving service in October, the church having been decorated with autumnal fruit and flowers. £7-10-0 was taken in the collection. The Rector took his choir to Shrewsbury for a treat,

Mary Hall, daughter of William Hall of Soudley, having passed every necessary examination at the first attempt, was qualified to act as School mistress. She was appointewd to be mistress of Shineton school at a salary of £80 a year and she would receive a pension on retiring.

A man named Morris had established himself as a carpenter at Soudley in Hope Bowdler parish, but on the border of ours, by building himself a galvanised iron shed which he used as a workshop and also as a dwelling. He was addicted to visiting the public houses in Church Stretton, and one evening he went down as usual, leaving his little stove alight. When he returned, he found that the building, which contained everything that he owned, had been burned down with all the contents, he was not insured. A subscription was raised to assist him, and including the proceeds of several concerts at Hope Bowdler, the sum of £26-14-0 was collected to give him a fresh start. Whether the shock sobered him, or whether all the advice, sympathy and encouragement he received had a good influence upon him I cannot say, but after the catastrophe he grew steadier.

On November 20th, during the run of the United Hounds, a hunted fox took refuge in the cellars of Ticklerton Court, fortunately when he emerged the hounds were pursuing a fresh fox.

At a winter auction at Shrewsbury Smithfield, a cow and a calf, the property of Major Hornby, topped the market at £28, nevertheless, £28 was not an excessively high figure.

The winter was very mild and there was practically no snow or frost. We picked a few primroses in the hedge banks around December.

Income tax was 1/2 in the pound. Poor rate on agricultural

land 9d in £1, on buildings 1/6 in £1. The purposes for which this rate was made and amount in the £1 levied for each purpose was: Relief of the poor and all other expenses of the Guardians 7d, County contributions 4d, overseers expenses 1d, education 6d – total 1/6.

Local prices: flour bread 6d the quartern, butter 1/- to 1/4 the pound, eggs 8-16 1/-, wheat 16/- a bag of 225lb, chickens 2/6 – 3/- each, ducks 3/- to 3/6 each, potatoes about 5/- a hundred-weight, mutton 10d a lb, beef and veal 9d – 1/- a lb, bacon and ham 1/- a lb, sultanas and raisins 6d a lb, rice 2d a lb, cod fish 4-8d a lb, sole 1/6 – 2/- a lb, lemon sole 10d – 1/3 a lb, cheese – cheddar and cheshire 10d – 1/- a lb.

Lucy Davies of Whitefields received a special card for having been a member of the Girls Friendly Society for 21 years, and one other member of our branch received a similar card. In 1912 the Church Stretton branch of the G F S had grown rather unwieldy and was divided into two. The three parts of Stretton with Woolstaston retained the name of the C S branch, while all the other parishes including our own were formed into the Rushbury branch.

The Rector gave a party at the Rectory to the Sunday School children and prizes to the most regular attendants.

Young Perkins, son of Mr Perkins of Hatton, took the small farm at Hatton and married in the spring, but his young wife died very sadly in November of an acute attack of Influenza.

1913

The Rector was away during Lent, his duty being taken by Mr Jardine.

The winter of 1912/13 was the mildest that I can ever remember, there was very little frost and snow fell on one day only, March 17th. Pyrus japonica and primroses began to bloom at Christmas and the fruit trees to bud in January, but it was also the wettest winter I can recollect and very bad for farming, gardening and all young stock. It rained nearly every day from October until the middle of May. The brook at Ticklerton was once impassable, which seldom occurs. At Eaton the water was several times out on the road and on one Sunday evening in February there was no service in church, the water being so deep in the road that no one could get to church. On two mornings the postman, when he reached Eaton, found the water too deep to walk through and had to hail Venables, who lives at the farm on the other side of the brook, and get him to fetch him across with his horse and trap. The Harton ford was impassable not once, as it usually is each winter, but over and over again.

In February Mr A Wood-Acton Esq, who had represented the district at C.S. on the County Council for 15 years, retired. There had been no contest in our district since 1888, in which year the

C C was created, when the post was keenly contested by our own Rector, Mr Holland Sandford, and Mr A Wood-Acton, the former gaining the election by 18 votes. When Mr H Sandford retired in 1898, Mr W-A was unopposed. On the present occasion the election was contested by Mr Beddows, Minton and Major Hornby of Bank House, Ticklerton. Maj H was supported by his uncle Mr W S Buddicom, by the labourers and most of the shopkeepers. Mr Beddows was supported by the farmers outside his Parish and by the whole of the Concervative gentry in the district, with the exception of W S B Esq, who worked up a political agitation against Maj H and provided 16 motors to carry voters to the polling station at Rushbury, Wistanstow and C S, while Maj H's friends had not one motor with which to help him. To this I attribute that Mr Beddows, a rather unpopular man, won the election by a majority of 39 votes out of an electorate of 1150 of whom 850 polled their votes.

After 12 years of office Mr Davies of Whitefields resigned the office of District Councillor. Mr Joseph Bebbington, Harton, was appointed in April.

Easter Sunday fell upon March 23rd, the earliest date but one upon which it can fall and the earliest day on which it has fallen for 57 years. In this neighbourhood Good Friday is always given as a holiday, and labourers usually set their potatoes, but could not do so this year because March 21st is too early to set potatoes.

The Rector gave a most handsome Easter gift to the church in the form of a set of embroidered veils and burses for the communion service in different colours assigned to the various seasons, fasts and festivals of the church.

The G F S members and other girls in the Parish were entertained to tea etc. at Ticklerton Court on February 28th, and the G F S candidates on April 18th.

According to an officially issued Parliamentary paper the births in Shropshire for the year 1912/13 amounted to 5,785, the marriages to 3,562 and deaths to 3,486.

The Archdeacon, after his usual tour of inspection, wrote to our Rector that the way in which our church is kept is a model to the Diocese, there not being so much as a tile displaced.

On May 26th occurred a most dreadful storm of thunder, lightning, rain and hail which, in less than half an hour, did incalculable damage. A small brook at Hope Bowdler in that short time became a raging torrent, threw down the wall of the Rectory garden, poured through the village, being 6' deep in the road swamped the blacksmiths and carpenters shops and literally carried away several gardens. Our pools at Soudley were converted temporarily into lakes, parts of the dam injured, sluices carried away and the wall in front of the large arch dividing Mr Benson's pool from ours destroyed, several tons of masonry being carried into the pool. The Ticklerton and Eaton brooks rose higher than they have ever done for 70 years, at Eaton Manor the torrent stopping at the doorstep. The rain and hail did equal damage, water poured into nearly every house and crops were ruined, everywhere gardens were devastated, young crops of grain destroyed, chickens and fowls washed away and drowned, a horse was struck by lightning. The hailstones, really larger than marbles, broke windows including 30 panes of glass at the back of Ticklerton Court, and were still lying about in heaps next morning. Two thunderbolts were reported to have been seen.

In or about the year 1889, in the month of May, there were frightful floods between Shrewsbury and Ludlow, and I can remember water pouring off the platform of the station and water deep in the street, at least one railway bridge was destroyed and passengers had to leave their train and walk to another, which was waiting on the other side of the broken bridge. About the year 1860, there was a hailstorm and the hail stones were said to be as large as pigeons eggs which destroyed sheep and cattle in the Corve Dale and broke nearly all the windows of Middlehope Hall, neither of these storms did as much damage in our neighbourhood as the one which took place in May 1913. George Williams remembers a worse flood 68 years ago when the big culvert under the lane between Mr Benson's pool and ours at Soudley was destroyed and the water was 5' deep in the kitchen of Lower Farm, Ticklerton but no one else living now can remember this flood.

Minnie Hall, daughter of W Hall The Alders, Soudley, was married to J Groom.

The summer was delightfully fine, but not very hot. The hay harvest was tolerable, but much of it was got in too green, the corn harvest was very poor, so much land could not be sown at all owing to the wet spring. Many young crops were ruined by the hail storm and a great deal of corn never ripened at all. There was little or no fruit, the hail having stripped the trees in May, with the exception of blackberries which were very abundant. The root crops were much better than had been anticipated. The Harvest Thanksgiving took place on October 12th, the church was prettily decorated, the Rector presented an embroidered fall of the pulpit desk, collections amounted to £8-9-6.

Our branch of the G F S was hospitably entertained at Millichope Park by Captain and Mrs Beckwith on June 24th, Emily Evans of the Parish received a framed picture, having been a member for 21 years.

The Rector entertained the Sunday School children to tea, he gave prizes to those who attended regularly. He took the choir to Shrewsbury for their treat and the afternoon was spent boating on the Severn.

A very successful pageant took place at Church Stretton in July, it was held in a charming glade at the back of the Hydro, the charming slopes of the Long Mynd forming a natural amphitheatre for the spectators. The pageant commenced with a charming fairy scene in which the prettiest children from our Parish and other neighbouring parishes took part as fairies etc. This was followed by scenes illustrating local history, Caractacus and the Romans, King Alfred's daughter founding a nunnery, Giraldus preaching a Crusade, Wild Humphrey at Stretton Fair, Morris dancing etc. James 11 visiting Stretton during a progress. Miss Buddicom took part in this scene as a "lady of quality". The pageant concluded with a march past and a tableau of all the characters, all singing Land of Hope and Glory. The pageant was well planned and owed a great deal to the beautiful surroundings. The weather was favourable and the attendance good. On the third and last day, Thursday, the market was practically deserted, the whole neighbourhood being at the pageant. £60 was cleared, half going to Stretton and half to Shrewsbury, several of the scenes having been arranged and acted by Shrewsbury people. These sums of money were devoted to charitable purposes.

In October a most violent hurricane swept through South Shropshire, little damage was done in our own Parish, at Ragdon a barn was blown down. The full force of the cyclone was felt in the Church Stretton valley where the track of the storm fortunately extending over a belt only a few hundred yards wide, could be traced by mangled trees, scattered branches, fragments of barns (one was carried nearly a mile) and houses with roofs, chimneys and windows in a wrecked condition. Fortunately the storm passed a little to the east of the town, but the 'crescent' in particular presented such a piteous spectacle that people came many miles to view such an unusual sight.

Deaths - in July Mrs Richard Jones of Chelmick valley, just outside the Parish, she and her husband had kept their Golden Wedding day the previous autumn. Mrs Poston, Heywood, died in December aged 75, she had been left a widow with a large family of young children, all of whom she brought up creditably.

In November a sad accident occurred to a Cardington man, a carpenter named Garrathy, who was working for Mr Hanbury Sparrow at New Hall farm, he was digging out a post hole close to a wall, and part of the wall fell on him, he was much hurt and died while being conveyed to hospital, he was 31 years of age.

Police cases at Church Stretton petty sessions. Herbert Humphries, Soudley, hawker was convicted of being drunk and told to pay costs. Mr Gatehouse, army cadet, staying at Eaton rectory was charged with riding a motor cycle to the danger of the public, i.e. at a terrific pace. He was represented by a solicitor and fined £1 and costs. Emily Short, school mistress at Hope Bowdler, was summonsed by the father of George Jarret, Soudley, who attends H B school, he had disobeyed the mistress and refused to hold out his hand to be caned, so Miss Short caned him across the legs, which is not allowed. He is a very naughty boy and everyone sympathised with Miss Short who was fined 6d and costs.

1898 to 1916 DIARIES

Mrs Buddicom had to undertake the unpleasant duty of causing to be evicted her tenants Daniel Speke and his wife from one of the three cottages known as Woodside cottages, they were higglers (door-to-door) by trade, they were in the cottages when they were bought by Mrs Buddicom and she kept them as long as she could, but they were thorough bad lots, dirty, thieving and drunken that the other tenants of the cottages would not put up with them, they would not go out peaceably, though offered £5 to do so, so they had to be evicted. The police would have had some trouble as they refused to budge, but the Relieving Officer came up in a motor, which he persuaded them to enter (they never having had a motor drive before) and having done so they were whisked off to Stretton, where they rent a room. This is the only time I can ever remember our having to evict a tenant.

Fred Hill, Ticklerton, had advertised for a farm labourer and engaged without reference a young man named Mansell, a few days later the police came to arrest him for stealing a bicycle from his last place. An exciting chase took place during which Mansell rushed through the Bank House kitchens and floundered through our pool, he escaped and made for Cardington Hill where a few days later he was found, half starved, hiding in a drain and arrested.

In October the United Hounds met at Ticklerton, a successful days cubbing followed. This pack killed 20 cubs during the 13 days of cubbing, a very good bag.

A very old resident gave up farming this year, W Robinson of Ticklerton Hall, he had come to this farm as a child (his father, old Cheshire Robinson) and after his father retired kept on the farm, and having lived in the same house for over 50 years, he had a remarkably successful stock sale, most extravagant prices being paid. He retired, with his wife, to the Gilberries near Gretton, which he owns.

At Barber's September Sheep sale, Mr Davies of Whitefields sold ewes at 41/6 each, J Cox at 45/- and Seabury, Hargrove, 31/-. Ewes were selling well and the top price at this sale being 54/- and the lowest 30/-. At Morriss's Craven Arms sale, R Wilding, Ragdon, won the first prize for a yearling Kerry ram which realised £42 and another yearling from his flock fetching £21.

There was a good deal of unrest about the countryside, which was inflamed by politicians who went about, specially among the farm hands. Lloyd George's act compelling all employees to insure against illness (the employers also having to contribute) was passed this year. It was singularly unpopular among all classes.

In July was offered for sale the Warren Estate, consisting of five farms, Harton Manor, Harton Farm, Wolverton and two at Alcaston in Acton Scott parish, each with adjoining portions of the Edge Wood. Only one farm was sold at the auction, though one the Alcaston farms was sold later. The Harton Manor was purchased by Miss Buddicom, 200 acres including 40 acres of Edge Wood. About the same time Mr Warren offered for sale the fine old refectory table, 14 feet long, the bench and carved screen behind it. It seemed a pity to move them from the house where they had rested for so long, but as they were to be sold, Miss Buddicom saved the table from the Americans by purchasing it and it was brought to Ticklerton Court. There is a sort of tradition repeated all over the neighbourhood in connection with this table, which is as follows. An immense oak was cut down, 'the Harton Hollow wood' and the three largest planks were made for three tables, the one formerly at Wolverton (now at Ticklerton Court), one at New Hall (and if it was the table that is there now, very inferior to ours) and the third, according to the story, 'was put to stop the weir'. The table appears to date from about 1600, so probably the story has been handed down ever since.

1914

The New Year was accompanied by a spell of very cold weather, frost, snow and 16 days of east wind. February was occupied by floods of rain, ploughing was achieved with great difficulty everywhere, and on some clay soils - not at all. May was bitterly cold and the late frosts did serious injury to the potato crop. In June was a terrific thunderstorm which killed 5 sheep belonging to Mr J Venables, Eaton, injury was done to some gardens, Eaton and Ticklerton brooks rose very high. July was fairly fine and the hay harvest was good, violent winds spoilt some fields of corn, otherwise the corn harvest was well got in and it was an exceptionally abundant crop. Blackberries, plums etc were an abundant crop, apples moderately so.

Police cases at Church Stretton Petty sessions. January 29th Edwin Duckett, Soudley, summoned for being drunk on Sandford Avenue, he was fined one shilling and costs. W Machin, Mount Flirt, was summoned for being drunk and using obscene language and for having given a false name and address, he was fined 10/- and costs or to go to prison for 7 days - he paid the fine. September, Bert Humphries and T Colley were summoned for being drunk, they were not fined but ordered to pay the costs

Our rector was away through Lent, the duty being taken by the Rev Boyer, who resided at the rectory during this period.

Mrs Buddicom of Ticklerton Court died on March 7th and was buried at Eaton-u-Heywood church on the 10th. Our rector came up from Brighton specially to take the service and was assisted by Mr Boyer and the Rev E Corbett-Winder, a nephew of Mrs Buddicom. The service was choral and the hymn 'Abide with me' was sung at the graveside. The grave had been beautifully lined with moss and flowers and 61 wreaths etc were sent by sympathisers. Besides relatives and friends, the churchyard was almost full of people from the estate, parish and neighbourhood who attended the funeral. In September Mr Buddicom had a beautiful marble angel erected to his wife's memory. In October, Mrs Kate Buddicom, fourth wife of the late Rev R J Buddicom died in Cheltenham aged 85. She was, by her wish, buried at Eaton-u-Heywood beside her husband.

The number of inhabitants now in Shropshire is stated in public statistics to be 264,000. The expenditure of the rural district council in the Church Stretton Union - 16 parishes - had been estimated at £1,250 for the year ending March 1914, but owing to unforseen damage to roads and bridges caused by the floods and storms, the sum was exceeded by £100.

On May 30th a new station for passenger traffic was opened at Church Stretton, the old station being converted into goods warehouses and goods yard.

The Royal Show, the finest agricultural show in England, took place in Shrewsbury on July 1, 2, 3 & 4. Champion prizes for sheep and fleeces were won by K Milne of Stanway Manor.

On July 3rd our King made a progress through Shrewsbury and visited the show. He was loyally and enthusiastically received, but he responded to the acclamations in a very stiff and ungracious manner. King George is the first reigning sovereign to visit the town since James 11.

In 1914 Alfred Kirkham married Miss Price from the Saplings. Annie Jones from Soudley Post office married a man named Eastment, employed by the County Council, who went to live at the Post Office with his wife as Post mistress. In December, Clara Corfield, Hatton, married Albert Edwards a sailor on HMS Dido.

In 1914 B Hanbury Sparrow Esq erected an ornate mural tablet in Eaton-u-Heywood church to his Father's memory.

The Harvest thanksgiving collection in October amounted to £9-13-2.

A 5 bay Dutch barn was erected at the Upper Farm, Ticklerton, property of R A Buddicom Esq. at a cost of £80. The price of wool, fleeces, at the July wool sales was from 9-15d per lb according to the quality of the wool.

The members and canditates of the G F S were entertained to tea at Ticklerton Court. Mr Friederichs gave his usual choir and Sunday school treats.

March 11th the United Hounds met at Marshbrook and drew the Acton Scott covers blank, they found in our Mousleys and hunted the fox through the Edge wood, over Hope Bowdler hills, down again to Rushbury where they killed after 50 minutes of the best. The United and neighbouring packs of hounds hunted through the parish several times through the season.

THE WAR

   The news of the war with Germany fell like a bombshell in our midst, a small temporary panic, the banks closed for a few days to prevent people drawing out their gold, and when they reopened it was to issue treasury notes of £1 and 10/- which had been hurredly printed to meet the emergency. A good deal of gold, however, continued to circulate in country districts. There was a frenzied rush of housekeepers to lay in stores, and this temporarily raised the price of provisions. Once the panic was over, prices dropped and did not rise considerably for 8 or 9 months, by which time food was 1/4 or 1/3 dearer than before the war.

   Many passenger trains were taken off during the mobilisation of the troops, but most were put on again in September, but it was never impossible to travel. It was indeed amazing how little the ordinary course of life was affected, we soon got used to seeing the trains and platforms thronged with khaki clad soldiers and to the new war regulations, the stringency of which were not felt in our quiet country district as it was not near the coast or large camps. We of course lived in a state of great excitement, specially during the first months when the Germans occupied Belgium and Northern France, despite the gallant efforts of our own troops. Nor shall we ever forget how horrified we were by the details of the unspeakable atrocities committed by the German army of invaders upon the civilian population in Belgium, as recorded in the newspapers and recounted by the Belgian refugees at Church Stretton.

   All local flower shows, pony shows, etc were cancelled and no balls took place this winter.

   In August a rest and training camp of 3000 men and 800 horses was established at Church Stretton for a short time. We saw the new Yeomanry recruits riding about our lanes, equally falling off into our Ticklerton brook, where the horses, often rough untrained animals, would pull up with disconcerting suddeness.

   Several families of Belgian refugees were entertained at Church Stretton, the surrounding parishes all contributing to their support. The voluntary aid department headquarters in Church Stretton began to collect, make garments etc for the soldiers and for the hospital. I undertook this duty in our parish, Mr Friederichs and Mrs Gatehouse each subscribed a £1 and Mrs Hamer of Wolverton 10/- to buy material and I provided the rest. 153 garments being made in the parish and sent to the VAD and to the Shropshire regiment in Flanders. Our schoolmistress and the children sent a large parcel of clothes to the children of the Belgian refugees in London.

   A small hospital of 30 beds was equipped at Church Stretton by local voluntary effort and maintained with very little help from government, which allowed only 2/- per day for each patient.

All labour, nursing and medical service was given free. At first only convalescents were treated but as time passed on the more serious cases were sent in.

The Prince of Wales started a fund to help DISTRESS and it soon reached £5 million, collections were held for it in every church, £11-6-8 was collected at our church, besides private subscription to the fund. It is very doubtful what was done with the money.

There was little unemployment for, besides the army and navy calling for recruits, numbers of men and women were needed for the factories, munitions work etc. The number of troops on the road was reduced to a negligible amount.

The dependants of soldiers and sailors were provided for on a scale that was certainly too lavish in the cases of labourers families. Women who had previously had to keep their families and husbands on 16/- a week, now were receiving double and having no husband at home to keep. This lavishness, though doubtless helpful to them for recruiting, must help to raise the taxes to huge proportions.

There was a great rush to join the colours, specially in the towns and amongst the sons of the county, scarcely a family among the upper classes being unrepresented in Shropshire, though indeed the same might be said for every class all over England. As Eaton is a purely agricultural parish there were not many in a position to enlist. Most of the farm labourers enlisted at once, thus leaving the farms with their sons, when they had any, to work their farms with only very old men or young lads to help them. Captain Beckwith, Millichope, was an energetic recruiter and most eligible men in the Munslow and Rushcote sides of the parish joined. Three sons of Mr & Mrs Gatehouse, who generally live in this parish, joined the army and were in all the most fierce fighting of Ypres, Hooge and Loos. Alec Gatehouse was wounded and was given the Military Cross. B Hanbury Sparrow had two sons in the army, Alan, the elder, went to the front with the Berkshires, which regiment suffered so badly that at last he was the only officer left of the regiment that first went out. At last he was badly wounded and also lost half his hand, he was mentioned in despatches and given the DSO. He later on rejoined his regiment and went back to the front. His younger brother, Brian, joined the Oxfordhire regiment and went out to Salonika in 1915. Major Hornby was at first instrumental in raising 3,000 special constables in London. He was then made Brigade major to the 7th Brigade under General Kinloch, and later made Lieutenant Colonel commanding the 8th York and Lancasters. In August 1915 he went out to the front with his regiment, his brother, Geoffrey, came with the 1st Canadian contingent and was killed at Ypres in May 1915. His sister Dorothy came with the Canadian nurses. Two nephews, J and C Carnsew with the 2nd Canadian contingent. Captain Friederichs, our Rector's brother, re-

joined the army. Others from our parish: Arthur Carter, Soudley, in the Shropshires. E Perkins, Hatton, in the RAMC. J Jones of Soudley Villa, RAMC. S Hartley of Ticklerton Hall, Shropshire Yeomanry. W Painter, formerly of Hatton, Canadian contingent. Sidney Rogers, a driver in the artillery from Heywood and Albert Edwards in HMS Grafton.

The late autumn and first part of winter, though very mild were exceptionally wet, indeed, it rained almost every day for months, this incessant rain is aspired by some to the firing of the big guns in elgium and France – artillery fire being popularly supposed to bring down rain from the clouds.

In an official publication of Novemebr 1914, it was stated that there were 12,500 men from Shropshire in the Shropshire regiments or other regiments. In 1911 there were 121,835 males, including old men and male babies, so that 10% of the male population of Shropshire are now under arms, a splendid record of patriotism.

1915

Mr Venables of Eaton Manor died on January 16th aged 74 and was buried at Eaton, his sons remained at the farm, also the deaf and dumb daughter. One of the sons, Clement, who had married Elizabeth Cox left the cottage where they had been living and went to the farm.

Mrs Hornby and Miss Buddicom got up a very successful concert in aid of the Church Stretton Belgian refugees. It took place on January 20th and the sum of £6-0-6 being taken. The seats were 2/- 1/- and 6d each. The greater part of the sum was taken by selling tickets beforehand and some at the door. There were no expenses, everything being given or lent. The programmes were printed and cost 3/6, and being sold at 1d each just covered their cost. Miss L Hayward lent the piano, the chairs and lamps were borrowed from Hope Bowdler parish room, Mr Robert Jones lent materials for the stage and gave 2 days for putting it up and taking it down. Mr Buddicom and Major Hornby lent three men to help with the school for two days. All the planks, chairs etc were fetched from Hope Bowdler and taken back by Mr Buddicom's pony and cart. Miss Buddicom did all the posters and the rehearsal was held at Ticklerton Court. Mrs Hornby lent their motor to bring up from Stretton Mr Burden who has a fine voice and sang delightfully. Mr Friederichs our rector acted as Chairman and did it very well. The concert commenced by the national songs of the allies given by the school children, followed by a piano duet given by Miss Buddicom and Miss Hayward. Other items on the programmme were songs by Mr Buddicom, Mr Burden, Miss Jones, the governess at Bank House, Mr T Croxton, Miss R Cleeton, Miss M Cox and Mr Robert Jones. Violin and cello solos by Miss G Hayward and Miss Short. Piano solos by Miss

Buddicom and Miss Elsie Childs. Recitations by Mr E Hall and Miss Doris Hall. The evening was a great success and was much enjoyed.

On February 2nd Mrs Hayward, school house, died. There was reason to fear that she had taken cold at the concert, the funeral was at Eaton.

On February 3rd the United Hunts met at Ticklerton, they had a good run, but did not kill. About this time, Miss Whitaker of Totterton Hall near Lydbury North, became 'Master of the United pack' to relieve the Master, Mr Connop, who joined the army, but she carried on hunting in a very perfunctory manner, just to keep things going.

At one period in March 1915 wheat was at 60/- a quarter.

In March a small rummage sale was held at Ticklerton Court, proceeds £3-7-6 were sent to Church Stretton hospital. Richard Jones of Chelmick Pools died at the age of 84, he was the oldest resident in the Hope Bowdler parish and he was a good thatcher.

In April, a national egg collection was organised to provide military hospitals with eggs, a great number was sent from our parish. Edwin Jones, our sexton, died after a long and painful illness. After one or two men had tried to undertake the work and failed, chiefly because it takes a lot of skill and strength for one man to ring a peal of three bells, Harry Hanson of New Hall Mill became our sexton and bell ringer.

In June Miss Ruth Hanbury Sparrow married Sir William Parker, Bart. a young officer in the new army. J Hartley of Harton married Miss Morgan.

In May, Mrs George of Ticklerton died, leaving a young family.

In July John Rogers of Heywood, who had been Mr Buddicom's coachman, died.

In November, Mrs Hill of the Lower Farm, Ticklerton, died. Miss Wade, who had been housekeeper to Mr Venables, married William Edwards, a roadman of the Turnpike Cottage, Birtley. Alice Jones of Heywood married Richard Morris, a carpenter at Soudley, and a daughter of Robert Jones, Hope Bowdler, married Wilfred Painter, formerly of Hatton who was in Canada when war broke out and came over with the Canadians.

Police cases at Church Stretton in 1915. Bert Humphries was summonsed for riding on the shafts without holding the reins. Tom Colley was summonsed for being drunk and was fined 7/6 and ordered to pay the costs.

The branch of the G F S girls were entertained at Acton Scott Hall, canditates and members of the Parish were also entertained at Ticklerton Court, and the Rector gave his treats to the choir and Sunday School children.

There was an excellent harvest, well got in. The Harvest Thanksgiving Service, the offertory amounted to £10-1-5.

1898 to 1916 DIARIES

In September the farmers of the district made a collection and had a jumble sale, chiefly of livestock, at Church Stretton where the sum of £220 was raised for the Red Cross. In the same month a Tricolor Day was held in Church Stretton in aid of the French Red Cross, small articles adorned with tricolors were sold for 3d. 6d and 1/-, and no less a sum than £29 was collected in the streets. £500 had been given for the several Belgian refugees in Church Stretton. By the end of 1915 little help was needed, one family being assisted out to Brazil where a post had been found for the husband. Other families also found work. One man was an iron worker who supported himself almost at once making ornamental objects, such as, candlesticks in wrought iron. He also made the new gates for the recreation ground and then became a munition worker in Shrewsbury.

The Rector was away for the winter months, the duty being taken by the Rev Charles Bryant of Church Stretton.

There was severe frost in November, followed by floods of rain in December. On December 27th a most severe gale swept over the country, hundreds of trees were blown down in the woods and a big larch fell down on the bridge over the brook at Eaton, doing much damage to the stonework. A great deal of damage was done everywhere, slates and tiles being blown down in all directions, Dutch barns blown crooked and even blown down. It was particularly tiresome that this should have occurred just at this time, labour being so scarce that it took months to make good the damage.

1916

Among the local sales of stock in January, the following can be given. Mr Hamer of Wolverton a cart mare £54. W Hall of Soudley a cow at £27-5-0. W Hartley of Ticklerton Hall a cow £26. J Hartley of Harton a cow £22-5-0. F Davies, Whitefields,, a Hereford cow £28-7-6. Ewes, top price at sale 75/-, lowest 50/-. W Downes, Common 59 and 60/-, John Cox 52/-, J Bebbington of Harton 50/- a ram. Stores 54/-.

The war, which optimists hoped would be over in May, continued to be the dominating factor. More men joined the army, but their numbers were insufficient. Instead of at once passing an act to bring in universal service, the Government dallied with the voluntary system, thereby wasting valuable time.

In September a national register was taken of all the men and women between the ages of 16 and 60, after this a voluntary scheme was drawn up, generally known as 'Lord Derby's Scheme', because he organised it. A number of groups were set out in order, fixed by ages to include all men, married or unmarried, 18 to 40. The men were persuaded or bullied into "attesting", i.e. to give their names to the recruiting authorities. Married men were promised that if they attested they would not be expected to join the army until all the unmarried men in England, whether they had attested or not, had done so. This promise was not well kept and much dissatisfaction was caused by this amongst the married men and their families.

A great number of men whose work was considered essential to the nation, such as munition workers, engine drivers, miners and millers, timber fellers, hauliers, waggoners, shepherds, cowmen and others engaged in husbandry were 'badged' and ordered to continue their work.

Postmen, employees in shops etc., were called up at once, and others who owned businesses had to replace employees with women and men over 40. In the end, the actual owner of the business, if under 40, had to join up, which usually meant closing down the business. Local tribunals were set up to adjudicate these cases, consider their merits and give exemptions where it was considered advisable. The Derby scheme did not bring enough men, so in 1916 an Act was passed rendering all men between 18 and 40, who were medically fit, liable to be called up to join the forces. The tribunals still continued to sit and exempt many necessary for work of national importance. In our district, anyhow, farms were left fairly undisturbed as far as the principal workers were concerned right up to the end of 1916. The great difficulty was the harvest, any extra labour being almost unobtainable. The Government professed to find labourers for the farmers, but in 1916 this did not work well.

In 1915/16 a great many changes, large and small, took place in our lives and conditions. I will name some. Women were employed in all kinds of work that had previously been considered suitable for men alone, one saw women in banks, chemists, shops and driving motors and motor lorries, distibuting parcels from motor transport, working in carpenters shops and forges, doing rough farmwork, window cleaners and a hundred other ways, especially in making munitions of war in munitions factories.

Many trains were taken off and cheap tickets were abolished. No photography or sketching was allowed, except by permit. Staying in hotels or apartments meant filling up a form that was sent to the police. All windows had to be darkened at sundown, so that no light might show to attract German Zeppelins. Motors and carriages were allowed very feeble lights, and in towns it was positively dangerous to go out after dark. The hours for which public houses and bars might be open for the sale of intoxicants were limited and it was forbidden for one person to treat another to a drink, this to prevent so much intemperance. A few heavy fines when these acts were first passed ensured general obedience.

It was almost impossible for anyone, except soldiers, doctors and nurses to leave England for the Continent. The postal services were not interrupted and letters and parcels reached the troops with astonishing speed.

1898 to 1916 DIARIES

A great many new and increased taxes were imposed, most trying of all was Income Tax which, in January 1916, was 2/6d plus 20% on the 2/6, in all 3/- in the pound. (In 1915 it was 1s3d plus 1/3 war tax) There was a small amusement tax on theatre tickets, a tax of one third their value of foreign motors, watches etc. Heavy taxes on beer, tobacco, tea, sugar, matches and other commodities. Increased taxes on motors. Postage rates were increased from 1d for 4oz to 1d an ounce and parcel post was increased by 1d in the pound. Most of these taxes, though of singularly small amounts, added up to a good deal as a whole. Also the cost of living, wages etc. were mounting all the time, in fact by the end of 1916 most of the principal foodstuffs had advanced from between 75% and 100% higher than before the war.

At this time the Diaries either ceased or have been lost, as no further records exist.

With the end of the Great War, the very large number of young men of the Parish who served in the forces was recorded on the War Memorial in Ticklerton, the details of which are on the following page.

THE WAR MEMORIAL

Brig Gen M L Hornby D.S.O
Maj A H Gatehouse
Capt G Gatehouse
Sap G Anson RE
Pte E Bradley KSLI
Pte W J Childs Labour Corps
Pte C Corfield RW Fusiliers

Pte R C Corfield KSLI
Pte E Dale KSLI
Gnr C S Downes RFA
P.O. A Edwards RN
Pte F T Edwards RWCKR
Pte G Francis KSLI
Pte E Goode KSLI
Pte A Hartley KSLI
Pte H Hughes SW Borderers
Pte G Jones RAMC
Pte T S Jones KSLI
Pte H Jones Lancs Reg
Spr J Lewis RE
Gnr R Morris RFA
Pte W Painter KSLI
Pte G H Perkins MG Corps
Trp J R Pitchford Shrops Yeomy
Spr S J E Rogers RE
Gnr G Sankey RFA

Lt Col A A Hanbury-Sparrow
Maj R Gatehouse
Capt C Hanbury-Sparrow
Gnr H Anson RFA
Pte R Cleeton KSOB
Pte H R Cleeton Lancs Fusiliers
Pte E S Childe Kings Liverpool
Rifles
Pte H Cox KSLI
Pte S Dickinson ASC
Pte J O Downes Dorset Reg
Pte D Edwards KSLI
Pte W Edwards RMLI
Pte J Francis RAMC
Pte F Gough KSLI
CSM C Hughes KOYLI
Pte E Jones SW Borderers
Pte W Jones
Pte P H Jones KSLI
Spr G Lewis RE
Spr D Merrilees RE
Pte S Morris KSLI
Drv A L Perkins RGA
Trp J E Perkins Shrops Yeomy
Pte P Poston Lancs Fusiliers
Pte E Sankey KSLI
Pte E Woodhouse KSLI

PARISH LIFE

CRAVEN ARMS TO MUCH WENLOCK RAILWAY

If one excludes wars and catastrophes like the Great Plague, there is nothing that would have affected the lives of the people of Eaton parish as much as the opening of the railway line from Cravens Arms to Presthope on 16th December 1867. This meant that as the Presthope to Much Wenlock section had been opened three years earlier, there was now a continuous line from Cravens Arms to Much Wenlock connecting with the main Shrewsbury to Hereford line.

The Shrewsbury to Ludlow line had been working since 1852 and, from 1853, went all the way to Hereford. But apart from those needing to make a long journey, its principal use would have been for business men and, to a certain extent, those attending the markets. It made little difference to the average villager, Church Stretton station was still a few miles away and it took time to get there, plus the cost of the tolls that were still operative at Hatton Gate until at least 1871.

The building of Harton station and a regular timetable of trains in each direction transformed the lives of a great many people. No longer were the long and tedious journeys on foot or by pony and trap necessary to obtain provisions, visit the shops and go to school for the older children. Harton station soon became busy with passengers, cattle, sheep and merchandise. It had a Stationmaster, he had his own cottage and the timetable was such that a train to Cravens Arms allowed just an hour for shopping before the return journey.

A train crossing Eaton railway bridge, c.1930.

A coal yard was soon established and instead of the long haul back from Stretton or, as it was in earlier days, from the wharfs in Shrewsbury, now it was a much simpler task for the farmers to collect their supplies, not only for the house but also for the steam engines now becoming common for driving the threshing machines. The threshed corn, in large sacks hired from the railway company, was now sent by rail to the corn merchants in nearby towns. The Estate farmers each had to give a statuary number of days work each year to their landlord, Squire Buddicom, Hanbury Sparrow and others, by hauling coal and wood. This was now less time-consuming, but it was an arrangement that persisted well into the 1930s.

The movement of sheep and cattle to the markets became much simpler. No longer were the flocks driven along the roads with all the hazards and time taken. Now, cattle trucks stood ready at the station and were hitched on to a regular train and arrived at market in no time.

The local school was no longer the natural limit of education, for older children could now easily attend higher schools in Much Wenlock or Shrewsbury.

Another village 'character' was added to the postman, schoolmaster (or schoolmistress) and shopkeeper - the Stationmaster. He became one of the community and when the time came for him to move on to another station or promotion, he would be given a farewell party and presented with a parting gift.

Before the railway was opened, hundreds of men were brought in to dig the cuttings, raise the embankments and lay the lines. They were not local men, they lived in temporary camps and there is little doubt that their presence accounted for the 3 or 4 pubs that blossomed and, no doubt, flourished, only to die again when the job was done and there was not sufficient local trade to sustain them - The Masons Arms and The Horshoes in Ticklerton, The Pheasant at Birtley and the Blue Bell at Hatton were all licensed at about the same period. Their existence must also have benefited the locals who did not now have to go all the way to Church Stretton if they wanted a change from their own home brewed beer and cider.

There is an interesting entry in the 1861 census. It shows that "131 woodsmen from Sedgley, Staffs" were living in tents in Eaton Parish. Were they brought in to clear the way for the railway line? It seems unlikely that such a large number would be needed, but what other explanation is there?

As cars, vans and lorries began to become more common from the 1920s, so the importance of the railway began to decline a little, it was still the main means of bulk transport, the daily milk train and passenger trains were in regular use. Just how valuable rail transport could be was illustrated time and again in bad weather conditions, none more so than in the very hard winter of 1947/8. All the roads in the Parish were blocked with snow, nothing could get out other than across the fields to the station and the train. For six weeks the only means of getting the milk and produce away and provisions in was by the trains.

The end of the railway came about with the Beeching Closures in the 1950s. The tracks were taken up, the bridges dismantled and the ground sold. Apart from looking on a map, the only way to see just where the line ran is, from a distance, when the local mist forms early some mornings, "it follows the old railway line", as the locals will tell you.

CIDER MAKING

Although today you would be hard put to find a cider apple tree in the Parish, let alone any orchards, yet there used to be enough local cider making for two mobile cider presses to do the rounds of the various farmers.

One belonging to Jack Miles, uncle to Tom Miles of Soudley, was probably the last one in use and after he died nobody else bothered. His old press was left abandoned behind a barn in Ticklerton until, eventually, it was taken to the Acton Scott Farm Museum and restored.

In addition to the apples grown locally, some farmers used to collect them from further afield, in the Corve Dale and other places. The apples were put in big heaps on the ground, often being picked over by pigs and hens. Jack Miles would arrive to start pressing, other farmers would go along and give a hand to each other in turn. Ticklerton Hall had very fine orchards of eating, cooking and cider apples. When their turn came, water was taken from Ticklerton Brook, before the bridge was built, and even though the Bank House sewage ran into the stream, it was reckoned to make better cider than water from the nearby ponds, which were too hard.

The apples were first pulped by two men turning handles, the pulp was then shovelled into layers or cheeses in the press, with matting between each layer with a framework around it. When it was full, they started turning the squeezers or press with long poles. The juice ran out into an open tub through a lead spout. The pure juice had a delicious taste, but too much soon had the effect of Epsom salts! It was mixed with water and put into large vats or barrels in the vast cellars beneath Ticklerton Hall.

Some special brews were made, beetroot being added to make it red and a little sweeter. Others used to have a piece of beef put in which, by the time it was ready to drink, had "been eaten away". Rats would sometimes fall in and drown, not being found until the vats were emptied. These did not seem to have any ill effects or spoil the taste!

PARISH LIFE

The choice of barrels was very important and each year, when
old whisky and brandy barrels were sent to Cravens Arms station
for sale, there was keen competition, plus a lot of sniffing of
the empty barrels, because a good barrel well saturated or steeped
with spirit would add considerably to the strength and flavour of
the final brew.

Cyril Perkins of Hatton was reckoned to make the best cider
around, and many are the tales of those who found they spent the
night in one of the barns after a few mugs, unable to make it
home. Mr Perkins used to reckon that after three or four years the
barrels had to be replaced, as the cider had taken everything out
of them, and they did nothing for the new brew.

FARMING

Until about 1860 all corn had to be threshed with flails and
then winnowed in a machine turned by a handle. Then came the barn
threshers, where the corn in the ear was put in the drum and turned by hand. Many people, in addition to farmers, had them. Edward
Hince who lived in a small cottage at Heywood was still using one
at the end of the 19th century.

George Williams, the last of the flail men?

PARISH LIFE

According to Phil Poston (in 1938) who was living at Heywood, the last person he remembers who still threshed with a flail was George Williams who used to travel round with one and thresh the corn that the women had been allowed to glean from the cornfields. He also thinks that his Mother (Poston's) was the last gleaner in the Parish. She then lived at the old Turnpike Cottage, Birtley, and gleaned the Hatton farms, where Williams would have used the threshing barn and probably winnowed it there too. The last time would have been in 1896 when she too moved to Heywood and never gleaned again.

Haymaking in Middleyard, 1893. C Bouchiere and men.

It was reckoned that two men threshing with flails in a barn all winter was no more expensive than to work with a machine, but soon after 1860, threshing machines had been developed and they used to be hauled from farm to farm by horses, with a stationary steam engine to drive them. By 1886 W Robinson of Ticklerton Hall had his own little steam driven threshing machine. This blew up one day when he was threshing peas for a neighbour. When the engine exploded, W Robinson Jun. was badly scalded about the legs and a workman named Breeze was struck by debris and had his leg broken in two places. The pea haulms then caught fire, then the stackyard and buildings. The pumps ran dry (it had been a long, dry summer) and they had to get water from the brook, a quarter of a mile away. 26 acres of hay and a building belonging to Mr Buddicom, some distance away, was also destroyed. They had great difficulty getting livestock out and a calf was burnt alive. The nearest fire engines were Shrewsbury and Ludlow, the Church Stretton engine had been sent away because of lack of funds to keep it.

The changeover from scythes in the cornfield began with the arrival of the reaping machine. Two brothers called Rogers from Chester bought one. The sheaves were thrown out loose and still had to be tied by hand. Self binders were rare up to the end of the 1890s.

Harvest time in the '30s.. l to r Henry Roberts, Winfield Attenborough, Mary Cushen, Evelyn Attenborough, Molly ?, Mrs R Attenborough, Ruth Attenborough, Ernest and Alfred Roberts.

The Wooldridge family from Wall used to operate threshing machines, going from farm to farm. The camp followers or casual labourers (down and outs) used to do all the rough work, straw, pavins (chaff) etc. and they would be given free cider each day. It was said that old Joe Wooldridge must have held the world record for cider drinking.

In the Second World War, in 1942, the District War Agricultural Committee, having done their best to deal with the enormous increase in threshing that the ploughing programme had brought about, laid down that no set of threshing tackle could stop at any farm for more than two days until every farm, large and small, had been visited.

PARISH LIFE

The first combine harvester - reaping, threshing and putting the corn in bags - was hired by Mr Young (or Mrs Amiss) at Lower House Farm, Ticklerton, in 1945. They were also the first in the Parish to introduce machine milking.

PLOUGHING

Ploughing and all field work was done with horses until the second world war, with one or two exceptions. In the 1914/18 war Wm Hartley at Ticklerton Hall had a tractor, but it was not a very successful venture and the only other one in the Parish until about 1938 was owned by Edward Cleeton at New Hall, but he only used it occasionally.

Farmers in the '30s had a hard lean time. Money was scarce and anyone who was not hard (or even tight) soon went down the drain and bankrupt. There were so many men out of work that at times when extra or casual labour was needed, farmers would sometimes have a new man starting each week because, with men coming knocking on the door for work, if they were not satisfactory, on they went and a new man took their place.

CHEESE MAKING

The Madeleys at Eaton Manor farm used to make and send a lot of cheeses to the Shrewsbury Cheese Fair. This took place every three weeks in the 1920s and '30s. Some extracts from account books of the period make interesting reading. The cheeses weighed 43-45lb and on January 10th 1924 they sent 57 cheeses at 1/4 a lb, two months later, on March 13th, 34 were sent but the price was down to 7d a lb.

In 1928 they sold a total of 450 cheeses in the year for £889. At this time butter was 1/7 a lb, a dressed chicken 3/6 and a couple of rabbits 2/8.

By 1930, when times were very hard, cheese was down to 6d or 7d and the year's turnover was down to only £722. The wages for a year paid to E Mansell were £84-10-0 and to E Williams, a lad, £27-19-0.

THE WOODS

The Edge Wood would have been part of the Long Forest and dates back to Norman times.

For centuries charcoal burning was carried on at various levels all along the Edge. These sites can still be clearly seen and where the ground has been levelled off, the earth is black. They were favourite places for rabbits to have their warrens and often used to run as much as 6' deep.

PARISH LIFE

Charcoal burning was still being carried on until just before the Second World War. One firm used to bring their own big metal kilns, but there were two local burners who still did it by hand in the old manner. They were Henry Addison and his son Billy who lived at Greystones Cottage, Birtley. Young Billy was "eleven to the dozen" and one day, cycling back from Marshbrook, going down Hatton Hollow, he fell off his bike into the hedge where a sharp stake went into his head and, sadly, killed him.

The Edge Wood was owned by Mr B Hanbury Sparrow and, before he died in 1936, part of his management policy was to carry out periodic felling to provide timber for the Estate use and, every two years, he would employ Sam Spencer of Craven Arms to bring his mobile steam engine driven saw bench to a field opposite Eaton Manor Farm to saw up the wood. It was then seasoned and used by the estate carpenter for building and house repairs. Mature oaks were also cut for sale. In earlier years, of course, all timber would have been cut by hand, using saw pits - very heavy work that used to command wages above the average.

His eldest son, Alan, inherited the estate but had not got his father's interest in it and felled nearly all the woodlands, mature and semi-mature trees. He did, however, start a replanting scheme.

Soon after the war, Alan Hanbury Sparrow sold the estate. Many tenants were able to buy their own properties but the bulk, including the woods, were bought by Charles Edwards. However, he did not keep them very long and in 1951 sold what was known as the 'Eaton and Rushbury Estate' which included New Hall and Eaton Manor Farms, cottages and woods in Eaton Parish. Noel Good, who had been rabbit catching all around the area when he came out of the army. bought a large section of the woods running from New Hall back towards Longville. In the years since then he has done an excellent job in replanting and managing them. It is said that if old Mr Hanbury Sparrow could come back and see them as they are today, he would appreciate what had been done.

Another activity connected with the woods was the periodic arrival of a particular Lancashire family (and sometimes other groups) of workers who used to live like gypsies in tents, they were called 'cloggers'. They used to fell alder (waller) trees, cut and shape them into clog bottoms, then move on.

At the top of Roman Bank and below the Edge wood, towards Harton, there were many limekilns, another trade that has died. And in the area around Claybrook farm blue, white and red clay was to be found, with brickmaking carried on there. On the old tithe maps, many of the field names show clearly where the different activities were carried on - Brickkiln Field (52) near Claybrook, Burnt Piece (422) near Eaton, Limekiln Piece (688) and a number of 'Limekiln' fields near Cuckoo's Nest.

PARISH LIFE

Mention of Cuckoo's Nest, which is near the top of Jacobs Ladder which runs up the hill beside Eaton Church, there used to be a small, isolated cottage of the same name. It became derelict and disappeared many years ago. When old Tom Carter, who once lived there, died, it was reckoned that his coffin must have been brought down to the church on a wheelbarrow, because only a single wheel mark showed down the hillside track.

THE SCHOOL

St Edith's School at Eaton.

An early record connected with education or schooling appears in 1817 when a Benjamin Wright M.D. left £400 to build a school-room at Rushbury (a neighbouring parish), and also included £5 to pay a schoolmaster to teach the poor children of Rushbury, Eaton and adjoining parishes each Sunday. A further £5 to a schoolmistress to teach children to knit and sew and £5 on December 1st for warm clothing. The remainder (?) to instruct 9 poor children of Rushbury and 3 of Eaton in reading, writing and common arithmetic.

In 1863 it was decided to have a school in Eaton and on April 15th of that year the Rev Robert J Buddicom and Ann, his wife, together with his brother William Barber Buddicom of Penbedre Hall, Flint conveyed an acre of Long Mousleys Field (tithe 263) as a site for a school for poor children and a residence for a leader.

PARISH LIFE

The school was called St Ediths and the census returns show the following occupants:

```
1871  John Marshall   - 26 National schoolmaster
      Jane      "      - 25 Schoolmistress
      Mary Roberts     - 21 S-in-law
      John Gordon      -  5 Boarder

1881  Edward Pennicot - 49 Schoolmaster
      Adela Marion "   - 18 School assistant
      Sarah Ann    "   - 25 D-in-law,housekeeper
      Bertram Lyle     - 11 mths gd/son
```

The schoolchildren - July 1897.
(back row) Mary Carter (head girl), Alfred Jones, George Roberts, G Anson, Ed Cleeton, John Morris, Tom Cleeton.
(second row) Mr Roberts (Schoolmaster) Lizzie Roberts, Eva Barlow, Ada Barlow, Bessie Cleeton, Jessie Easthope, Mary Cleeton, Miss L Davies of Whitefields.
(third row) Kittie Barlow, Lucie Gardiner, Alice Barlow, Polly Jones, Dottie Stephens, Mabel Gardiner.
(fourth row) Edwin Jones, Robert Jones, George Barlow, Alfred Roberts, Dick Cleeton, Jasper Jones.

By 1897 Mr Roberts was the schoolmaster, assisted by Miss Lucy Davies of Whitefields and in the July there were 13 girls and 12 boys. By the Summer of 1900 there were 18 boys and just 6 girls attending. Edwin Jones, George Thomas, Richard and Mary Cleeton were given prizes by Miss Lilian Buddicom for the best attendance records.

Mr Roberts left the school in 1908 and though kindhearted, it is recorded that *"he had not been a very efficient master"*. He was, nevertheless, given a handsome presentation. He was succeeded by Miss Short. She lived with her sister, who lodged with the Jasper Jones family in the Hope Bowdler School house, where one of the conditions of being a tenant was that you had to board the school teacher. Norman Jones of Chelmick Valley was born there and the family remained in residence until 1930 when his father, Jasper, built his house in Chelmick Valley.

The Eaton school house, not being needed, was occupied by Mr Edwards, an insurance agent, who lived there rent free on condition that his wife played the organ in church. The rent was paid by the church out of the Church warden's funds at £4 a year. This continued until 1922, it was then raised to £5 until 1953. The rent for '54/5 was £30, after which payment ceased.

In 1915, Miss Short married Mr Rowe, the schoolmaster at Cardington, and her successor was Miss Kelly, described as "a clever teacher".

The school children were given parties at Christmas, and at other times of the year too, by the Rector, the Buddicoms at Ticklerton Court and the Hornbys at the Bank House. Gifts of sweets or an orange were much prized. Good attendance was also rewarded each year with special prizes. The school was also used for Sunday School, and attendance was looked upon as being more or less compulsory. Here again prize books were given for good attendance and there was an annual outing to Shrewsbury – a great treat.

One day in 1925 a terrific gale was raging, and the pupils were horrified to see the toll rope of the single bell in the belfry suddenly disappear up into the roof. Moments later there was an almighty crack as the bell and belfry tower crashed down on to the roof and somersaulted into the girl's playground which, because of the bad weather, fortunately was empty.

The school closed soon afterwards and the children had to go to Hope Bowdler, where the school remained open until 1948, or take the train from Harton Road station to Rushbury school.

In 1931 the old school building became a Men's Club, the Rector being the first President. He presented some guns and pistols and they used to challenge teams from Rushbury, Marshbrook, Church Stretton etc. to shooting matches. There was also a small billiards table. The Club closed down in 1939, reopening again for a short while after the war. Today it is a private house.

FOLKLORE

A large number of books have been written, many in great detail, on the subjects referred to in the following pages. These particular extracts have been gathered from the relatively small area in and around this Parish, and were either said by or believed by many of the people who lived there. Where the origin is known, it is included.

CURES

Many of these local medical cures are well known in different parts of the country, but villagers used to take them seriously and, who knows, some may still do so.

LIVER complaints. Carry a potato, tied in the bend of the leg, under the knee. It will become quite hard and yellow.

CANCER. Make an infusion of Red clover, strain and then drink. Also eat lots of honey.

RHEUMATISM 1. Take a chair without a seat. Put a bucket of cold water under the chair. Sit the patient on the chair, wrapped up in blankets, put a white hot brick in the bucket and the steam rising will act as a steam bath.

2. Carry a potato in the pocket.

CONSUMPTION. A boy with T.B. was advised to swallow a live frog. There were two men who were 'Lungish', they walked about the cornfields at harvest time, picking up small live frogs and swallowing them down as a cure.

BOILS & SPRAINS. Comfrey, take the whole plant, chop up stalks and leaves, wrap in linen and apply as a poultice. This was said to work for either humans or animals.

WHOOPING COUGH. 1. Mrs Groom of Hisbeach tells how when her Gwenny had whooping cough badly, an old woman told her to get a hairy caterpillar, put it in a little bag, and tie it round the childs neck. By the time the caterpillar was dead, the whooping cough would be cured.(c1914)

2. Take a hair from the cross on a donkey's back, put it in water and then drink it. (Cleeton)

PILES. Take a wisp of hay, put it in a bucket. Pour boiling water on it and sit on the bucket. The steam is 'sharp', but will cure the piles.

FLU. Strew rue on beds to keep away the flu.

WARTS. 1. Steal a bit of beef, rub it on the wart and bury the beef. By the time the beef has decomposed, the wart will have gone.

2. Take a piece of wood and bury it at the crossroads. The idea being that someone will walk over it and 'catch' the wart. (Edward Hall)

3. Teddy Hall (1925) had a very bad 'rough old wart' on his knee. He fell down and tore it. A lady staying at the Sandford Hotel where he was working saw it, gave him a pin to bury, and said he was to tell nobody about it and it would go. He did as he was told and a few weeks later the wart had disappeared.

HYSTERICS. Beat the bare back with nettles.

COUGH. To cure a cough, put a piece of white chalk in each shoe, in a day or two the cough will be cured.

GENERAL DEBILITY. As a cure, drink milk that a ferret has been drinking from. (A ferret is a very tenacious animal for life and so gives tenacity of life by sympathetic means)

MANURE. George Seabury of Common Farm, caught his arm on a piece of barbed wire, made a great tear right down the inner side of his arm, from armpit to elbow, in places nearly to the bone. He gathered up manure off the field and plastered it over the wound. Two days later he soaked it off and it was already almost healed. He put on so much manure and stunk so much that his father would not have him sit with them. This was quite a common cure for cuts, but one wonders why patients did not suffer from tetanus.

SAYINGS and PROVERBS

The many sayings and proverbs of Shropshire have been well documented elsewhere. Here are a few that were collected from people living in the Parish.

BIRTHS. A new born baby "mun go up before they go down". (Mrs Attenborough)

FOLKLORE

If there is no higher room/attic, someone must get on a chair and lift the infant up to the ceiling.

BEDS. It is said that people cannot die in beds made of pheasant or pigeon feathers.

BATS. Bats clinging to the outside of a window pane is a sign of death coming. This happened when Lilian Buddicom's father had his accident on Pikes Bank and, although he did not actually die, he was at death's door for weeks. Mr Duncan, who was with him, was killed on the spot. However, it happened again in 1922 when both her Father and husband died..

WINTER PINE.or House leek was sometimes used as a poultice for earache. Also, said to be lucky on houses and especially on roofs of cow houses and pig sties.

BLIND BALLS or Puff balls. In a season when there are many 'puff balls' there won't be many mushrooms.

RED CAMPION or Thunderflower. It is said that if the flowers are picked, a thunderstorm will come on.

FLOPPY DOCKS or Foxgloves. A girl known by Miss Auden, when her grandmother was ill, asked the Doctor if she might give her grand-mother some 'Floppy dock tea'. The Doctor, thinking that 'Floppy docks' were some sort of docks said "It won't do her any harm". But it did, the girl made the 'tea' too strong and the grandmother died. The girl was aquitted.

ELDER. Unlucky to bring into the house to burn. If a cow is in calf, the cow will cast her calf (W Hall). But it was not unlucky to make patterns on door steps with the juice of elder. (see 'Superstitions')

OAKS. Oaks are supposed to keep lightning away (though they are so often struck). The 'acorn' still used as a pendant on blinds, presumably to appease THOR, the God of thunder.

GOOD FRIDAY. Unlucky to work on Good Friday, but lucky to plant potatoes on that day.

GOATS. Lucky to let goats run with cattle, said to prevent cows casting their calves (Perkins had one in 1938). Some people think the goat eats up herbs that are injurious to cattle.

FOLKLORE

PREMATURE BIRTH. If an animal is born prematurely, it will generally live until the date it should have been born, and then die on that date (Hall 1930).

BIRTH MARKS. When Harold Hall's mother was expecting and 'near her time', she went into the garden for a cabbage and, unknown to her, her husband had set a trap for rabbits. A black rabbit that was caught in the trap sprung up and startled her. Harold was born with a birth mark that looked like a rabbit. He carried the mark all his life.

SWEDES. Swedes should be sown when the moon is waxing.

BACON. Women must not cure bacon or make pork pies when expecting or at menstruation periods for, if they do, the meat will go sour. Also, bacon must not be cured when moon is waxing because, when cooked, it will run away to fat.

FRIDAY. Harvest must not be started on a Friday. Also applies to starting any work or job on a Friday.

LAMB. If a lamb or young pig dies, it is usual not to bury it but hang it up in a tree until 'it fades away'. (Mrs Pugh) This was frowned upon by the authorities and in 1939 a local man was fined 10/- for doing this.

FOALS. When a foal is born it has a second or 'false' tongue which drops out. This must be found and nailed up in the stable, otherwise the foal will have no luck. (Mrs Pugh)

SOME LOCAL EXPRESSIONS

"Har bin' 'ee?"- How are you.

"I'll warm your jacket for you" - punish, beat.

"Straight up twelve" - midday.

"They leaping beans be that profligate" - runner beans are so prolific.

"At twice" - in two periods.

"How long do you think the acorns will take to grow into trees?
"I reckon you'll be ready for your coffin afore they'll be ready to make the boards".

FOLKLORE

After a splendid harvest, a man asked a notorious grumbling farmer - "Well, anyhow, Holmes you can't complain THIS year". Holmes replied, grudgingly, "Well, a' dunno - there bain't no bad hay for the coos".

Alfred Cox was tossed by a bull and Mrs Cox, discussing the affair, said "By all I hear tell, it ain't done Alfred no good".

"I never said nowt o' the sort" or even "I didn't never say nowt o' the sort". (double negatives)

"The bull is gand quiet".

"People shouldn't go mumping and gumping about this and that, they should speak out straight". (at meetings)

"Back o' nine". - after nine o'clock.

A Father, after his son had been keeping company with a young girl for some years and when their engagement was announced said "Ah,(yes) they've hung up their sign".

A man who had done a good days work in the harvest field said, when the farmer came by, "Well, I reckon I've arned my wages today" The farmer replied,"Ay, but that binna enough, I want ye to arn a bit for me too".

"My first job when I left school was JAGGING coal about with mi dad's coal pony for one und another". (carting coal to different people)

"'E tuk mi poultry money and 'e canna BARGE upon me that way now". (put upon)

"We are closing down the fruit centre today" Ted Hall replied "At last, as the shoemakers wife said when she threw it at him".

Ronnie Cox, talking of a disobedient dog said "Ah, he's unforbidden, but he'll larn in time".

"Shaping for 21" - approaching 21 years old.

A. "You must a got up early today"
B. "Well I didna get up afore I was awake".

"I'm better, but not exactly eating carrots".

FOLKLORE

"We talked on old times and that's the best kind of talk there be".

"I just speak to my neighbour about her fowls stavaging about in my garding. But she gives me forty words for free, so I goes off and leaves her, and now we don't speak no more".

"Ay, I've bin on the Perch". A man who had been ill.

PROVERBS

"A still bee gathers no honey"

"Pointin' at the Poomp wunna clean oot the well".

"Caradoc's got 'is cap on"- a sign of bad weather.

"Where parsley flourishes, the Mistress wears the breeches".

"Like a Bridgnorth election - all on one side".

"Pigs may fly, but they're unlikely birds".

"It's neither mi eye nae mi elbow" i.e. it's between the two, a compromise.

"A green something is better than a ripe nothing".

"If you hear anything new on a Friday, it will add another wrinkle to your face".

"If you go to Church Stretton.
 You spen more than you getten".

"If the ice bears soon before Christmas, it wunna bear a duck after".

"If you buy a green dress, you'll soon wear a black one".

"One years seeds make seven years weeds".

PERQUISITES

Today, newspapers are full of the 'perks' that are on offer to all sorts of people in all sorts of business, but there is nothing new in this. Shropshire country folk have always had their own particular brand, and here are a few of them.

FOLKLORE

PIG KILLER. The man who kills the pig, claims the snout. In old days a snout was long enough to provide a meal, now the snout of most improved breeds is very small. T Miles (an old pig killer) used to try to take the sweetbreads as well.

TIMBER FELLERS. He has the right, by custom, to the big chips of the trees that he fells, as well as any dead wood in the tops.

FENCES. The man who pleaches a fence has the right to:
    1. The old stakes he may find in the hedge (good for firelighting).
    2. Any big thorn or other bushes which may do for firewood, but he may not take sapling oaks etc.
    3. Any high growing hazels - for pea sticks etc.

CAULS. If there was a caul at a birth, the midwife would carefully preserve it or sometimes part with it for a considerable price.
    "Cauls were often stolen by midwives as they were saleable for as much as 20 guineas for one, as they are not common".
    Possession of a caul is said to be good for eloquence.
    Also, supposed to protect sailors from drowning.

SHEEP BUTCHER. He claimed the 'Pluck' (viz. liver, lights and head). If the owner of the sheep wanted them, he had to pay the butcher something extra.

POTATOES. Labourers often had a piece of potato ground on the farm. 800 yards was the usual amount. The farmer ploughed and manured the ground, but the labourer would provide the seed potatoes, set them and lift them up in his own time.

HARVEST TIME. When rabbits were driven into the middle of a corn field, the labourers claimed the rabbits that they knocked down with sticks. All those the farmer shot or were killed by his dogs belonged to him.

SUPERSTITIONS

    There were many people who believed in them, and even those who pretended to take no notice, would always be very careful not to flout them.

CLATTERING GAP/GLAT, near Hill Top, on the Wenlock Edge. A murder had been committed on that spot and the body dragged through the hedge. Presumably the intention being to bury the body later. An attempt was made to disguise the gap in the hedge with thorn and branches, but in vain. The next morning the gap was there again and a passing traveller saw the body and raised the alarm. For years all attempts to mend the hedge (by growing a new one) failed and the gap was always there. (Chronicle 16/7/1954

Another version of the haunted spot was given by Mr H Shenton of Church Stretton, who tells a tale of 1835 when William Corfield, gamekeeper for Moses Benson of Lutwyche Hall, was shot dead in the Edge Wood near Five Chimneys. A John Thomas of Hughley was charged with the murder.

Sometimes the clattering of horses hooves were heard near the spot, but no horse was ever seen - hence the name 'Clattering Gap'.

CHURCH CLOCK. In some churches the Church clock is stopped during the service because of the belief that, if the clock struck during the singing of a hymn, a parishioner will die during the following week.

PATTERNS on threshholds and hearth stones.

Until the end of the 19th century there were many farmhouses and cottages that had their doorstep decorated with green patterns. They were said "to keep the evil away or out" though, more often they were made for 'Good luck'. They were also 'laid' on the hearthstone to stop the Devil from coming down the chimney. They were to be found on stone steps leading to bedrooms, on the flagstones in kitchens and dairies too.

The patterns were made by taking a bunch of elder leaves, squeezing them, and rubbing the patterns on the stones with the leaves, when the pigment will make bright green patterns. They lasted for weeks, even months and could be washed, though the colour then fades. Dock leaves and oak were occasionally used. The most interesting patterns are with loops, with its suggestion of a winding thread to keep witches away. The following are examples of patterns used by some local people.

The pattern should be done without taking the hand off the stone. This pattern was seen at Ticklerton Court 1897-1900

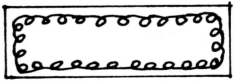

The one below was done by Hetty Miles (Heywood) Doorstep and hearthstone.

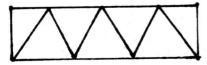

FOLKLORE

Mrs Eastment, Soudley Post Office.

 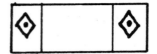 

Mrs Lewis, The Alders, Soudley on stone steps leading to bedrooms.

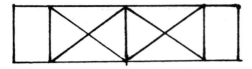

Mrs Miles, Sycamore Cottage.

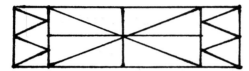

Flagstone patterns.

WORDS

The 'Shropshire Word Book' by Georgina Jackson is well known and very comprehensive, there are other publications too, but some of the words here were recorded locally and may contribute to the very special vocabulary of Shropshire words.

AG - portion (ag of sand or of a hedge).
AGAINST - by the time. "I'll have the kittle bilin' against you are ready for tea".
BANTERING - of a bargain, beating down the price. "He's not the sort of man to banter us down".
BATTER (or N) - a bank or wall sloping outwards from top to bottom.
BE - his "That be hisn"
BIGGUTED - has a high opinion of himself.
BIGSORTED - arrogant, uppish
BING - the passage behind the boosy where the cattle were fed.
BOOSY - feeding place in a cow barn.
BREVETTING - looking for, hunting about.

FOLKLORE

BUTTY — mate or companion.
CANT — tattle.
CHAUSE — drive away "chause the hens off".
CHIS PIT (cheese pit) a small round wooden cheese mould, about 12" diameter, with drainage holes in the bottom.
CLEM — to starve, hunger or cold.
COMMUNING — "He is communing at the door with rabbit skins".
COUCHED — lying, e.g. rabbits.
CROSSLONKARD — awkward (in disposition).
DECORDED — parted, describing how two people had parted company.
DOTE — to desire a thing.
DOUT — to extinguish, put out.
DREARING — "To take a good straightforward walk may do one good, but DREARING about the barn and yards all day, don't do me no good, nohow".
ESH — white ashes from the grate.
ESPEN — hustle, harrass. "A wild dog will ESPEN the ship".(sheep) "Now mi lad, dunna ye ESPEN the coos".
FALTER — to become ill or show signs of extreme old age.
FLEM — a channel from the main stream to a water mill.
FOWAN — resembles, "He fowans his Mother".
FROMMET — away from "Come away frommet the rick".
FRUM — early, used as an expression 'Frum taters".
GALLOUS — mischevious (of boys).
GLEEDY — glowing, of a fire.
GODFATHER — a piece of wood fastened against a post to strengthen it.
GORSTERING — masterful (pugnacious)   "I don't reckon nought on 'er, 'ers a GORSTERING piece".
GRUB SPEWS — worm casts. "They GRUB SPEWS do blunt the knives terrible".(mowing).
GYVER — swank.
HELE — cover potatoes.
HIGGLER — man who buys old iron, rabbits etc and sells again.
HOTTEN — to heat. "I'll HOTTEN up the tea with hot water".
JACOBS LADDER — a small home made ladder with the strips of wood nailed on the outside of the long side pieces.
JAG — selling in small quantities.
JO or GAO — lines or cords for driving horses when chain harrowing etc.
KALE — spill over or upset. "Don't let the pan KALE over". " KALED the chair over".
LING — to carry, "ling hay".
MAULING — hard or difficult work.
MOGGED — timber inserted among bricks without design to give strength to the building — not proper b/w style.
MOIDERED or MOITHERED — confused, bothered.
MOILY — dirty, wet or sticky soil.

FOLKLORE

MULLOCK – dirt.
NARKING – amazing. "Its very NARKING". or "Her bin allus NARKING at 'im" – nagging.
NASH – a scythe, because the best makers were Isaac Nash of Worcestershire. The scythe was introduced in about 1800, when it superceded the sickle.
OLOPPERS – curious bone in a sheep's leg, used in the past as apple corers.
ORDAIN – order, usually a master's order.
PATENT – ill, suffering. "She'd bin very PATENT all the winter". (about a woman who'd died in her sleep)
PEART – in lively health.
PITCHIN' – a piece of cobbled yard.
PITTERING – peering or seeking about.
PLITCH – a stay placed against a post.
POWER – a quantity. "A POWER o' folk in th' church".
RANK of manure – heap.
RAWLING – rough "RAWLING old saucepan".
RICE STICK – for knocking down apples.
ROMPIN KITLINS – Golden sovereigns "My son has got all my ROMPIN KITLINS off me". Perhaps in reference to the rampant lion and unicorn of the Royal Arms on sovereigns.
SCROOGE CUT – square cut.
SHARP – "Pretty sharp", in rather lively health.
SKIPPET an iron bowl attached to a long handle for cleaning out gutters.
SLIPE – slippery. "The roads were that SLIPE, I couldna' get".
SNIVE – swarming.
STAVAGING – rushing about, doing damage.
STITCH – a division between cow stalls.
TALENT – loft of hay above stable, a space left to pull down hay.
TALON – rough loft for hay over a cowhouse.
TAUNTING – urging, "Kept on TAUNTING her Mother to give her a new dress".
TROLLY or DOBBIN – light cart or wagon.
'UNT – (pronounced h'oont) a mole.
URCHIN – hedgehog.
UNWED – not weeded.
WER – a hoar frost – "Wer frost".
WHIFFLE – light snow. "There was a bit o' snow WHIFFLING around".
YEAZEL – hazel.
YORKS – twisted hay bands tied below the knees.

PARISH SCRAPBOOK

There are many pieces of information that do not warrant a special chapter but are, nevertheless, what local history is all about. They are included here, in no particular order, for the enjoyment (or enlightenment) of the reader.

WALL WAKES - were held on a date early in August. They were discontinued just before the War. There used to be sports, stalls with cakes, gingerbread etc., barrels of beer and a good deal of drunkenness. Respectable people avoided the Wakes and, over the years, they gradually disappeared. The 'sports day' at Wall on August Bank Holiday Monday took the place of the old Wall Wakes.

MILESTONE - at the top of the Sandford Avenue, on the way to Hope Bowdler, there used to be a milestone which read, (on the left side) "Wenlock 11 To Wynnstay Arms" (The Wynnstay Arms has been the Gaskell Arms since about 1840) and, on the right side it read "Stretton 1 To The Market Hall"

TITHES at Hope Bowdler. The Rev Marsh was the last parson in the area to collect the tithes in kind. He used to ride round the cornfields marking his every 10th sheaf. The tithe barn stood where the Hope Bowdler school was later built. Mr Marsh also had animals brought to him as part of the tithes due but, in practice, the farmers generally bought them back again.

FUNERAL - Bill Holford tells about the funeral of Richard Wilding (1854-1934) of Ragdon. Ragdon Farm was then occupied by his son and old Mr Wilding, who had married again, was living at Little Stretton. He had 'ordained' that he should be taken to Hope Bowdler churchyard in his own wagon, drawn by his old mare, and passing his old home. This was done and his coffin was placed on his farm wagon and taken up the steep Hough lane - Wyrestych - to Ragdon, where the wagon halted for 5 minutes (and no doubt took refreshment!) and then on to Hope Bowdler, by way of Chelmick, across the top fields. A man called Minton from the Hough was one of the bearers and the others were Ragdon workmen.

ROBERT JONES (in 1938) was nearly 80, and had been a carpenter until sometime during the Great War. He had learned his trade from his great grandfather, Richard Galliers (Gallears). There were, in Hope Bowdler, a pair of tiny cottages (now called 'Thatchers'), occupied by Amos Mawn and the Galliers and, at one time, it was said that there were 24 children in the two cottages.

Robert Jones' father was a carpenter to Mr Pinches at Ticklerton, so the tradition of family service was carried on when his son worked for the Buddicoms. His sons were all builders. Robert Jones, as a boy, had gleaned at Lower House Farm, then occupied by a man called Mason. Another person who gleaned there was 'old Betty Amis'. The fritillaries - mournful widows - the very dark, old fashioned fritillary flowers, whose dark heads look like widow's bonnets, that were to be found in the Ticklerton Court garden came from her.

Mr W F Duncan, c.1890, at the Bank House front door..

FATAL ACCIDENT - Mr Duncan, who lived at the Bank House and was described as a 'toff', was travelling (in 1891) in a pony and trap with Wm Squire Buddicom down Pikes Bank, Hope Bowdler, when they were involved in an accident. In the crash Mr Duncan was fatally injured, and Mr Buddicom had a shaft through his stomach, he survived, but he lay at Hope Bowdler Rectory for several weeks in a critical condition, before being moved home. He suffered from the wound until he died.

TITTY CARTER - a nickname he acquired because he suckled his mammy until he was two.

WATERCRESS WILLY - Bill Holford's nickname. Also, Blackberry Bill.

CHELMICK VALLEY - The Rev Marsh (of Hope Bowdler) had a long dispute with Thomas Humphreys (1796-1884), a woodsman who 'squatted' on so called common land in the valley, and built two cottages -

one for himself and the other for his daughter Mrs Breeze. Mr Marsh questioned his right to build and would go during the day, while Humphreys was at work, and take the furniture out of the house and put it on the roadway, then put locks on the doors. Humphreys would come back at night, break the locks off and put his furniture back. One day when the Rector was reading the Commandments in church and came to the last *"Thou shalt not covert thy neighbours house"*, Humphreys jumped up and called out *"Then why do you covert mine?"*. It ended in a lawsuit with the defeat of Mr Marsh. Breeze, the husband of Humphreys daughter, married several times. He was 83 when he married for the last time. She was quite young when he married her, and she was still living during the first world war. Her neice, Emily Breeze, was in service at Ticklerton Court. Both cottages were poorly built and were condemned, though they were still occupied until new homes could be found for them.

PHILIP POSTON said, in 1948, that he was 76. Until 1947 he had been a sub-postmaster for 35 years. His district was Upper Heywood, Chelmick Valley, Chelmick, the Hough, Ragdon and Dryhill. He used to walk at least 40 miles a week. He reckoned he must have called 10,000 times at Ragdon. He found delivering the daily newspapers a great trial as, although there might be no letters to leave, he still had to deliver the paper daily. He was paid 6/11 a week in 1912, when he left it was 44/-. He began to report local news for the Shrewsbury Chronicle in 1922, but had been doing this for the Wellington Journal for much longer. He knew shorthand and attended weddings, funerals and other functions.

ERNEST MARSH also delivered letters in this district for at least 45 years - his round included Lilywood, Stone Acton, The Gutter, Middle Hill, Woodgate, The Common, Claybrook, Saplings and Whitefields

BERT HUMPHRIES was a haulier and lived in a tin shed near Stonehouse Farm, Soudley. He was the strongest man around for his size. He owned a vicious black mare - Kit. Harold Hall's father had a smallholding at Birtley and used to let a field to Bert for his horse. He (Bert) would ask the two lads to go and give his horse some water, one used to go to the top of the field and attract the horse's attention, while the other put the water through the gate. They dare not go in on their own. He was a marvellous old man, but could be nasty too. There is a story told of how, one day, a man on a new bike rode up behind him and startled him, Bert swung round and put his stick through the spokes and took them all out.

TOM COLLEY was a postman who lived at Heywood by the old Chapel. He used to get very drunk. One night he went to a dance at the

PARISH SCRAPBOOK

Hope Bowdler village Hall and took a great big bag of kippers with him. He was offering them to everyone when the parson, Rev Percy Mathews, asked him to leave. Tom said *'You'd better come with me Rector'*. *'Yes, I'll come through the door with you'*. *'That's just what I want, I want to pin one on yer'* said Bert. He did not know that Percy Mathews had been a brilliant amateur boxer, so perhaps it went the other way, as Bert did not come back in again.

JACK LEWIS, father of Ken Lewis the Church Stretton postman, was chauffeur to the Buddicoms, and drove one of the first cars in the village.

JOHN ROGERS - Buddicom's coachman for many years, lived in one of the little cottages on Heywood. His pension, when he retired, was to continue living there, rent free.

FLOODS - In 1886 there was a great flood in May, the rain poured in torrents from Tuesday to Saturday, the May Fair was ruined. The 'old reservoir' in Carding Mill valley was broken, and several railway bridges at Church Stretton were damaged. The passengers had to get off the train and walk past the broken bridges and get on another train that was waiting. Water was pouring off the the platform at the station.

RABBITS (pre Second World War) There were a terrific number of rabbits around, the Edge Wood was literally snithing with them. They were some of the best around, running out at 6lb a couple. From half a mile away, below the Edge Wood, you could see clearly the runs on the hillside. Some farmers used to pay part of their rent with rabbits. From a stall in Market Street, Craven Arms old Mrs J P Wood would buy and sell rabbits, poultry and fish too.

STORM 22nd July 1807 Note in the Baptism register 1759-1812 by Richard Fleming, Curate.
"A most Awful and Tremendous Storm of Thunder and lightning, hail and rain. Hail fell in the neighbourhood from 4 to 5 inches in length, resembling broken jagged ice. The wheat cut off at the head, windows destroyed everywhere the hail could reach. Fruit and gardens nearly destroyed. In fact, it was an Awful Visitation. May it ever be remembered in this neighbourhood."

MEAD is older than wine. Plato tells us that Paris, in the Garden of Zeus was drunk, not with wine, but with nectar, for wine 'was not yet known'. Plato also says that mead was used as a libetic before the cultivation of the vine.
Mr (or Mrs) James of Hatton Gate made mead by steeping a honeycomb in water and fermenting it with yeast. It was better if pure honey was used. They used to sell it from there until 1930.

CLAY - When some repairs were done at The Hollies, Heywood they found that the chimney breast had been built with clay instead of mortar. The interior walls of the old barn at Upper Heywood and Lane End cottage were put together with clay. Ted Hall said that when learning the building trade and chimneys were being built, dung was mixed with the mortar for plastering inside, this made a smooth face which soot would not stick to. The rough mortar that masons line a chimney with nowadays (1940) comes off with the heat, leaving a rough surface for the soot to stick to.

The following is a description of a small farmhouse kitchen, that was recorded in 1939.

The kitchen:
1. Flitches of bacon lying on the bacon cratches.
   Hams in muslin bags hanging from the ceiling.
2. Bladders of lard hanging on the wall.
3. Long pieces of seaweed, brought back from an outing to Llandudno, now used as a weather glass.
4. There is a high oak 'press', drawers below, cupboard above. On side of cupboard hangs an accordion.
5. In contrast, on a small table stands a wireless set.
6. A well filled bookshelf, religious books, school prizes and 6d records.
7. A basket of clean washing on the floor.
8. On a shelf a goose wing and a quill of duck's feathers, both used for dusting.
9. Photos of family, enlarged.
10. Grandfather clock.
11. Two country oak chairs.
12. No welsh dresser, as is usual.
13. Rag rug.
14. Over high mantle shelf are brackets for a gun. Japan tea caddies, probably relics of Christmas gifts.
15. No china dogs or cows, such as are often seen.

EATON PARISH ROOM - Opened on 6th December 1930 by The Hon Mrs Rotton, with a whist drive and dance - tickets 2/6. The 'Church Stretton Elite Band' played.

SHOOTING - When there were shoots at Eaton or Ticklerton, young lads were engaged as 'stops', they were sent out to walk, quietly, up and down the edge of the woods to keep the birds in. They were paid 2/6. The beaters got 5/- plus a picnic lunch and a bottle of beer.

ROOKS On the left hand side going from Ticklerton to Birtley, just beyond the Bank House, was a large rookery. In May each year it was customary to have a shoot. The dead birds were given to each house in the village – Tom Attenborough can always remember rook pie, he said it was delicious.

CRICKET used to be played in the field below Birtley house, opposite the old rookery. It was founded by Mr Platt of Soudley. The Hall boys, Harold and Leonard, Joe Groom and his son Ted, and others levelled the ground, flayed it, took the turf off. They had a good team and played in matches as far as Edgton, Downton, Acton Burnell, All Stretton and Millichope. It closed in the late 1930s.

The Village Cricket team in the '30s.
(back row) Tom Attenborough, Harold Hall, Henry Bolton, Ben Ward, Doug Hardy
(front row) Leonard Hall, Eric Groom, Ted Hall, Joe Groom, Charlie Parry, Ted Groom.

SECOND WORLD WAR It is hard to remember that an almost cavalier attitude prevailed when war was declared in 1939.

Tom Attenborough was on a cycling holiday with two friends when war was declared on September 3rd. They were on their way home and it was a Saturday. They went to the pub at Wall and said what about joining up? See you in the village on Monday. They set off for Shrewsbury and went to the Army recruiting office. There was nobody there, so Tom joined the queue outside the RAF place. He was accepted but, before actually joining he had to square up his job, so it was October before he went – he was in for six years. His brother, Winfield, was still at School and his mother still lived in Ticklerton. When he came home on leave he found everyone seemed to be managing pretty well, except for the likes of tea and sugar. Otherwise there was not much deterioration in living standards, thanks to large gardens and local farmers,

STONE AGE finds have been made around Eaton.

In 1954 Michael Hartley of Claybrook Farm found the butt end of a ground and polished flint axe lying on top of ground he had just ploughed.

Tom Attenborough's father found a flat perforated stone disc, possibly a spindle whorl, on the surface of a sunken water-washed track in the Edge Wood. It is roughly circular, 1 " diameter and " thick, with a straight drilled hole " diameter in the centre.

Axe heads have been found at The Saplings by Bob Pugh and at Common Farm by E Meredith.

PLOUGH SUNDAY used to be celebrated in Eaton Church with an old fashioned horse plough, offered by a local farmer, being blessed by the Rector.

PLOUGH MONDAY was once kept in a very different spirit. The young men would take the plough round the parish, collecting money for a 'spree' at night. If any one of the houses were unfriendly or so unwise as to refuse to contribute, they would plough up the lawn!

SIMNEL SUNDAY or as it was also known, Midlent Mothering Sunday, used to be when farm servants who had been hired for the year, were allowed to go home on Mothering Sunday. They were generally provided with a cake by their employer to take to their mother.

It might be just a good farmhouse cake or a genuine Shropshire Simnel cake. This was a rich plum cake, enclosed in a pastry crust, flavoured with saffron, and the upper edge scalloped round. It was first boiled, then brushed over with egg, and finally baked. It looked rather like a flat pork pie.

Rev Holland Sandford, 1823 - 1904

PARISH SCRAPBOOK

HOLLAND SANDFORD

The arrival of Richard Sandford as Vicar to Eaton Church in 1831 was to have a significant impact for, as a wealthy man, he not only rebuilt the Vicarage but also provided a bridge over the brook. He was, himself, Patron of the Church and there is little doubt that he gave of himself to the Church and the parishoners during the 29 years he was the incumbent. When he died in 1860, aged 69, his son Holland took over the living.

Holland Sandford was 37 when he was inducted. He was an M.A. Humphrey Sandford, another member of the family, was now Patron of the Church, in fact the Sandford family retained the Patronage for more than the next one hundred and twenty five years.

Early in the 13th century the Rectorial status of Eaton was removed by Wenlock Priory and all incumbents thereafter were Vicars until, in 1868, the long awaited change was made and Rev Holland Sandford was made Rector, with all the benefits and status that involved.

Although he was Rector for 40 years, little has been written about him in local documents. The Church prospered in his time. In 1869 he replaced the medieval bell that had become cracked.

He was, apparently, an eccentric gentleman, a man of high intellect, a batchelor, who must have found it lonely at the isolated Eaton Rectory. At times he had a housekeeper as well as a servant living in but, by the 1881 census, the only other person recorded as being resident there was Mary Vaughan, a general servant.

He was frequently seen to be riding his horse or driving his gig into Church Stretton. On his journey he used the new road constructed in open fields between the old Hazler Turnpike and the point where it joined the old Hazler road and crossed the Watling Street. There was neither a hedge nor trees to protect the traveller and, although he all too frequently complained to those in high places, his complaints went unheeded. He then took matters into his own hands, formed a committee of local gentry and others with the object of planting trees along either side of the new road to add shade and beauty to it.

There are records of the countless meetings of one Committee or another to determine what sort of trees should be planted, how far apart they should be, who should supply them etc. There are copies of the hundreds of letters to Royalty, the nobility and business men throughout the country, inviting them to allow a commemorative tree to be planted in their name. Most people accepted, but many were confused, not being sure if they were expected to "pay for the honour" or not. Lime trees were finally chosen, and among the many famous names, no lesser person than the Prince of Wales agreed to have one planted in his name.

The scheme was extended to include the main west/east street of Church Stretton and, on 19th December 1884, the official naming of "Sandford Avenue" took place. It was a grand occasion, for not only Church Stretton, but also for the surrounding district too. The official opening was celebrated with a luncheon with more than 40 gentlemen present and the Committee minutes record that "a convivial time ensued".

Vandalism, often considered a modern disease, reared its ugly head on Saturday night, 3rd January 1885, when it was found that *"6 of the lime trees had been mutilated by being cut with a knife – not the work of Boys, but of lubberly louts from 17 to 20"*. A reward of £5 to find the culprits was offered, the police called in, bills printed and advertisements placed in the 'Evening News' and 'Wellington Journal'. All to no avail.

The trees were *"dressed by covering the injured parts by clay and matting, in the hope that they may outlive the injuries inflicted on them"*.

Today, a great many of the original trees are still standing, bearing proud witness to this one particular public act of Holland Sandford, that has ensured the family name is both remembered and renowned for ever.

His health began to fail and, in 1899, he was taken seriously ill. He had to give up most of his duties. In March 1900 he was removed to the Asylum in Church Streton. All his books and furniture were sold by public auction. By the autumn it was obvious he would not recover his health enough to return to his duties and, after nearly 2 years without there being a regular incumbent at Eaton, the Patron – Humphrey Sandford – appointed the Rev C G N Friederichs to the living. His brother was Rector at Acton Scott, a neighbouring parish.

Holland Sandford lived another 4 years and was buried in Eaton Churchyard, alongside his Father, on December 26th 1904, before a very large congregation.

The Official opening and naming of "Sandford Avenue" 19th December 1884

CONCLUSION

It is not really possible to write a conclusion to a book such as this, as history and reminiscences are on-going. However, it is worth pausing and reflecting on what obvious changes there have been, as we enter the last decade of the 20th century.

In the 150 years since the first fullt census was carried out, many of the houses have disappeared and new ones have been built, yet there are only three more houses (64) today than were listed in the 1841 census summary.(see opposite) But when it comes to compare the number of people who lived there, the difference is far more marked. The totals in the table opposite include 146 children under 18, leaving 105 men and 90 women — 195. There are now 83 men and 68 women — 151 listed on the 1990 electoral roll. There is no record of how many children there are today, but it is probably less than one third of the 1841 figure.

In 1871, the census showed that all but 74 of the 322 people in Eaton parish were born in Shropshire, of whom no less than 163 were born either in Eaton or an adjoining parish. How many of today's residents were born in the Parish? — perhaps a dozen. The details from 120 years ago make interesting reading.

1871 — birth places of inhabitants of Eaton.

Parish	99	Hereford	6	Worcester	1
Adjoining parish	64	Cheshire	24	Lancashire	1
Other Shropshire	85	Rutland	2	Lincolnshire	4
Unknown	13	Nottinghamshire	2	Devonshire	1
Others	13	Montgomeryshire	3	Gloucestershire	2
		Berkshire	1	Essex	1

There is no doubt that the make-up of the people is quite different today, but have we progressed? There is now no public house, no shop or post office and no trains. The number of farms have dwindled, there is no cider making and, apart from the farmers themselves, there are very few people who live,work and earn their living in the parish. There is still the Church, the Village Hall and amidst the hustle of modern day living, there is still the unspoilt and unchanged countryside.

In this book there have been glimpses of life and of the people who lived, worked and died in the Parish, but this is, and can only be, a tiny fraction of the history of past centuries.

Finally, stand once again on the Ragleth Hill and look out over Eaton-under-Heywood, you can still hear the silence, the peace and the quiet.

APPENDIX ONE

CENSUS 1841 — 1881

The following pages contain details extracted from the five '10 year' census returns. The vast majority of houses have been located and marked on the 'Field Maps', showing all those that were in existence in 1840, together with the owners at that time. It has been possible to identify the majority of the occupants of each house during the 40 year period but, with many of the cottages, it has not always been possible to be certain exactly 'who lived where', and in these cases the names have been set in *italics*. All that can be said for certain is that they were all living in the Parish in the appropriate year.

Against each tithe number, the relevant page number of the map upon which it appears is given in brackets.

The summary of the 1841 census shows:-

	Houses	Male	Female
EATON	12	46	31
TICKLERTON	40	109	102
HATTON	9	32	22
	61	187	155

No 1 CUCKOOS NEST Tithe No 390 (map p44)

1841

William Bullock	- 59 Ag Lab
Mary "	- 50
Charles "	- 10

1851

William Bullock	- 70 Farmer 17 acres
Mary "	- 60
Thomas "	- 15

1861

Thomas Carter	- 46 Small farmer
Martha "	- 37
George "	- 9
Harriet "	- 6
Herbert "	- 4

1871 uninhabited

1881

Edward Owen	- 64 Farmer 17 acres
Elizabeth "	- 60
Thomas "	- 14
Richard "	- 8

No 2 EATON TOWNSHIP Tithe No 405 (map p44) Owner Maria Eaton

1841

James Jones	- 45 Hoopmaker
Ann "	- 45
Samuel "	- 65 Ag Lab
Sarah "	- 55
Ann Poston	- 12

1851

| Sarah Jones | - 72 Widow Lab wife |

No 3 VICARAGE Tithe No 403 (map p44)

1841

Richard Sandford   - 43 Vicar
James Newall   - 18 Male servant
Sarah Gwilliam   - 60 Female servant

1851

Richard Sandford   - 59 Vicar
Elizabeth Morgan   - 40 Servant
W Fewtrell?   - 36 Handyman
Thomas Jones   - 44 House servant

1861

Holland Sandford   - 37 Vicar
Martha Evans   - 23 Cook,widow

Elizabeth Langford - 18 General servant

1871

Holland Sandford   - 47 Rector
Sarah Horton   - 36 Housekeeper
Frances Edwards   - 18 Housemaid

1881

Holland Sandford   - 57 Rector
Mary Vaughan   - 27 Servant

1990 F Warrington, now known as The Cedars

No 4 EATON Tithe No 412 (map p44) Eaton Manor/Church Farm Owner Maria Eaton

1841

Joseph Jones   - 40 Farmer
Sarah   "   - 40
Sarah   "   - 13
John   "   - 11
Thomas   "   - 6
Richard   "   - 4
Maria   "   - 3
June   "   - 6mths
Thomas Corfield   - 50 Asst,on farm
Richard Evans   -   Male servant
Edward Harley   -   Male servant
Thomas Jones   -   Male servant

1851

Richard Cleeton   - 22 Farmer, 222 acres
Maria   "   - 24 Sister
Mary Dunne   - 14 Servant
Samuel Dodd   - 30 House servant
Thomas Blakeway   - 19 House servant
Frederick Downes   - 16 House servant
Daniel Howells   - 11 House servant

1861

Richard Cleeton   - 31 Farmer
Sarah   "   - 30
George Beddoes   - 22 Nephew
Mary Francis   - 22 General servant
Timothy Hince   - 22 Farm servant
Thomas Jones   - 36 Farm servant
Thomas Higgins   - 19 Farm servant
Edwin May   - 13 Servant

1871

Richard Cleeton   - 41 Farmer 210 acres
Sarah   "   - 43
Sarah Ann "   - 8
Ernest Beddoes   - 13 Nephew,scholar
Jane Owen   - 20 General servant
Timothy Hince   - 36 Waggoner
John   "   - 18 Cowman
William Spragge   - 13 Waggoner's boy

1881 unoccupied, owned by J Loxdale Warren
1895-1934 J Venables
1934- J H Madeley 1990- A W D Madeley

No 5 EATON Tithe No 352 (map p44) Eaton Cottage Owner Maria Eaton

1841

William Dunne   - 43 Ag Lab
Mary   "   - 44
Mary   "   - 4
Sarah   "   - 11 mths

1851

William Hughson   - 34 Lab
Sarah   "   - 28
Mary   "   - 9
Ellen   "   - 4
William   - 2
William George   - 42 Lab
Thomas Harrison   - 25 Visitor & labourer

1861

```
  ?   Harvey        - 41 Ag lab
Hannah    "         - 47
Hannah    "         -  2
Martha Child        - 87 formerly lab wife
```

1871

```
William Reynolds    - 25 Gamekeeper
Fanny     "         - 25
Agnes     "         -  1
```

1881

```
James Bowen         - 37 Ag lab
Mary     "          - 34
Robert   "          -  8
Nellie   "          -  4
Ann      "          -  3
Edwin    "          -  1
Annie Miles         - 22 formerly Dom serv
James    "          -  3 illeg son
Richard Russell     - 38 Ag lab visitor
```

1990 R R Child

No 6 Tithe No 317 (map p44) Whitefields/Eatonglebe

1841

```
William Bray        - 52 Farmer
Thomas    "         - 54
John      "         - 15
Henry     "         - 13
William   "         -  3
Richard   "         -  9
Mary      "         - 78
```

1851

```
William Bray        - 61 Farmer 52 acres
Thomas    "         - 65 Brother - Ag Lab
Sarah     "         - 35 House servant
William   "         - 13 Nephew plouhgboy
Henry     "         -  7 Labourer's son
```

1861

```
William Bray        - 67 Farmer 100 acres
Thomas    "         - 70 Brother
John      "         - 38 Nephew
Harvey    "         - 20 Nephew
Ann       "         -  3 Neice
```

1871

```
John Faulkner       - 37 Farmer 160 acres
Jane      "         - 35
William   "         - 17
Anne      "         - 15
Louisa    "         - 13
Sarah     "         - 11
Martha    "         -  9
John      "         -  7
Catherine "         -  4
Ada       "         -  2
John Thomas         - 19 Waggoner
```

1881

```
John Home           - 53 Farmer 140 acres
Mary     "          - 46
John     "          - 26
Ann      "          - 24
William" "          - 21
Margaret "          - 15
Mary     "          - 11
Caroline Rudd       - 21 Farmer's daughter
Beatrice  "         - 18      "       "
George Grainger     - 14 Servant
```

Hanbury Sparrow bought it from the church

1888-1917 F Davies

1917-1941 W Pugh

1975 J D Lawton

No 7 Tithe No 381 (map p44) Lilywood Owner Maria Eaton

1841

Charles Hayes	- 45	Farmer
Sarah "	- 45	
John "	- 15	
Sarah "	- 11	
William "	- 13	
Hannah "	- 9	
Mary "	- 7	
Martha Batley	- 15	Female servant
Andrew Hughes	- 20	Male servant

1851

Charles Hayes	- 61	Farmer 85 acres
Sarah "	- 61	
William "	- 24	
Sarah "	- 21	
Hannah "	- 19	
Mary "	- 17	
Richard Lawton	- 32	House servant
Thomas Possit?	- 17	House servant

1861

Edward Pritchard	- 26	Farmer
Hannah "	- 29	
George "	- 3	
Mary "	- 4 mths	
Sarah Hayes	- 70	m-in-law
Mary ?	- 9	Scholar
John ?	- 10	
Edwin Blakeway	- 18	Carter
? "	- 13	General servant

1871

Cornelius Jones	- 57	Farmer 34 acres
Esther "	- 53	
Edward "	- 23	
Esther "	- 14	
Cornelius "	- 11	
Mary Hopper	- 28	dght,,lab's wife
John "	- 8 mths	g/son

1881

Cornelius Jones	- 65	Farmer 40 acres
Esther "	- 61	
Edward "	- 28	Ag Lab
Mary "	- 28	D-in-law
Cornelius "	- 21	Ag Lab
Edward "	- 7	g/son
Thomas "	- 5	
John "	- 4	
Arthur "	- 2	
George "	- 4 mths	

1895-1900 J Robinson
1900-1909 W Pugh
1909-1917 J Lewis
1917-1941 S Jones
Demolished

No 8 Tithe No 432 (map p44) New Hall Farm Owner Maria Eaton

1841

William Hayes	- 50	Farmer
? "	- 20	
Thomas "	- 12	
Margaret "	- 50	
Ann "	- 80	
John Preece	- 20	Male servant
John Wood	- 20	Male servant
Elizabeth Barker	- 20	Female servant
Sarah Goodman	- 15	Female servant

1851

Thomas Hince	- 33	Farmer 200 acres
Mary "	- 27	
Margaret "	- 4	
Henrietta "	- 1	
William Hayes	- 62	Father-in-law
Martha Cadwallader	- 26	Servant
William Broom	- 26	House servant
Richard Colley	- 18	House servant
John Fox	- 14	House servant
William Mason	- 13	House servant
Thomas Taylor	- 26	House servant

1861

Thomas Hince	- 43	Farmer
Mary "	- 37	
Margaret "	- 14	
Henrietta "	- 11	
Harriet "	- 9	
Martha "	- 7	
Frederick "	- 3	
William Hayes	- 74	f-in-law,farmer
John Gittins	- 33	Milller
Edwin May	- 19	Carter
William Downes	- 13	General Servant
Daniel Parton	- 48	General servant
Caroline Carter	- 20	Servant

1871

Mary Hince	- 47	Farmer 200 acres
Eva "	- 47	Farmer's dghter
Frederick	- 13	Scholar
Thomas "	- 18	Scholar
William Hayes	- 82	f-in-law
Annie Davies	- 5	visitor
Edward Mason	- 31	Farm servant
George Williams	- 30	Farm servant
William Wilson	- 15	Farm servant

1881

Thomas Cleeton	- 46	Farmer 197 acres
Jane "	- 20	Housekeeper
Sarah Francis	- 19	Servant
William Cartwright	- 21	Farm servant
Edwin Williams	- 16	Farm servant

1888-1926 T Cleeton
1926-1934 Mrs M Cleeton
1934-1941 E Cleeton
1957 Bought by Mrs Whitaker, then to Mrs Treasure
1990 Mrs E M Treasure

No 9 Tithe No 431 (map p44) New Hall Mill Owner Maria Eaton

1841

John Edwards	- 73	Miller
Thomas "	- 33	"
John Hatfield	- 15	
Ann Chandler	- 45	Female servant

1851

William Harris	- 49	Miller
Martha "	- 53	
Caroline "	- 25	
William "	- 16	
Mary "	- 12	

1861

unoccupied

1871

James Rooke	- 29	Miller
Sarah "	- 32	
Alice "	- 6	
Annie "	- 4	
Robert "	- 6 weeks	
George Harris	- 26	Miller's asst

1881

Henry Oliver	- 46	Miller
Eleanor "	- 45	
Henry "	- 9	
Emily Jones	- 16	Neice

1888-1900 T Morris

1900-1913 T Anson

Derelict

No 10 HARTON Tithe No 480 (map p54) Harton Manor Farm Owner Thomas Dunne

1841

Ann Ward	- 45	Farmer
Frances "	- 12	
Elizabeth "	- 8	
Frances Lewis	- 45	
Susannah "	- 50	
John Paston	- 25	Male servant
John Humphries	- 17	
Samuel Thomas	- 14	
Jane Humphries	- 15	
William Finder	- 25	Saddler

1851

Thomas Farmer	- 35	Farmer - 175 acres
Mary "	- 35	
Abigail "	- 7	
Mary Eliza	- 5	
Margaret "	- 3	
Thomas "	- 1	
James Richards	- 23	Servant
Elizabeth Reynolds	- 16	House servant
John Evans	- 28	House servant
George Taylor	- 28	House servant
William Roberts	- 13	House servant

1861

Thomas Farmer	- 48	Farmer
Mary "	- 48	
Mary	- 15	
Margaret	- 13	
Thomas	- 11	
Samuel Bright	- 52	Bailiff
Sarah Lewis	- 16	General Servant
Edward Henry	- 23	General servant
James Edwards	- 17	Servant
Robert Parton	- 14	Servant

1871

Thomas Farmer	- 21	Farmer
Mary "	- 25	Sister
Margaret "	- 23	"
Samuel Bright	- 62	Uncle
William Davies	- 31	Waggoner
William Adams	- 40	Workman
William Edwards	- 12	Waggoner's boy

1881

Edmund Bounds	- 62	Farmer 170 acres
Sarah "	- 61	
Edwin "	- 25	
Amelia Shuker	- 8	g/daughter-scholar
Sarah Williams	- 16	General servant
Edward Speake	- 26	Farm servant
Herbert Beavan	- 19	Farm servant

1891 Wm Bebington
1913 L Buddicom
1926-41 W J Parry
1941 Sold to Mr Jenks, Mr Morgan Edwards bailiff,
1956 Bought by E Meredith
1957 Bought by Mrs Treasure (Mrs Whitaker lived there)
     It was then empty for 2 years
1990 G Perkins

No 11 HARTON Tithe No 460 (map p54) Harton Farm Owner Thomas Dunne

1841

Ann Medlicott	- 55	Farmer
Elisha "	- 25	
Margaret "	- 35	
Elizabeth Spencer	- 15	
Joseph Speak	- 20	Ag Lab
Edward Williams	- 15	Ag Lab
William James	- 15	Ag Lab
Thomas Bennet	- 10	Apprentice

1851

Ann Medlicott	- 68	Farmer - 170 acres
Margaret "	- 40	Daughter-in-law
Thomas ?Yells	- 14	
Thomas ?Yells	- 38	Farmer
William Rea	- 32	House servant
Edward James	- 42	House servant
William Bright	- 30	House servant
George Williams	- 10	House servant

1861

John Lewis	- 40	Farmer
Martha "	- 38	
Mildred Harris	- 15	
John Goodman	- 17	Groom
Edward Lewis	- 13	General servant
? Yells	- 22	Visitor

1871

Thomas Weatherell	- 33	Farmer 172 acres
Emily "	- 34	Sister
Caroline Crowther	- 17	Servant
James Preece	- 25	Farm servant
Henry Lewis	- 22	Farm servant

1881

Samuel Trickett	- 47	Farmer 172 acres
Mary "	- 42	
Mary "	- 13	Scholar
Lydia "	- 12	
Samuel "	- 12	
Harriet Corfield	- 22	General servant
Job Heath	- 48	Farm servant
Thomas Hughes	- 18	Farm servant

1891 Richard Corfield
1912 J F Hartley
     F Hartley
     K F Hartley
1990 K J Embrey

No 12 WOLVERTON Tithe No 511 (map p54) Wolverton Manor Farm Owner John Blockley

1841

George Minshull	- 29	Farmer
Thomas James	- 20	Ag Lab
Thomas Law	- 25	Ag Lab
Mary Evan	- 25	Female servant
William Sias	- 14	Ag Lab
Ann Bebbington	- 15	Female servant

1851

Benjamin Beddowes	- 40	Farmer - 306 acres
Ann "	- 39	
Benjamin "	- 9	
James "	- 8	
John "	- 5	
George "	- 3 mths	
Martha Cadwallader	- 19	Servant
Maria Sankey	- 22	House servant
George Venables	- 17	House servant
Thomas Meredith	- 13	House servant
John Jokien?	- 27	House servant

1861

Benjamin Beddowes	- 50	Farmer
Ann "	- 49	
Elizabeth "	- 21	
James "	- 18	
John "	- 16	
Hubert "	- 14	
George "	- 10	
Sarah "	- 8	
Martha Morris	- 22	Visitor
Sarah "	- 19	"
John Thomas	- 63	Carter
Richard Bright	- 21	Carter
John Richards	- 20	Carter

1871

Samuel Hotchkiss	- 36	Farmer 303 acres
Emma "	- 31	
Ann Reynolds	- 8	step-daughter
Fanny Griffiths	- 20	Dairymaid
Emma Hall	- 17	General Servant
Thomas Bright	- 22	Farm servant
Edwin Smith	- 18	Farm servant

1881

Richard Medlicott	- 60	Farmer 319 acres
Elizabeth "	- 50	
Mary "	- 27	
Richard "	- 22	
Ann "	- 22	
John "	- 17	

Wolverton Manor Farm contd

```
William Medlicott    - 14
Kate       "         - 13
Emma       "         - 10
Richard Francis      - 48 Farm servant, widower
```

```
1891 John Parry
1929-39 Hamers
1956 T E Lowe
1970 C Edwards, a dealer from Wrexham
1983 R Orme
```

No 13 Tithe 218 (map p54) Railway Cottage

1871

```
Richard Duncan    - 30 Agent for G W R
Mary       "      - 25
John       "      - 60 Father,farm lab
John Whitehead    -  1 Nephew
```

1881

```
Richard Duncan    - 40 Stationmaster
Mary       "      - 35
John Whitehead    - 11 Nephew
Selina Allen      - 43 Wife's sister,cook
```

1891

```
Richard Duncan    - 50 Stationmaster
```

No 14 Tithe No 262 (map p60) St Edith's School
       Land given 15/4/1863 - closed 1925/6

1871

```
John Marshall    - 26 Nat schoolmaster
Jane       "     - 25 School mistress
Mary Roberts     - 21 s-in-law
John Gordon      -  5 Boarder
```

1881

```
Edward Pennicot  - 49 Schoolmaster
Adela Marion "   - 18 School assistant
Sarah Ann    "   - 25 d-in-law,hsekeeper
Bertram Lyle     - 11 mths gd/son
```

No 15 TICKLERTON Tithe No 152 (map p60) Upper House Farm Owner William Pinches

1841

```
Robert Everall   - 50 Farmer
Mary       "     - 50
Richard    "     - 25
John       "     - 20
Martha     "     - 17
Sarah      "     - 15
William    "     - 14
Robert     "     - 13
Ann        "     - 10
James      "     -  7
Mary Jones       - 15 Female servant
William Carter   - 18 Male servant
John Tench       - 14 Ag Lab
```

1851

```
John Edwards     - 62 Farmer 272 acres
Mary       "     - 66
Edward Bright    - 22 Farm bailiff
Emma Edwards     - 17 Dairymaid
Edwin Williams   - 16 House servant
Bridget White    - 15 House servant
Richard Robinson - 12 Ploughboy
```

1861   (no census return)

1871

```
John Home        - 42 Farmer 256 acres
Mary A "         - 37
John   "         - 16
Ann    "         - 14
Selina "         - 12
William "        - 11
Margaret "       -  6
Mary   "         -  1
John Edward      - 29 Servant/workman
```

1881

```
Joseph Manley    - 39 Farmer 249 acres
Esther    "      - 38
Elizabeth "      - 22
Joseph    "      - 18
John Hince       - 26 Farm servant
Alfred Blakeway  - 13 Farm servant
Mary A Kitson    - 15 Domestic servant
```

Upper House Farm contd

John Jones	- 21	Waggoner
Lucy Richards	- 18	Dairymaid
Harry Evans	- 13	Waggoner's boy

1891 Wm Hill
1900 John Cox
Harry Cox (sold by R Buddicom 1953)
1990 H and G Cox

No 16 TICKLERTON Tithe No 189 (map p60) Lower House Farm

1841

John Hyde	- 35	Farmer
William "	- 35	
lizabeth "	- 30	
Mary "	- 25	
Elizabeth Harvey	- 20	Female servant
William Jones	- 15	Male servant
Aquilla Griffiths	- 15	Male servant
Edwin Harley	- 14	Male servant
George Goodman	- 11	Male servant

1851

Thomas Gallears	- 31	Farmer 237 acres
Adah "	- 24	
William "	- 4	
Ann "	- 2	
Richard "	- 27	Farm Bailiff
Hannah Carter	- 16	Housemaid
Richard Adams	- 17	House servant
Thomas F ?	- 16	House servant
Richard Jones	- 14	House servant

1861

John Shuker	- 26	Farmer 200 acres
Ann "	- 34	
Sarah Groves	- 12	Wife's daughter
George Shuker	- 1 mth	
Elizabeth Roberts	- 19	Dairymaid
Emma Downes	- 12	Housemaid
George Shuker	- 23	Farm bailiff
Thomas Musson	- 20	Waggoner
John Rogers	- 18	Waggoner
George Belkbinder	-	Groom
William Thierson	- 10	General servant

1871

George Garfit	- 25	Farmer 320 acres
Mark "	- 59	Father, Rector of Coninsby, landowner
Frances "	- 47	Step-mother,
Francis "	- 10	Scholar
Emma Green	- 24	Servant/cook
Nearid? Smith	- 20	Housemaid

1881

John Hartley	- 64	Farmer 300 acres
Eleanor "	- 62	
Hannah "	- 20	
Amos "	- 16	
Edwin Bowen	- 19	Farm servant
John Hughes	- 16	Farm servant

1895-1905 James Hill
1905-1917 Mary Hill
1917-1922 F & Lizzie Hill
1926-1941 A & H Roberts
1953 Mrs Harrison and J Young
1953 Sold by R Buddicom
1990 E Young

No 17 TICKLERTON Tithe No 258 (map p60) Ticklerton Hall Farm Owner Edward Downes

1841

William Downes	- 55	Farmer
Ann "	- 55	
Mary "	- 20	
Susannah "	- 15	
Thomas "	- 25	
Hannah Edwards	- 20	Farm Servant
Mary Haines	- 15	Farm Servant
Josiah Price	- 25	Male Servant
James "	- 20	Male Servant
William Speak	- 25	Male Servant
Richard Giddings	- 12	

1851

William Darcey	- 27	Farmer 336 acres
Mary "	- 37	
Mary Bone	- 27	House servant
James Dean	- 28	Farm bailiff

1861

Samuel Medlicott	- 62	Farmer 300 acres
Susannah "	- 62	
Frederick "	- 28	
William "	- 20	
Susannah "	- 17	
Ann Bright	- 29	Farmers daughter
Elizabeth Bright		
Emma Howells	- 16	House servant
William Humphries	- 22	Farm servant
John Williams	- 22	Farm servant
Thomas "	- 14	Farm labourer

1871

William Robinson	- 37	Farmer 258 acres
Catherine "	- 38	
William "	- 15	
Joseph "	- 9	Scholar
Esther "	- 7	
Isabella "	- 1	
Eliz Whittingham	- 75	widow, m-in-law,
John Meredith	- 60	Servant/workman
Samuel "	- 21	Waggoner
Thomas Carter	- 16	Waggoner's boy
Margaret "	- 17	Dairymaid
Jane Speake	- 15	Nursemaid

1881

William Robinson	- 47	Farmer 300 acres
Catherine "	- 48	
William "	- 26	
Joseph "	- 18	
Esther "	- 16	
Isabella "	- 11	
Harry "	- 7	
Hannah Brunt	- 15	Servant
William Sprag	- 22	Farm labourer

1929 Mrs Mary Roberts
1990 W A Shaw

No 18 TICKLERTON Tithe No 155 (map p60) Ticklerton Court Owner Wm Pinches

1841

Mary Pinches	- 70	
William "	- 35	
Mary "	- 30	
Elizabeth "	- 30	
Ann Bird	- 60	
Frances Carnfield	- 25	Female servant
Sarah Getten	- 30	Female servant
Elizabeth Dukes	- 13	Female servant
William Howell	- 25	Male servant
Edward Tennant?	- 15	Male servant

1851 unoccupied Rev R J Buddicom living at Smethcote

```
1861                                    1871

Isabelle Latouche   - 30 Lady          William G Harrison - 55 Servant/butler
Eleanor Biggs       - 28 Lady          Harriet      "     - 48 Housekeeper
Sarah Gibson        - 34 General servant  Charles Williams - 31 Coachman
Henry Taylor        - 16 General servant  James Perkins    - 24 Footman
Patrick Boor        - 53 General servant  Emma Richards    - 23 Kitchenmaid
                                       Susan Lewis        - 18 Housemaid

1881

William Squire Buddicom- 41 Land agent,Income derived from land
Rev R J Buddicom
Eliz Haughton "     - 37
Robert Arthur "     -  6
Lilian Holland"     -  2
Elizabeth Barrow    - 21 Housemaid
Elizabeth Price     - 17 Nurse

1891-1922 William Squire Buddicom
1922-1938 Lilian Hayward
1941 Brig Gen A M Tyler, CMG,DSO,JP.
1953 Sold to J Young
1990 J P Young
```

No 19 TICKLERTON Tithe No 253 (map p60) Hisbeach - semi-detached Owner John Griffith

```
1841                                    1851

Edward Griffiths    - 67 Mason         William Jones      - 38 Ag Lab
Keziah              - 64               Hannah      "      - 31
                                       John        "      -  7
                                       Henry       "      -  4
                                       Samuel      "      -  3
                                       Esther      "      -  6 days
                                       Elizabeth Cook     -  1
                                       Keziah Griffiths   - 75 widower,visitor

1861                                    1871

Keziah Griffiths    - 86 Shoemaker     Elizabeth Amies    - 78 form.Dom Servant
                                       Arthur Howells     - 10 gt/nephew
                                       John Fox           -  3 Boarder

HISBEACH - semi-detached

1861                                    1871

William Carter      - 36 Labourer      Willaim Carter     - 45 Farm labourer
Mary        "       - 33               Mary        "      - 44
Thomas      "       -  5               Ann         "      - 12
Ann         "       -  3               William     "      - 10
William     "       -  1               Betsy       "      -  7
                                       Eliza       "      -  5
                                       George      "      -  1

1881

William Carter      - 52 Ag Lab
Mary        "       - 50
Eliza       "       - 17
George      "       - 11

1990 W Russell
```

No 20 TICKLERTON   Tithe No 255 (map p60) one time 'The Masons Arms' Owner Ed Downes

1841

```
Henry Goode       - 50
Ann      "        - 40
Mary     "        -  7
Sarah    "        -  5
Thomas   "        -  4
Elizabeth "       -  2
John     "        -  6 mths
```

1851

```
William Downes    - 69 Farmer 5 acres
Ann      "        - 68
Mary Garton       - 18 Servant
```

1861

```
William Downes    - 79 retired farmer
Ann      "        - 77
Ellen Evans       - 18 General servant
```

1871

```
Edwin Harley      - 43 Publican
Eliza    "        - 43
John     "        - 15
Mary     "        - 13
Edwin    "        - 11
Eliza    "        -  5
Margaret "        - 5mths
Amy      "        -  2
William Rogers    - 20 Lodger/labourer
Richard Hughes    - 20 Lodger/labourer
```

1881

```
William Harley    - 53 Widower, ag lab
Edwin Goode       - 27 Stepson, ag lab
Robert Roberts    - 10 gd/son
```

1929 Thos Attenborough
1990 G Rose, now known as Hill View

No 21 TICKLERTON Tithe No 257 (map p60) Blacksmiths Owner Wm Pinches

1841

```
Francis Wall      - 30 Blacksmith
Maria    "        - 70
Sarah Morgan      - 20
James Underlow    - 25
Thomas  ?         - 20
William Langford  - 15
```

1851

```
Francis Wall      - 42 Blacksmith
Martha   "        - 26
William  "        -  3
Mary     "        - 10 mths
Thomas Evans      - 22 Journeyman b/smith
Harriet Cantrell  - 13 Visitor
Thomas Lewis      - 18 Journeyman b/smith
Thomas Wenlock    - 12 Errand boy
```

1861

```
Francis Wall      - 52 Blacksmith
Martha   "        - 39
William  "        - 13 Scholar
Mary     "        - 10 Frances Wall - 8
John     "        -  6 Richard   "   - 4
```

1871

```
Thomas Price      - 50 Blacksmith
Mary     "        - 47
Richard  "        - 17
John     "        - 14
```

1881

```
Edwin Evans       - 41 Blacksmith
Eliza    "        - 38
Mary Ellen "      -  5
Emily    "        -  3
Edwin    "        -  8 mths
Thomas Tisdale    - 15 Blacksmith's apprentice
```

1929 S H Rowe, Blacksmith
1990 G W Hesbrook, now known as The Forge Cottage

<u>No 22 TICKLERTON</u> Tithe No 174 (map p60) Bank House, one time The Horseshoes public house
                  Owner John Griffith

1841   1851

William Jones   - 35 Sheep merchant   Benjamin Purslow   - 33 Innkeeper
William   "   - 1?   Elizabeth   "   - 26
Richard   "   - 12   Sarah   "   - 3 mths
Mary   "   - 78   Fanny   "   - 22 Sister, annuitant
?   "   - 27   Thomas Evans   - 22 House servant
Martin Tipton   - 15   Elizabeth Harris   - 16 House servant
George Willis   - 20   William Morral   - 21 Timber haulier
                                                 Jesse Robinson   - 15 Timber haulier
                                                 Eliza Jackman   - 12 Visitor, scholar
                                                 Mary Carter   - 60 Lab wife

1861   1871

Edward Downes   - 52 Farmer 45 acres   William Green   - 52 Farm bailiff
Jane   "   - 54   Sam   "   - 42
Thomas "   - 19   Marshall   "   - 16 Groom
Richard "   - 9   Eliza   "   - 11
Mary   "   - 13   Richard   "   - 9
                                                 Charles   "   - 7
                                                 William   "   - 5
                                                 Adam Jeffrey   - 23 Servant/waggoner
                                                 Thomas Wainwright   - 19 Cowman
                                                 Alfred   "   - 18 under Waggoner

1881

George Parrish   - 54 Farmer 131 acres Cattle dealer
Elizabeth M "   - 45
Mary Ann   "   - 17
George   "   - 14
Alice Maude "   - 4
Ellen Bettison   - 24 Wife's sister, annuitant
Elizabeth Norton   - 30 Visitor
James Waters   - 23 General servant

1895   H Jones
1900/5 The Misses Holt
1909/13 Major Hornby
1917/29 Brig Gen Leyland
1934/41 H P Carver
1990   D W Bigley

<u>No 23 BIRTLEY</u> Tithe No 162 (map p60) Pheasant Inn/Birtley Villa/Pheasant Cottage
                Owner John Hide

1841   1851

Richard Carter   - 25 Ag Lab   William Owen   - 55 Lic, Victualler
Mary   "   - 50   Ann   "   - 60
Thomas "   - 25   William   "   - 36 Labourer
Sarah   "   - 10   John Pinches   - 36 Visitor, labourer
Elizabeth "   - 7

1861   1871

William Owen   - 78 Lic, Victualler   Richard Davies   - 56 Publican
Ann   "   - 78   Sarah   "   - 61
William "   - 48 Labourer

1881

Richard Davies   - 66 Farmer 30 acres
Sarah   "   - 69

1882 Edward and Mary Hall
1908 Mrs Sarah Hall
1949 Harold Hall
1990 R Phillips

No 24 BIRTLEY Tithe No 170 (map p60) opposite Pheasant Inn

1841   1851

Richard Pitches?   - 30 Ag Lab   Richard Nicholls - 42 Labourer
Charlotte   "   - 30   Charlotte   "   - 41
                                      Henry Avan?   - 50 Visitor, lawyer
                                      Bernard "   - 19   "   "

1861

William Jones   - 36 Labourer
Ann   "   - 30

Demolished

No 25 BIRTLEY Tithe No 163 (map p60) Greystones Owner John Robinson

1841   1851

John Roberts   - 30 Ag Lab   John Roberts   - 39 Ag lab
Mary   "   - 33   Mary   "   - 39
                                      Benjamin Owen   - 39 Visitor, lawyer
                                      Hugh   "   - 18   "   "

1861   1871

Edwin Harley   - 33   John Lewis   - 27 Farm labourer
Eliza   "   - 33   Margaret "   - 25
George   "   - 13   Mary   "   - 2
John   "   - 5   Benjamin "   - 1 mth
Mary   "   - 3
Edwin   "   - 1

1881

Maria Corfield   - 40 Timber feller's wife
Edward   "   - 7
Sarah   "   - 4
Mary   "   - 2
Clara   "   - 3mths

1990 K Johnson

No 26 BIRTLEY/HATTON Tithe No 662 (map p60) Owner Rev Powell

1841   1851

Thomas Roberts   - 60   Thomas Roberts   - 70 Carrier, soldier
Sarah   "   - 50   Sarah   "   - 61
William   "   - 6   George   "   - 3
Mary Chiney?   - 20   Thomas   "   - 38 Son, labourer

```
1861                                    1871

Thomas Roberts    - 45 Labourer         Thomas Roberts    - 57 Labourer
George    "       - 13                  Margaret   "      - 48
Margaret "        - 38                  George     "      - 23 Labourer
Charles  "        -  3                  Charles    "      - 11 Scholar
George Lewis      -  9 wife's illeg son Charlotte  "      -  7
Elizabeth Jones   - 61 Mother           Elizabeth Lewis   - 77 Widow,m-in-law
                                        James      "      - 21 Stepson,cowman

1881

Thomas Roberts    - 67 Ag Lab
Margaret "        - 58
Charles  "        - 21
Charlotte "       - 18 Dressmaker
George Lewis      -  3 gd/son
```

1990 W Bason, now rebuilt and known as New House

No 27 HATTON GATE Tithe No 557 (map p72)

```
1851                                    1861

Sarah Hill        - 42 Toll collector   Sarah Hill        - 51 Grocer
Catherine "       -  3                  Catherine "       - 13 Scholar
Eliza     "       -  1                  Philip Burgess    - 52 Lodger,glazier
Philip Burgess    - 43 Visitor,glazier/painter

1871                                    1881

Sarah Hill        - 61 Tollgate keeper  Richard Bowyer    - 46 Ag lab
Philip Burgess    - 63 Boarder,glazier  Elizabeth  "      - 45
                                        Rebecca Evans     - 12 step-daughter
```

No 28 HATTON Tithe No 654 (map p72) Upper Farm Owner William Wynne

```
1841                                    1851

William Wall      - 35 Farmer           William Wall      - 49 Farmer 200 acres
Frances  "        - 30                  Joanna    "       - 45
John     "        -  7mths              John      "       - 10
Jane Harris       - 20 Female Servant   Elizabeth "       -  3
Sarah Hughes      - 13 Female Servant   Edward Chisolm    - 25 House servant
Jeremiah Wall     - 20 Male Servant     Edward Jones      - 18 House servant
Joseph Humphries  - 15 Male Servant     Thomas Downes     - 15 House servant
John Titley?      - 13                  Ann Perry         - 15 House servant

1861                                    1871

William Wall      - 59 Farmer 200 acres John Wall         - 28 Farmer 200 acres
Frances   "       - 59                  Eliza    "        - 22 Sister
John      "       - 20                  Fanny    "        - 65 Mother
Mary      "       - 18                  Samuel Lewis      - 22 Waggoner
John Aston        - 32 Farm servant     William Evason    - 22 Cowman
Thomas Carter     - 18 Farm servant     Herbert Turner    - 13 Waggoner's boy
James Wainwright  - 13 Farm servant
Matilda Williams  - 15 General servant

1881                                    1909-1941 E Perkins and C Perkins

Mary Wall         - 33 Farmer's wife    1990 J Perkins
Arthur "          -  3
John   "          -  4mths
Isabella Lewis    - 16 General servant
George Williams   - 40 Ag lab
Jeremiah Rough    - 14 Farm servant
```

No 29 HATTON Tithe No 652 (map p72) semi-detached, One time The Blue Bell and Workhouse

1841

Name		Age	Occupation
Alice Benbow		- 40	Beerseller
Mathew	"	- 20	Ag Lab
Mary	"	- 15	
Harriet	"	- 10	
William	"	- 10	
John	"	- 8	
Joseph	"	- 7	
Charles	"	- 4	
Richard	"	- 4	
Richard Felling		- 36	Bricklayer
John Carter		- 35	Lab

1851

Name		Age	Occupation
Alice Benbow		- 53	Lic.Victualler
Harriet	"	- 20	
Mathew	"	- 33	Form.farm bailiff
Edward	"	- 28	Labourer
Richard	"	- 11	
Margaret Edwards		- 31	Miller's wife
Frances	"	- 4	gd/son
John	"	- 2	gd/son
Sarah	"	- 8 mths	gd/daughter

1861

Name		Age	Occupation
Cornelius Jones		- 45	Labourer
Esther	"	- 42	
Elizabeth	"	- 15	
Eliza	"	- 13	
Jane	"	- 3	
Esther	"	- 3	
Cornelius	"	- 1	

1871

Name		Age	Occupation
Joseph Jones		- 80	form Farmer
Sarah	"	- 71	
Richard	"	- 33	Carpenter
Maria	"	- 30	Dressmaker
George	"	- 28	Stone mason
George	"	- 4	gd/son

1881

Name	Age	Occupation
Richard Jones	- 44	Carpenter
Mary Faulkner	- 22	Neice, housekeeper
George Jones	- 14	

No 29 HATTON Tithe No 652 (map p72) semi-detached

1841

Name		Age	Occupation
Francis Harris		- 25	Ag Lab
Mary	"	- 30	
Mary	"	- 9	
William	"	- 5	
Thomas	"	- 3	
Samuel	"	- 1	

1851

Uninhabited

1861

Name		Age	Occupation
Evan Edwards		- 35	Gamekeeper
Mary Ann	"	- 31	
Emma	"	- 7	
Richard	"	- 5	
Mary	"	- 3	
Elizabeth	"	- 2	
William	"	- 1	

1881

Name		Age	Occupation
Sarah Poston		- 38	Widow,Par,relief
John	"	- 11	
Philip	"	- 8	
Susan	"	- 6	
Druey?	"	- 4	
Annie	"	- 2	

1990 D Fryatt, now known as Hatton Cottage

No 30 HATTON Tithe No 585 (map p72) Manor Farm Owner Rev Powell

1841

Name		Age
Elizabeth Howells		- 45
Mary	"	- 25
John	"	- 5
Sarah	"	- 1

1851

Name		Age	Occupation
Susannah Evans		- 40	Farmer 96 acres
John	"	- 17	
William	"	- 13	
Jane	"	- 11	
Mary	"	- 9	
George	"	- 6	
Sophia	"	- 4	
Mary Calkin		- 12	Servant

1861

John Faulkner	- 32	Farmer 110 acres
Mary "	- 32	
Elizabeth "	- 7	
Emma "	- 4	
William "	- 1	
Ellen Davies	- 23	House servant
Richard Cadwallader	- 14	Farm servant
John Jeffries	- 15	Carter

1871

William Hale	- 29	Farmer 88 acres
Elizabeth "	- 37	
Thomas "	- 10	
William "	- 7	
Ann "	- 5	
Sarah "	- 2	
John "	- 9 mths	

1881

John Pinches	- 65	Widower,farmer 100 acres
John "	- 32	
Mathew Ruff	- 16	Farm servant
Fanny Bedlam	- 21	General servant

1990 P Norbury

No 31 HATTON Tithe No 650 (map p72) Middle Farm

1841

James Rawlins	- 45	Farmer
John "	- 20	

1851

Joyce Rawlins	- 60	Farmer 40 acres
John "	- 32	
Alice "	- 30	d-in-law
Thomas Bennett	- 14	House servant

1861

John Rawlins	- 41	Farmer 67 acres
Alice "	- 40	
William "	- 10	
Harriet "	- 8	
Eliza "	- 6	
John "	- 4	
James "	- 2	
Edwin Gardner	- 12	General servant

1871

John Rawlins	- 51	Farmer 68 acres
Alice "	- 50	
William "	- 19	
Harriet "	- 18	
Eliza "	- 16	
John "	- 14	
James "	- 13	

1881

John Rawlins	- 61	Farmer 69 acres
Alice "	- 60	
William "	- 28	
Harriet "	- 26	
James "	- 23	

1891 John Rawlins

1990 C Perkins

No 32 HATTON Tithe No 653 (map p72) Lower Farm Owner Henry Mytton

1841

William Evans	- 55	
Susan "	- 30	
John "	- 7	
Susan "	- 5	
William "	- 3	
Jane "	- 1	
Hannah Lewis	- 14	F S
John Jones	- 12	M S

1851

Edward Jones	- 54	Farmer 200 acres
Sarah "	- 51	
Anne Marie "	- 23	
Edward "	- 17	
Emma "	- 17	
John "	- 12	
William Maund	- 16	Cordwainer
Thomas Hughes	- 22	House servant
William Jones	- 20	House servant
William Ward	- 15	House servant

1861

```
John Jones         - 22 Farmer 200 acres
Sarah      "       - 61 Mother
Ann Bright         - 36 General servant
Richard Pugh       - 19 Carter
George Gardner     - 14 Servant
```

1871

```
Joseph Manley      - 48 Farmer 200 acres
Esther    "        - 47
Thomas    "        - 22
Samuel    "        - 20
John      "        - 18
Ellen Smith        - 30 Dairymaid
Margaret Hughes    - 16 Housemaid
Mary Bennion       - 19 Visitor
```

1881

```
Samuel Manley      - 30 Farmer 200 acres
Sarah       "      - 32
Alice Lloyd        - 13 General servant
William Jackson    - 20 Farm servant
Emanuel Reynolds   - 19 Farm servant
```

```
1891 Samuel Manley
1909-1941 E Jones
1990 R Jones
```

No 33 HATTON GROVE Tithe No 596 (map p72)

1841

```
Benjamin Downes    - 60 Farmer
Elizabeth   "      - 50
Frances     "      - 14
Anthea      "      - 10
Eliza       "      -  8
Philip Poston      -  8
```

1851

```
Benjamin Downes    - 72 Farmer 20 acres
Elizabeth   "      - 64
Fanny       "      - 22
Philip Poston      - 17 House servant
Sarah Owen         -  9 gd/daughter
James Bliss        - 23 Visitor,lawyer
William    "       - 29    "        "
```

1861

```
Edward Benbow      - 38 Farmer 20 acres
Fanny       "      - 33
Elizabeth   "      -  6
Alice       "      -  5
Fanny       "      -  4
Benjamin    "      -  2
Philp Poston       - 27 Labourer
Percy Downes       - 82 Widower
```

1871

```
Edward Benbow      - 48 Farmer 20 acres
Fanny       "      - 45
Alice       "      - 15
Benjamin    "      - 12
Emma        "      -  9
Harriet     "      -  7
```

1881

```
Hallen Jones       - 49 Ag lab
Mary      "        - 50
Louisa    "        - 15
Edwin Cleeton      -  2 Boarder
```

No 34 HATTON No location

1841

```
Samuel Bennett     - 65 Ag Lab
Sarah      "       - 65
Richard    "       - 40 Ag Lab
Samuel     "       - 50 Ag Lab
```

1851
Uninhabited

```
1861                                    1871

John Wainwright    - 52 Labourer       John Wainwright    - 62 Labourer
Emma       "       - 31                Emma       "       - 42 wife
Thomas     "       -  9                Emily      "       - 15 Scholar
Alfred     "       -  8                Edwin      "       - 12
?essiah    "       -  5                Mary       "       - 10
Edwin      "       -  2                Charles    "       -  7
Mary       "       - 1mth              Robert     "       -  5
                                       Joseph     "       -  2

   1881

John Wainwright    - 72 Ag lab
Emma       "       - 52
Charles    "       - 17
Joseph     "       - 11
Elizabeth  "       -  9
Arthur     "       -  5
```

No 35/6 SOUDLEY Tithe 124 (map p76) Owner William Pinches - semi-detached

```
1841                                   1851

James Parry    - 35 Ag Lab             Sarah Jones        - 72 Widow, lab wife
Phoebe   "     - 57


1861                                   1871

Walter Lewis   - 29 Tailor             Walter Lewis   - 44 Tailor,Post/master
Eliza    "     - 37                    Elizabeth "    - 48
Ann      "     -  4
George   "     -  2


1881

Walter Lewis   - 50 Tailor
Elizabeth "    - 56
```

1891 Walter Lewis

1908 known as Post Office Cottage No 1,Now, Soudley Cottage

semi-detached with above

```
1841                                   1851

Benjamin Speak  - 46 Ag Lab              ?  Harley    -    Ag lab
Mary      "     - 48                   Ann       "    - 24
Elizabeth "     - 22                   Elizabeth "    - 10mths
Mary      "     - 16
John      "     -  7


1861                                   1871

John Marston   - 40 Labourer           Edward Cleeton  - 40 Cottager 6 acres
Mary     "     - 33                    Elizabeth "     - 48
Lucy     "     -  2                    Charles   "     - 13
                                       Henry     "     - 12
                                       Richard   "     - 11
                                       Sarah     "     -  9
                                       Thomas    "     -  6
```

1881

```
Richard Layton        - 70 Ag lab
Sarah      "          - 60
```

1908 known as No 2 Post Office Cottages, A Humphreys

Known as Pool Cottage when sold 9/1/1953, now Soudley Cottage

1990 N Brown

No 37 SOUDLEY Tithe No 138 (map p76) Wayside Cottages Owner William Pinches

1841

```
Thomas Hughes      - 60 Ag Lab
Mary Williams      - 30
Ann Haswell        - 30
John Williams      - 13
Thomas "           -  9
Betsy  "           -  7
George "           -  3 mths
```

1851

```
Charles Hughes     - 36 Labourer
Cicely  "          - 34
Ann Meyrick        - 28 Servant, sister
Benjamin Colley    - 15 Servant
Edwin Hughes       -  3 mths
Thomas Griffith    - 74 Lodger, pig butcher
```

1861

```
Charles Hughes     - 46 Labourer
Cicely  "          - 46
Edwin   "          - 10
John    "          -  8
William "          -  5
```

1871

```
Charles Hughes     - 56 Labourer
Cicely  "          - 55
Edwin   "          - 20 Shoemaker
```

1881

```
Charles Hughes     - 67 Farmer 10 acres
Cicely  "            65
```

1908 known as Nos 1 (E Goode) & 2 (Mrs Evans) Soudley Cottages

1953 Mrs Miles No 1 T Miles No 2 Sold 9/1/53

1990 G Frampton

No 38 SOUDLEY Tithe No 139 (map p76) Yew Tree Cottage Owner William Pinches

1841

```
John Wilkes        - 30 Ag Lab
Ann    "           - 35
Thomas Goodman     - 40 Ag Lab
```

1851

```
Thomas Goodman     - 51 Ag lab
Mary      "        - 45
Elizabeth "        - 23
Dinah     "        -  5
Ellen     "        -  3
Thomas Hughes      - 72 f-in-law, lawyer
```

1861

```
Thomas Goodman     - 62 Ag lab
Mary      "        - 54
Ellen     "        - 12
Charles Marston    - 26 Bailiff
George Williams    - 20 Ag lab
```

1871

```
Thomas Goodman     - 69 Farm labourer
Mary      "        - 63
Dinah     "        - 25
Mary      "        -  2 gd/daughter
Elizabeth Williams - 35 step-dghtr, cook
```

1881

```
Thomas Goodman      - 81 Widower,Ag lab
Elizabeth Williams  - 45 step-daughter,housekeeper
George Jones        - 38 s-in-law,bricklayer
Dinah        "      - 35
Mary         "      - 12
Thomas       "      -  2
Eleanor      "      -  1
```

1953 Hugh & Clara Hughes   30/8/54 bought by Hughes

1990 L Bretherton

No 39 SOUDLEY Tithe No 140 (map p76) Owner William Pinches

1841

```
Richard Williams    - 50 Ag Lab
Sarah      "        - 43
Thomas     "        -  8
```

1851

```
James Sheffield     - 47 Stonemason
Thomas      "       - 18 Labourer
Sarah       "       - 14
```

1861

```
John Marston        - 22 Labourer
Ann        "        - 22
John       "        -  1
```

1871

```
John Harley         - 54 Labourer
Ann        "        - 78 Mother,widow
Maria      "        - 55 Sister
```

1881

```
Thomas Harley       - 28 Ag lab
Eliza      "        - 23
Elizabeth  "        -  2
Eleanor    "        -  6 mths
```

Demolished

No 40 SOUDLEY Tithe No 142/4(map p76) The Alders (semi-detached) Owner William Pinches

1841

```
Thomas Griffith     - 65 Farmer
Ciceley Colley      - 25 F S
Benjamin   "        -  5
William    "        - 25 Ag Lab
```

1851

```
Edward Higginson    - 45 Horsebreaker
Frances     "       - 39
Ann         "       -  7
Mary        "       -  1
Edward      "       -  1
```

1861

```
John Rogers         - 54 Farmer19 acres
Ann        "        - 61
```

1871

```
John Rogers         - 64 Farmer 25 acres
Ann        "        - 70
```

1881

```
Ann Rogers          - 79 Widow,annuitant
```

1953 J Lewis let with 4,225 acres

The Alders (semi-detached) with above

1841

```
David Lewis         - 54 Ag Lab
Elizabeth "         - 48
Ellen     "         - 11
John      "         -  2
Eliza     "         -  8 mths
```

1851

```
David Lewis         - 65 Lab form farmer
Elizabeth "         - 57
John      "         - 11 Gd/son
Eliza     "         -  9 Gd/daughter
James     "         -  3 Gd/son
```

1861

John Lewis	- 23	Ag lab
Sarah "	- 23	
Thomas "	- 1	

1881

Thomas Harley	*- 25*	*Ag lab*
Elizabeth "	*- 23*	
Eliz Harrington	*- 84*	*Lodger,knitter*

1908 W Hall

1953 Sold for £29,000 (derelict) 11/4/53

1990 K Holloway

<u>No 40A SOUDLEY</u> No location

1841

Mary Morgan	- 62
George "	- 23

1861

Thomas Carter	- 46	Labourer
Mary "	- 71	Widow
Elizabeth "	- 29	
William "	- 9	
Thomas Williams	- 10	Boarder,scholar

1881

Thomas Carter	- 66	Ag Labourer

1871

Eliz Harrington	*- 73*	*Ret hsekeeper*
John Wall	*- 18*	*Serv,jy/man tailor*
George Purslow	*- 18*	*Apprentice tailor*

1851

Richard Carter	- 64	Labourer
Thomas "	- 32	
William "	- 27	
James "	- 25	
Sarah "	- 22	
Mary "	- 41	Visitor
Ann Dodd	- 71	Widow, lab wife
Hannah Downes	- 18	Servant

1871

Thomas Carter	- 56	Ag Labourer

<u>No 41 SOUDLEY</u> Tithe No 128 (map p76) Stone House Farm Owner William Pinches

1841

William Cox	- 65	Ag Lab
Frances "	- 50	
Margaret "	- 22	
Ann "	- 20	
John "	- 15	
Maria "	- 10	
Edward "	- 25	

1861

William Cox	- 50	Labourer
Margaret "	- 40	
Mary "	- 25	
Sarah "	- 18	
Ann "	- 15	
Elizabeth "	- 12	
John "	- 10	
William "	- 8	
Frances "	- 11 mths	

1851

William Cox	- 76	Farmer 26 acres
John "	- 25	
Maria "	- 23	
Harriet Evans	- 15	Servant

1871

Margaret Cox	- 55	charw/m,sempstress
Fanny "	- 10	daughter/scholar
Evan Edwards	- 42	Boarder,gamekeeper
Elizabeth "	- 10	Boarder

1881

Margaret Cox   - 64 Charwoman

1908 E Duckett, 51 acres

1953 Sold to J Platt 26/10/53 9.79 acres

1990 S Dade

<u>No 42 SOUDLEY</u> Tithe No 133 (map p76) Owner William Pinches

1841				1851			
Thomas Bennet	- 54 Ag Lab			*Thomas Williams*	*- 33 Ag lab*		
Ann "	- 49			*Elizabeth "*	*- 34*		
Henry "	- 25			*Jane Beddowes*	*- 12*		
Ann "	- 13			*Eliza "*	*- 9*		
Sarah "	- 6			*Elizabeth "*	*- 7*		
William "	- 4			*Elizabeth Downes*	*- 67 Visitor, annuitant*		

1861				1871			
John Flind	- 56 Ag lab			Thomas Goode	- 32 Stone mason		
Sarah "	- 30			Martha "	- 32		
Elizabeth "	- 6			Henry "	- 3		
Ann "	- 4			Emanuel "	- 1		
Martha "	- 1						
Thomas Sheffield	- 29 Boarder, labourer						

1881

Thomas Goode	- 41 Widower, stone mason
Henry "	- 13
Emanuel "	- 11
Catherine "	- 6

Demolished

<u>No 43 SOUDLEY</u> Tithe No 132 (map p76) Owner William Pinches

1841				1851			
William Parton	- 33 Ag lab			Thomas Pugh	- 30 Railway labourer		
Elizabeth "	- 36			Emma "	- 40		
David "	- 6			Emma "	- 2		
John "	- 4						
William "	- 2						

Demolished

<u>No location SOUDLEY</u> probably beside No 43

1841				1851			
Richard Poston	- 20 Blacksmith			James ?	- 45		
Ann "	- 20						

1861

William Bradley	*- 44 Miller*
Sarah "	*- 36*
Sarah "	*- 12*
Jane "	*- 7*
Charles "	*- 3*
Eliza "	*- 1*

Demolished

No 44 SOUDLEY Tithe No 126 (map p76) ?Court House? Owner John Griffith

1841			1851		
Richard Dodd	- 55 Ag Lab		John Dodd	- 42 Ag lab	
Ann "	- 60		Margaret "	- 33	
Hannah Downes	- 9		John "	- 1	

1861			1871		
John Smith	- 32 Labourer		*Richard Carter*	*- 58 Ratcatcher*	
Mary "	- 48		*Sarah "*	*- 64*	
Eleanor "	- 9		*Thomas "*	*- 27 Labourer*	
Richard Cadwallader	- 40 Labourer		*John "*	*- 25*	
			Sarah "	*- 7 Gd/daughter*	

1881

John Faulkner   *- 60 Widower,builder*
Mary Rinn   *- 50 Housekeeper*

Demolished

No 45 HEIGHWOOD Tithe No 97 (map p76) Owner Ann Duckett

1841			1851		
Ann Duckett	- 49		Ann Duckett	- 58 form Masons wife	
Elizabeth "	- 18		Elizabeth "	- 28 Dressmaker	
Ann "	- 15		Ann "	- 23 Dressmaker	
Sarah "	- 10		Sarah "	- 20 Dressmaker	

1861			1871		
Ann Duckett	- 66 Staymaker		Ann Duckett	- 40 Dressmaker	
Ann "	- 32 Dressmaker		Sarah "	- 38	
Sarah "	- 29 Dressmaker		Ann Lewis	- 14 neice,scholar	

1881

Thomas Adams   *- 44 Ag lab*
Ann "   *- 42*
Mary "   *- 11*
Ellen "   *- 5*

1990 Now known as Poston's Cottage

No 46 HEIGHWOOD Tithe No 100 (map p76) Owner Ann Duckett

1841			1851		
Josiah Duckett	- 35 Mason		Josiah Duckett	- 48 Stone mason	
Martha "	- 30		Martha "	- 45	
George "	- 8		George "	- 17	
Josiah "	- 5		James "	- 13	
Jane "	- 3		Sarah "	- 11	
Sarah "	- 2		Susannah "	- 10	
Susannah "	- 2 mths		Richard "	- 6	
			?assiah "	- 5	

1861	Unoccupied		1871		
			Sarah Bray	*- 58 Farming 10 acres*	
			William "	*- 33 Labourer*	
			Mary "	*- 34 d-in-law*	
			Henry Greaves	*- 9*	

1881

John Edwards   - 38 Ag lab
Ann   "   - 34
Edwin   "   - 9
Mary   "   - 7
William   "   - 2

1908 John Rogers

1953 Mrs Miles Known as Sycamore Cottage,Now derelict

<u>No 47 HEIGHWOOD</u> Tithe No 101 (map p76) Owner Richard Collins

1841

Thomas Harris   - 35 Wheelwright
Maria   "   - 30
Martha   "   - 10
Mary   "   - 2
John   "   - 7mths
Francis Smout   - 15 Wheelwright

1851

Thomas Harris   - 46 Wheelwright
Maria   "   - 42
Mary   "   - 12
John   "   - 10
Lucy Ann "   - 8
Thomas   "   - 6
Maria   "   - 4
Fanny   "   - 4
Emily   "   - 9 mths
Mary Lucas   - 82 m-in-law

1861

Thomas Evans   - 32 Blacksmith
Mary   "   - 28
William   "   - 8
Emma   "   - 4

1871

Edwin Pritchard   - 36 Lawyer
Hannah   "   - 39 Wife,milliner
George   "   - 13 Scholar
Mary   "   - 10
Annie   "   - 8
Sarah   "   - 4
Edwin   "   - 2

1881

William Hall   - 28 Ag lab
Mary   "   - 30
Edward   "   - 1

1990 D Gillette, now known as Yewrigg Cottage

<u>No 48 HEIGHWOOD</u> Tithe No 105 (map p76) Owner William Pinches

1841

Cornelius Jones   - 25 Ag Lab
Esther   "   - 22
John   "   - 1
Maria   "   - 64
Elizabeth "   - 20

1851

Cornelius Jones   - 33 Thatcher
Esther   "   - 33
Mary   "   - 8
Edward   "   - 4
Eliza   "   - 2
Elizabeth   - 1

1861   Unoccupied

1871

John Cox   - 46 Labourer
Fanny "   - 40 Sempstress
Edward "   - 8 Scholar
Mary   "   - 6 Scholar

1881

Andrew Hughes   - 60 Farmer 20 acres
Jane   "   - 46
William   "   - 13
Sarah   "   - 11
George   "   - 8
Martha   "   - 6
James   "   - 3

1908 Mr Abbott 1953 C Oliver
Known as Fir Tree Cottage, Now demolished

No 49 <u>HEIGHWOOD</u> Tithe No 95 (map p76) Owner George Harris

1841   1851

George Harris   - 77 Mason   George Harris   - 50 Stone mason
Martha   "   - 69   Ann   "   - 49
Joseph   "   - 41   Edward   "   - 20
Mary   "   - 39   Ann   "   - 13
George   "   - 34

1861   1871

George Harris   - 85 Stone mason   Ann Harris   - 28 Charwoman
Ann   "   - 54   Joseph "   - 8
Mary   "   - 8
Ann   "   - 23

1881   Uninhabited

1908 Gep Whittingham Jones Known as Soudley Villa

1953 Mr A E Taylor

1990 G Young Now known as Quarry Cottage

No 50 <u>TICKLERTON</u> Tithe No 93 (map p76) One time The Barracks/Sebastopol
                       Owner James Ellson

1841   1851

John Ellson   - 28   John Ellson   - 35 Lawyer
Jane   "   - 30   Jane   "   - 42
William "   - 4   James   "   - 11
Ann   "   - 2   Mary E "   - 9
James   "   - 6mths   Wedard "   - 2
                                       Richard Wilkes   - 37 Cordwainer,lodger
                                       Stephen Clutterbuck- 15 Scholar
                                       Eleanor Ellson   - 82 m-in-law

1861   1871

John Ellson   - 46 Carpenter   John Ellson   - 58 Carpenter
Jane   "   - 50   Jane   "   - 62
William "   - 23 Lawyer
Edwin   "   - 12 Scholar
George Jackson   - 23 Lodger,carter
Mary   "   - 18
George "   - 5mths

1881

John Ellson   - 68

1908 Mrs Barlow and Mrs Speke

1990 O Seabury Now known as WOODSIDE COTTAGES (one of three)

No 51 <u>TICKLERTON</u> Tithe No 94 (map p76)

1841   1851

James Ellson   - 70 Lawyer   Samuel Harris   - 35 Stone mason
Clementine "   - 70   Harriet "   - 33
                                       Sarah   "   - 6
                                       Isabella "   - 5
                                       Jane   "   - 3
                                       Alice   "   - 1

1861

William Hughson	- 42
Sarah "	- 39
Ellen "	- 13
Sarah "	- 7
Jane "	- 4

1871

Francis George	- 73 Stone mason
Margaret "	- 77

1881

Samuel Harris	*- 65 Bricklayer*
Harriet "	*- 64*
Richard "	*- 28*
Betsy "	*- 24*

Also Woodside Cottage one of three

No 52 HEIGHWOOD Tithe No 15 (map p76) Mount Flirt Owner Robert Devizes

1841

Francis Wilkinson	- 45 Farmer
Ann "	- 38
Mary "	- 17
Richard "	- 9
Sarah "	- 6
Ann "	- 2
Thomas Jaber?	- 26 M S
? ?	- 14 F S

1851

William Hotchkiss	- 47 Farmer 60 acres
Sarah "	- 33
Frances Heighway	- 20 House servant
Thomas Adams	- 17 House servant

1861

Philip Pritchard	- 32 Farmer 60 acres
Elizabeth "	- 27
John "	- 2
Ann "	- 8days
Maria Mapp	- 48 Mother-in-law
Ann Carter	- 16 General servant
George Lewis	- 13 General servant

1871

Thomas Corfield	- 42 Farmer 55 acres
Mary "	- 30
Edith "	- 3
Hubert "	- 2
William "	- 1
Robert "	- 3 days
Thomas "	- 3 days
Jane Lewis	- 17 Servant

1881

John Downes ?

1891 Edwin Corfield

1990 G Mitchell

No 53 THE HOLLIES Tithe No 62 (map p76) Owner John Bridgwater

1841

Thomas Faulkner	- 50 Farmer
Mary "	- 49
John "	- 15
Martha Carter	- 16

1851

John Smith	- 26 Farmer 60 acres
Mary "	- 37
Mary Ann "	- 1
Thomas Burd	- 12 House servant

1861

William Burgess	- 60 Farmer 58 acres
Martha "	- 54
William "	- 15
Elizabeth "	- 10

1871

Edward Height	- 35 Farmer 50 acres
Elizabeth "	- 35 Wife
Edward "	- 8
William "	- 6

1881

Francis Davies	- 71 Farmer 65 acres
Harriet "	- 64
Richard "	- 35
Emma "	- 25
Lucy Ann Gittins	- 7 gd daughter

1908 J Grainger 63 acres

1929 Geo Hotchkiss

1953 W R Edwards Sold 8/10/54 66.4 acres to W Edwards

1990 R Cox

<u>No 54 HEIGHWOOD</u> Tithe No 23 (map p76) Owner Martha Harris

1841

| Martha Harris | - 75 |
| William " | - 44 Ag Lab |

1851

Joseph Harris	- 51 Stone mason
Mary "	- 49
George "	- 45 Brother

1861

Joseph Harris	- 61 Stone mason
Mary "	- 59
George "	- 59 Brother,mason

1871

| Joseph Harris | - 71 widower,ret mason |
| George " | - 12 Scholar,visitor |

1881   Uninhabited

1938 Knocked down and used to build Meadowbrook.

<u>No 55 HEIGHWOOD</u> Tithe No 24 (map p76) Owner Eliza Harris

1841

Elizabeth Harris	- 70
Samuel "	- 25 Mason
Thomas George "	- 25 Wheelwright
Ann "	- 31
Elizabeth "	- 2

1851

Edward Rogers	- 33 Ag lab
Mary "	- 34
John "	- 8
Sarah "	- 7
Ann "	- 4
Mary "	- 2

1861

Edward Rogers	- 45 Labourer
Mary "	- 45
Ann "	- 14
Mary "	- 12
John Hince	- 9 Boarder,scholar
Sarah Grice	- 81 Visitor

1871

Edward Rogers	- 53 Gardener
Mary "	- 54
John "	- 28 Coachman
Sarah "	- 26 Dressmaker
Ann "	- 24 Cook, unemployed
Mary "	- 22

1881

| Edward Rogers | - 63 Gardener |
| Mary " | - 64 |

<u>No 56 HEIGHWOOD</u> Tithe No 26 (map p76) Owner George Harris Jun

1841

George Harris	- 40 Mason		
Ann "	- 40		
Rose "	- 16	Mary Harris	- 12
Edward "	- 8	Elizabeth "	- 6
Ann "	- 4	Thomas "	- 1

1851

William Carter	"	- 28	Carpenter
Sarah	"	- 56	m-in-law
James	"	- 9	
Mary	"	- 8	

1861

Thomas Blakeway	"	- 33	Carter
Emma	"	- 22	
John Rea		- 2	illeg son

1871

Edward Hince	"	- 36	Farm labourer
Mary	"	- 30	
Sarah	"	- 8	Edwin Hince - 6
Alice	"	- 4	Mary " - 2
Emily	"	- 2 mths	

1881   Uninhabited

1990 J Teague known as Lane End

No 57 HEIGHWOOD Tithe No 28 (map p76) Owner William Pinches

1841

Thomas Wenlock		- 55	Ag Lab
Ann	"	- 60	
Ellen	"	- 20	
Thomas	"	- 4	
Walter Lewis		- 8	

1851

Thomas Wenlock		- 69	Labourer
Ann	"	- 73	
Richard Williams		- 52	Cordwainer
Helen	"	- 33	
Thomas	"	- 4	Grandson

1861

Richard Williams		- 61	Shoemaker
Ellen	"	- 42	
Thomas Wenlock		- 79	Lodger

1871

Richard Williams		- 70	Shoemaker
Ellen	"	- 58	

1881

Richard Williams		- 77	Boot & shoemaker,widower

1908 G Jones
1953 T Holland (15½ acres) now known as Greenfields

1990 P Everingham

No 58 HEIGHWOOD Tithe No 43 (map p76) Owner John Hazwell

1841

Thomas Yapp		- 50	Ag Lab
Mary	"	- 50	

1851

Thomas Yapp		- 64	Ag lab
Mary	"	- 64	
Eliza	"	- 25	
Thomas George		- 15	
Edwin	"	- 8	

1861

Thomas Yapp		- 81	Labourer
Mary	"	- 82	
William Wellings		- 11	g/son,visitor

1871

Thomas Yapp		- 90	Widower
Hannah Beddoes		- 66	Dau,widow,

1881   Uninhabited
             Site of Methodist Chapel?

<u>No 59 COMMON</u> Tithe No 1 (map p76) Common Farm Owner William Pinches

1841

```
John Wilding      - 65 Farmer
Mary     "        - 70
William Tuck      -  9
Richard Child     - 20 Male Servant
? Hughes          - 14 Male Servant
Samuel Evans      - 12 Male Servant
Sarah Ridge       - 20 Female Servant
```

1851

```
Thomas Rogers     - 40 Ag lab
Sarah     "       - 31
Mary      "       -  6
Sarah     "       - 11 mths
```

1861

```
Robert Rogers     - 50 Farmer 114 acres
Sarah     "       - 44
Richard   "       - 17
John      "       - 15
Sarah     "       - 14
Thomas    "       - 14
?         "       - 10
William   "       -  8
Alfred    "       -  5
Emily     "       -  3
Charles           -  3 mths
Thomas Dickson    - 80 Labourer
```

1871   unoccupied

1881

```
Henry Downes      - 60 Farmer 116 acres
Amy       "       - 50
William   "       - 14
John      "       - 70 Brother
Sarah     "       - 62 Sister-in-law
William   "       - 27 Nephew
Henry     "       - 23 Nephew
William   "       -  3 grandson
```

1908 W Downes 110 acres
1929 Thos Seabury
1954 George Seabury (116 acres)
1957 E Meredith
1983 G Preece

<u>No 60 CLAYBROOK</u> Tithe No 288 (map p76) Owner William Pinches

1841

```
Philip Hince      - 58 Farmer
Elizabeth "       - 41
John      "       - 20
Philip    "       - 18
Mary      "       - 15
Timothy   "       - 11
Edward    "       -  9
James     "       -  7
```

1851

```
William Burgess   - 60 Farmer - 112 acres
Martha    "       - 43
Mary      "       - 11
Jane      "       -  8
William   "       -  6
Martha    "       -  3
Elizabeth Bunger  -  6 mths
William Briggs    - 18 Servant
Henry Lewis       - 14 House servant
```

1861   unoccupied

1871

```
William Mason     - 70 Farmer 125 acres
Jane Ownes        - 35 Housekeeper
Thomas Adams      - 38 Cowman
William Cox       - 15 Waggoner
```

1881

```
John Cox            - 29 Labourer
Leonora "           - 28
Edward  "           -  3
Arthur Sydney       -  1
```

```
1891 Wm Kirkham
1929 Edward Cox      Sold 4/10/52
1954 Thos A Hartley 111 acres
1990 R Hartley
```

<u>No 61</u> Tithe No 306 (map p76) The Saplings

1861

```
George Grainger     - 56 Farmer
Esther     "        - 58
George     "        - 26
Samuel Hughes       - 15 Servant
```

1871

```
Joseph Bromley      - 51 Farmer 85 acres
Mary        "       - 49
Eliza       "       - 16
Benjamin    "       - 11 Scholar
William     "       -  7 Scholar
George Williams     - 60 Workman
Francis Danks       - 26 Boarder,farrier
```

1881

```
Joseph Bromley      - 62 Farmer 84 acres
Mary        "       - 59
Eliza       "       - 26
Thomas      "       -  7 gd/son
Edwin Rowson        - 10 Farm servant
Francis Danks       - 35 Lodger,vet surgeon
```

1953 R Pugh 129 acres

APPENDIX TWO

ST EDITH'S CHURCH

Eaton — under — Heywood

Shropshire

The following is a record of the Family names found on the tombstones, stone slabs, floor and walls of the Church.

Summary of the number of memorial stones recorded for each century.

17th century — 3

18th century — 35

19th century — 111

20th century — 65

No date — 4

Pages 224 — 248 compiled by Lilian Buddicom c.1915 and transcribed from the written notes, together with pages 249-254, in March 1989 by Alan Dakers.

In Church yard between porch and tower - flat stone of sandstone, raised on pedestals.

BENEATH THIS STONE
Lie the Remains of Richard Duckett Junior late of Chatwell
    Lawn He died Febry 11th 1847(?) aged 52(?) years
?He had long felt ? that earth was not his...nor earthly objects his best portion??

A ridged flat stone - E S

Flat stone   I H

Fixed to S wall (outside)
Sandstone monument

Near this place
lies the body of
STEPHEN OXENBOLD
    late of
    TICKLERTON
who departed this life
    December 26th
    Anno Domini 1767
            aged 53

Flat stone -
            J H
        Ann Hammonds
    died June 18 1863
        Aged 27

4 flat stones, ridged and lipped

E H - T H - I H - 'no letters'

Outside tower door, flat stone

Here lyeth the Body of
John Oxenbold who de
parted this life May the
23d Anno Dom 1725 in the
48th Year of his age
ALSO
on the North side this
Stone was interred the
Body of Mary Wife of
John Oxenbold late of
Ticklerton. She died June
24th 17(??69) Aged (?) years

        ALSO
    In Memory of Ann
the Wife of Francis Wainwright
    she departed this life
        January 4th 1788
        Aged 82 years

Inside church
Chancel inside communion rails, paving stones

    Mary Lutley Spin. D of
    Bartholomew Lutley Esq. and
Margaret his Wife departed this
    life June 24th Anno Dom 1724
            ? ? 55

HERE
    terr'd the Body
of Philip Lutley Esqe
Son & Heir of Bartholomew
Lutley Esqe Obiit 29th Octr
Anno Dom 1731

IOHES IENKS HUIUS
ECCLAE VICARIUS
OBIIT DEC.19.1695
AETAT PLUS 90
IOCOSA UXOR EIUS
OBIIT FEB 28 -79

"Coat of arms"

Here lye the Bodies of Bartholomew Lutley
of Lawton on the County of Salop Esqe, and
Margaret his Wife; she was the Daughter of
Herbert Jenks of Newhall in the County of
Salop Esqe; and departed this life the secondof May 1674 Aged 35.
Bartholomew dyed
the 15th December 1716. in the 80th year of
his Age And was Son and Heir of Adam
Lutley of Brome Croft Castle in the County of
Salop Esqe. They left two sons and four
Daughters (viz) Philip and Adam, Elizabeth,
Margaret, Mary and Magdalen Philip married
Penelope the Daughter of Richard Barneby
of Brockhampton in the County of Hereford
Esqe Adam married Hester the Daughter
of Richard Wredenhall of Doronton in the
County of Salop Gent Elizabeth was
Married to Thomas Barodenym of Llanasop
in the County of Flint Esqe Margaret was
Married to Herbert Howorth of Burghill in
the County of Hereford Esqe.

In centre of pavement of Nave

Here Lyeth ye
Body of Willm
Pinches of Tick
lerton who De
parted this
Life June ye 12th
Anno Dom 17
52 Aged 74

Here lyeth the
Body of Mary
Pinches Wife of
William Pinches
of Ticklerton
who Departed
this Life Novmr
the 27th Anno
Dom 1724

Chancel, below Communion Rails from the left

Here Lyeth ye Body
of Thomas Ward
who Departed this
Life the 17th of June
Anno Domini 1709
Aged 14 years

Here lyeth the
body of Henry
Newnham late of
Longvill who was
inter'd Feb the 3
Annod 1697

  "Coat of Arms"

Here lyeth the Body of
Richd Ward Jun late (of?)
Harton Gent; Who Departed
this life May ye 29
1730: Aged 40:
Also
The Body of Mrs Margaret
Ward wife to the above
Mentioned Mr Richard Ward
who died 9th April
1768 Aged 73

Here lyes the Body of
Lucretia Daughter of Justinian
Barrow of ye City of London
M.D: widow of the late
Revd. Henry Hibbin B.D.
Rector of the Second Portion
of Wadesdon in the County
of Bucks; Sometime Fellow
of Balliol Colledge in Oxford
she departed this Life Augst
14th 1729 Aged 69

Small brass let into the stone slab

Exivia Richardi Hancock
Evangelii ministri fidelis
omnibus quas
deposuit martii 26
1692

Centre of nave
(Stone slabs with oval inlays of black marble)

Humphrey Pinches
late of Shrewsbury
died March 1st 1805
aged 81
Elizabeth his wife
died July 31st 1807
also aged 81

Here lieth the Body of
Thomas Pinches
late of Shrewsbury
died May 17th 1797
aged 44

In Memory of MARY
wife of William Pinches
late of Ticklerton
died June 12th 1752
aged 74
Mary his wife
died November 27th 1724
aged 39

In Memory of
William Pinches of Ticklerton
he departed this life the 12
of June Anno Dom 1752
aged 74 years

In Vestry, West Wall (Tower)

This stone is Erected
by a sincerely attached Daughter
to the Memory of
The Revd RICHARD FLEMING A.B.
of Worcester College, Oxford
and for many years the faithful Pastor
of this and the neighbouring
Parish of Easthope
who died at the Vicarage, Eaton
the 20th day of December 1819
aged 65 years
Only the actions of the just
smell sweet and blossom in the dust

South pavement leading to tower

Here lieth the Body of
Richard Pinches
son of Richard and Mary
diedOct 20th 1789 aged 36
also Elizabeth Pinches
his sister
late of Harton
who died March 6th 1822
aged 72

In Memory
of
Joseph Hammonds
died Decr 8th 1822
Aged 85 years
MEMENTO MORI
--

Edward Hammonds
died Feby 11th 1818 Aged 37

In Memory of Thomas
The son of John Hide and
Elizabeth his Wife He died
May 14th 1809 Aged 3 yrs
Alas he's gone and like a spotless
dove
To increase the number of the
blest above
Secure of peace his soul is gone
to rest
To the eternal mansions of the
blest

Sacred
to the
Memory of
Elizabeth Fleming
an
Exemplar
of
Christian Piety
and
Of every duty
both
Public and Private
Obiit April 6th 1812
Aetatis snee 44

Sacred
To the memory of
Elizabeth the wife of
John Hide who departed
this life June 29th 1840
aged 63 years

With ancious thoughts she did
attend
The cares of worthy wife and Friend
With patience bore afflictions rod
'Till summoned here to meet
her God

Vestry, East Wall

IN MEMORY OF
Richard Smout late of
the Spellar:in this Parish
He died June 13th 1825
Aged 93 years

Also here lies the body of

Ann his Wife She died July

13th 1819 Aged 79 years
we

IN MEMORY OF
Ann the Wife of
FRANCIS SMOUT
of Upper Millichope who
departed this life April 16th
1813 - Aged 39 years

Francis the son of Francis
and Ann Smout He died
Jun 12th 1807 Aged 8 months

To
the Memory of
John Hide late of the
HOLLIES IN THIS PARISH
He died Jan 2nd 1797 aged 89 yrs
Also Here Lieth the Body of
JAMES HIDE
He died July 7th 1753 Aged 47
Prepare for Death pray let us all
We know not when the Lord will
call

In Memory
of
John Hide late of
Ticklerton he Died April
the 19th 1830 Aged 78 years
Here to our grief doth lie our
friend
Left us behind some tears to spend
Tho loss to us Death was his gain
In heaven we trust his soul
remains

NEAR THIS PLACE
lie the body of Martha
Sister to the said Richard
Smout She died July 27th
1825 Aged 81 years

Time was we stood where though of
now
And vie wd the dead as though oft
we
Ere long thou wilt lie as low as

And others fiand to look on thee

Near this Place
lie the remains of
FRANCIS SMOUT
Senior late of Upper
MILLICHOPE
He died Septr 29th 1847
Aged 79 Years
Here doth three corpes lie
The Husband,Wife and Child so dea
Wrapt up in Clay they must remain
Till Christ shall raise them up
again

THIS
Stone is erected
to the Memory of
Elizabeth Rachel and
Frances the Daughters of
RICHARD & SUSANNAH
Duckett of Haywood in
this Parish   Elizabeth
died Sept Ye 20th 1819 aged
28 years, Rachel died
May 17th 1822 Aged 29 years
Frances died May 28th 1807
9 months
Blessed are the dead that
die in the Lord

In Memory
of
Elizth Daughter of Timy and
Elizth Smout of Gretton
died Nov 10th 1829
Aged 3 Years 10 months
This lowly bud so young and fair
Called hence by Early doom
Just come to show how sweet a flower
In Paradise would bloom

In Memory of
Richard Duckett
who died Feb 25
1830 Aged 73
also Susannah his
wife who died June
22nd 1830 Aged 64
In love and peace they livd
together
Till God did call one from the
other
Till the last trumpet it will Aged
sound
The all in judgment rise therefore
In hopes of pleasure evermore
Also
Mary Daughter of
Richard & Susannah Duckett
died April 11th 1834

S wall of chancel

Here lies interred
the Body of Philip Lutley Esq
Lord of the Mannour of Eton and Patron
of the Church Son and Heir of Bartholomew
Lutley Esqr late of Lawton in the County
and Margaret his Wife who also are interred here
He was a most affectionate husband, a most prudent
The prudent Father & sincere Friend who living was
a dying lamented by all that knew him. He married
Penelope only Daughter and Heir of Richard Barneby
of Brockhampton in the County of Hereford Esqr
by whom he had two sons Jenkes & Bartholomew
Richard, four daughters Isabella, Penelope, Margaret
and Sarah all living. He departed this life the 20th of
October in the 64th year of his life, Ann Dom 1721

To the Memory of Jenkes Lutley of Lawton
in the County of Salop Esqr who dyed the 27th day
of January in the 35th year of his age Ann Dom 1743

Also Penelope Lutley of Henwick in the County
of Worcester Wife of the aforesaid Philip Lutley
Esqr who dyed the 7th of March in the 60th year
of her Age 1745

This Chancel was Beautified and the Burial
Vault built at the Charge of the Above mentioned
Jenkes Lutley Esqr in the Year 1743

To The Glory of God
and in loving memory of
ISABELLA FRIEDERICHS
who died at Acton Scott Rectory
June 30th 1906
in the 69th Year of her Age
also her son
Captain Duncan Alexander Friederichs
of the Royal Engineers
Born November 7th 1869
Captain Friederichs served in the Egyptian Campaign
of 1898, and was present at the Battle of Omdurman
and the taking of Khartoum. He was mentioned in
dispatches, received the medal and clasp.
After passing through the Staff College with great
distinction he was appointed D.A.A.G. at the
Irish Headquarters in Dublin.
In January 1906 he was appointed Adjutant of the
Field Force in the Somaliland Campaign
He fell gloriously in action on the heights near
Hassan Hgaz, July 17th 1901 while rescuing and
endeavouring to convey, on his horse, to a place
of safety, a wounded non-commissioned officer.
This memorial is erected by the
Rev C G N Friederichs, Rector of this Parish
to the memory of his beloved Mother and Brother.

To the glory of God in loving memory of
Arthur Sparrow
late of Preen Manor Shrewsbury, F.S.A.
Lord of the Manor of Eaton under Haywood, D.L.& J.P.
for the County of Salop and J.P. for the County of Stafford
who died the 21st January 1898 aged 71 years
This memorial is erected by his son
Alan Bertram Hanbury Sparrow
(erected in 1914)

South wall of Nave

UNDERNEATH
ARE DEPOSITED
THE REMAINS OF
JOSEPH COOKE
(late of Aston Mill
in the Parish of Munslow)
WHO DIED SEPTEMBER 22nd
1851 Aged 76 years

Near this place repose
the remains of MARY
wife of JOSEPH COOKE
of ASTON MILL
in the Parish of Munslow
who departed this life
26th Feb 1826
aged 41 years
Her sufferings here were long and
great
Which wean'd her from this earth
But in them she found a happy
state
and most Celestial Birth

In Memory of
JOHN PINCHES
who died Decr 16th 1740
aged 58
Ann his wife
died Novr 7th 1767
aged 51
Richard their son
died July 21st 1757 Aged 25

Near this place
lieth the Body of
WILLIAM PINCHES
(late of Harton in the Parish)
who died Feby 6th 1808
in the 88th Year
of his Age

Near this place
Lies Interd the Mortal Remains
of JOSEPH MATTHEWS; he died
April 16th 1782: Aged 46 years
Farewell vain world I have had enough of thee
And little care I what thou sayest of mercy
Thy smile I corte not, nor thy Frowns I fear,
My hope's in Christ, my Head lies easy here

West window

In memory of Elizabeth youngest daughter of William
and Mary Pinches of Ticklerton and wife of Robert Joseph
Buddicom Rector of Smethcote, she died May 16th 1859

N side wall, chancel below communion rails

Underneath lie the remains
of the Revd Thomas Gwynn, A.M.
late Vicar of this Parish, died May 2nd 1799
aged 33 years
If honest worth, with Charity combined,
Deserve the dear remembrance of Mankind,
Here may the worthy drop the tender tear,
For such was his desert who slumbers here

Beneath is interrd
The Body of Mary
The Wife of Richd
Ward Sen of Harton
Gent who died Feb 23rd
1728 Aetat 65
And also the Body of
Richd Ward Husband
to ye above mentiond
Mary Ward who died Mch 20
1735/6 Aged 79
They had issue four sons viz: Adam
Edward, Richard, Thomas. And five
Daughters viz: Beaty, Hannah, Mary, Irene, Abigail

In a vault underneath
are deposited the mortal remains of
WILLIAM PINCHES
late of Ticklerton Gentleman
who departed this life November 19th 1818
Aged 67 years

Also of Mary his wife
who died February 13th 1844
Aged 74 years

In memory of
William Pinches, Gentleman
only son of

William and Mary Pinches
of Ticklerton
He died November 29th 1849
aged 47 years
"And they mourned over him,
saying, alas my brother"

Sacred to the memory of
Mary
Daughter of William and Mary
Pinches
of Ticklerton
who died and was interred at
Portobello near Edinburgh
September 12th 1846
aged 40 years

CHURCH YARD East Corner
(Angel)
In Memory of
Elizabeth Haughton
the beloved wife of
William Squire Buddicom
who entered into rest
March 7th 1914 aged 71 years

(Ledger)
Here lieth the Body of
William Pinches
late of Ticklerton
who died Nov 28th 1849 aged 47

Marble cross & ledger)
"God is Love"
(Latin phrase)
In loving memory of the Rev Robert Joseph Buddicom M.A.
died at Redlap 11th July 1895, aged 80

Here lieth the body of Elizabeth Buddicom
late of Ticklerton
who died at Smethcote Rectory May 16th 1859
aged 51 years

(Headstone)
In Memory of
Charlotte Nichols
of the Parish who
Died Jan 11th 1859
Aged 49 years
Prepare for death, pray let
us all
We know not when the Lord
will call
Also of Richard Nichols
husband of the above
who died October 3rd 1889
aged 78 years

(Headstone)
In Memory of
Ada
Daughter of Richard and Eliza Ray
who died Jan 4th
Aged 17 years
for to me to live is Christ and to
die is gain

(Headstone)
In Loving Memory
Emma Davies
(of Whitefields)
who died August 20th 1908

aged 54 years
"With Christ, which is far
better"

(Headstone)
In memory of
Dafny, Daughter of Thomas
and Mary Yapp of Haywood died
July 8th 1836 in the 18th Year of
her age
A Father who to me was dear
A Mother who is very near
Five sisters and a brother too
And yet for Christ I bade them
adieu

(Headstone)
Sacred
to the Memory of
Josiah Duckett
late of Haywood who died
June 13th 1855, aged 52 years
also Martha the beloved
wife of the above who died
April 2nd 1858, aged 52 years
also Jane daughter of the above
who died May 13th 1858 aged 20
years
also Richard son of the above
who died Feb 22nd 1866 aged 21 years
Blessed are the dead who die in
the Lord

(Headstone)
Sacred
to the Memory of
William Hamlett
who departed this life
April 10th 1849
aged 60 years
"Blessed are the dead which die
in the Lord"

(adjoining are 3 small headstones)
```
J D    R D  M D
1858   1866 1858
```

(Ledger)
In affectionate remembrance of
John Preece late of Upper Millichope
who departed this life November 17th
1870 aged 67 years

Tomorrow I will seek the Lord
the foolish heart will say
Tomorrow may no time afford
O seek the Lord today
call

(on reverse side)
Sacred to the Memory of
Martha the beloved wife of
John Preece late of Upper
Millichope in this Parish
who departed this life
June 23rd 1864 aged 63 years
Prepare for death pray let us all
We know not when the Lord doth

In memory of
Henry son of
John & Martha Preece
late of Upper Millichope
who died Feb 1st 1871
aged 25 years

In memory of
Elizabeth the wife of
Richard Harris
late of the Hollies   she died
April 8th 1809 aged 51/4 years

To the sacred memory of
Anne the daughter of
John & Martha Preece
who departed this life January 10th
1856 aged 20 years
also
of William the son of
John & Martha Preece
who departed this life December 31st
1860 aged 26 years
also
of John the son of
John & Martha Preece
who departed this life August 10th
1867 aged 28 years
Prepare for death pray let us all
We know not when the Lord doth call

Here lyeth ye
Body of John Batley
who Departed this
life November ye 12
anno domini 1738
aged 40(?) years

(Headstone)
In loving Memory of
William Rawlings
of Hatton
died July 15th 1897
aged 46 years
With Christ which is far better
also of
James Rawlings
died June 16th 1902
aged 44 years
Peace perfect peace, with loved ones
far away
In Jesus keeping we are safe and they

(flat stone near yew tree)
Beneath this stone
lie the remains of
Frances the daughter of
Thomas and Sarah
Rogers of Haywood
She died Oct 7th 1840
aged 15 months
This lovely bud so young and fair
called hence by early doom
Just come to show how sweet a
flower
In Paradise would bloom

(Headstone)
In affectionate remembrance of
Joseph Manley
of Manor Farm,East Wall
late of Ticklerton
who met with his death
by being thrown from his trap
May 5th 1887 in his 65th year
also of Esther
the beloved wife of the above
who died December 8th 1886
in her 64th year
Not gone from memory
not gone from love
But gone to Our Father's home above

(Headstone)
In affectionate remembrance of
John Wainwright
of Hatton
who died April 8th 1888
aged 79 years
Thy will be done

(Cross)
In affectionate remembrance of
Joseph Jones (late of Eaton)
who died January 5th 1879
aged 90 years
also Sarah Jones
wife of the above
who died Febrauary 12th 1881
aged 80 years
Through much tribulation ye shall
enter the Kingdom of Heaven

(Ledger)
Sacred to the memory of James
son of Benjamin and Ann Beddoes of
Wolverton
who departed this life January 18
1809 in the 81st year of his age
"James a servant of God and of the
Lord Jesus Christ"

(Headstone)
In loving memory of
Sarah Ann
wife of Samuel Manley (of Hatton)
who died October 15th 1896
aged 49 years
Not gone from memory,
Not gone from love
But gone to the Father's home above
Also of Samuel Manley
(late of Hatton farm)
who died November 8th 1906 aged 55 years
Also Mary Trickett Manley,
daughter of the above
who died March 26th 1907 aged 23 years
And with the morn those angel faces smile
which I have loved long since and last awhile

(Rustic cross)
In affectionate remembrance of
Helen Downes
of Upper Millichope
who departed this life Jan 22nd
1892
In the 68th year of her age
Come unto me and I will give you
rest

(Ledger)
Sacred to the memory of John
son of William & Mary Carter
(of the Wetmoor) who died Oct 4th
1866 aged 24 years
Looking for the mercy of our Lord
Jesus Christ unto eternal life

(Marble cross)
Frederick Downes
of Upper Millichope
died July 13th 1879
aged 23 years
Blessed are the dead that die
in the Lord

(Headstone)
Sacred
the memory of
Elizabeth wife of
Timothy Smout of Gretton
She departed of this life
Nov 4th 1852 aged 71 years
also to the memory of

(Headstone,chipped)
To
the memory of
Ann
The daughter of Timothy and
Elizabeth Smout of Gretton
She died May 19th 184-
a   years

Timothy Smout of Gretton
who died August 15th 1812
aged 84 years

(Behind this large headstone
are two flat slabs marked 'T' & 'E S')

(Flat slab)
Beneath this stone
Lieth the remains of Timothy
Son of Richard and Mary Smout of
Wall He died May 8th 1808 aged 2 years

weep   not with
nor you   day
If
To   by friends
     with Christ in perfect bliss to
dwell
(Behind this headstone is a flat
slab marked 'A S')

In memory of Sarah Smout
She was born May 18th
In the year 1821
And died June 10th 1822

Suffer the little children to come
unto me and forbid them
not for of such is the
Kingdom of Heaven

(Square Cox,S.side)
In memory of
William Cox
Late of Soudley who died
March 3oth 1860
aged 86 years

(Top,S.)
also William
Son of William and Frances Cox
who died May 7th 1865
aged 55 years
In memory of Mary who died
Oct 26th 1874 at Rowton aged 59

(E. side)
Also of Margaret
Daughter of William and Frances
Cox who died November 28th 1862
Aged 48 years

(Top,E.)
We all do   as a leaf

(N.side)
In memory of Frances Cox wife of
William Cox of Soudley
who died July 25th 1848
aged 61 years

(Top,N.)
Sacred to the memory of
Ann Codlings daughter of William
and Frances Cox who died
at Bewdley November 14th 1862
aged 44 years

W.side)
Also
Edward son of Willm
and Frances Cox
who died Sep 29 1851
aged 45

(Top,W.)
In memory of
Sarah Cox
who died July 27th 1880
aged 58 years
Though lost to sight to many dear

(Headstone)
In affectionate remembrance of
John Rawlings of Hatton
died July 2nd 1894
aged 76 years
God is our refuge and strength
also of
Alice wife of the above
died April 9th 1905
aged 84 years
He giveth His beloved sleep

(Small stone near centre Yew)
Sacred to the memory of
John son of William and
Mary Bullock who departed
this life November 1st 1845
Aged 10 years
Morn not for me my parents dear
Nor lightly shed a tear
For I am gone but just before
To meet my Saviour dear

(Slab near E window)
In memory of Francis the son of
Fr   Preen and Elizabeth his
W   Life
            nd Suckered
Mother   ight for 1
   l Coli   to a place of Rest
Alfo M   dyed ye 31
of Decemr 176- Aged 5 years
              Wife of
Frances Preen who departed this
life 20th Jany 1780 Aged 40

(Upright stone)
In loving memory of
William Downes
of Middlehope
who died February 10 1895
aged 80 years
Blessed are they that die in the Lord
Also of Mary Wife of the above
who died September 30th 1903
Aged 88 years
Gone but not forgotten

(Big flat stones near
S Chancel window)
Here is interred ye Body
of Thomas Palmer of
Ticklerton Gent who
Departed this life
Augt ye 6th 1732 Aged 41

Here lies interred the body of
William Palmer of Ticklerton Gent
who departed this life
May ye 20 1701

(Headstone)
SACRED to the Memory of
Elizabeth the Wife of
William Webster
she died April 16th 1839
Aged 39 years

(Cross)
In affectionate memory of John
The third and loving son of
Joseph and Esther Manley
of Ticklerton
Who died August 12th 1881
Aged 28 years
In the midst of life we are
in death

(Upright stone)
In affectionate remembrance of
Edward Downes
Who died at Upper Middlechope
January 18th 1888
aged 76
Verily there is but one step
Between us and Death

(Stone, top worn away)
          of
  illiam Palmer Gent
late of Ticklerton
who died September 24
1777 Aged 55

Here lieth ye Body
of Samuel Martyn who departed
this life March 12 Anno
Dom 17-- Aged 20

(Headstone)
SACRED to the Memory of
William Webster
of Middlehope
he died March 16th 1846
Aged 48 years

Here o'er our virtuous Parents Dust we leave a stone to tell
They so on earth fulfilled their Trust, as now in Heaven do dwell
So that altho' we feel the loss of these so dear our Friends
Their Life well spent while here they was, Hath gained a better end

---

(Marble cross)
In Memory of
Nellie
youngest and dearly loved child of
Richard and Elizabeth Medlicot
of Wolverton
who died August 20th 1878 Aged 5 years
Safe in the arms of Jesus

(Headstone)
Sacred to the Memory of
Mary Wife of Richard Smout of Wall
who died Nov 25 1843 Aged 66 years

Sacred to the Memory of
Richard Smout at Wall
died March 19th 1858 Aged 80 years
A loving Husband
A tender Father
A sincere Friend
And a good neighbour

(Stones behind)
'R S' 'M x S' 'M x S'

(Headstone)
In affectionate remembrance of
Eleanor Wife of John Hartley
Born July 24th 1818
Died July 27th 1884
"I know that my redeemer liveth"
also of the above
John Hartley
Born March 8th 1817
Died July 3rd 1890
also of Hannah their daughter
Born March 7th 1861
Died May 5th 1890
God is love

(Marble cross)
In loving memory of the
Rev Holland Sandford M.A.
Rector of the Parish for 40 years
Born June 2nd 1823
Died November 23rd 1904

(Headstone near churchyard wall)
Sacred to the memory of
Margaret
Wife of William Hayes of New Hall
(in this parish)
who died Dec 23rd 1845 Aged 61 years
Dear as thou wast and justly dear
We will not weep for thee Our ehought
shall check the starting tear, it is
that thou art free and thus shall
faith's consoling power the tears of
love restrain Oh that save thy
passing hour could wish thee here again

also of William Hayes
Husband of the above
who died Aug 7th 1873
Aged 85 years

Sacred to the Memory of
Mary Dautr of Richd and Mary
Smout of Wall
who died July 12th 1839
Aged 31 years
Blessed are the dead which
die in the Lord

(Marble cross)
In loving memory of
Edward Wilson
who died Dec 2nd 1891
aged 31 years
In the midst of life we are
in death

(Ledger)
Beneath this stone rest the
remains of the Rev Richard
Sandford M.A. for twenty eight
years Vicar of this Parish and
fourth son of the late Folliot
Sandford Esquire of the Isle of
Rossall in this County
He departed this life on the 2nd
day of January 1860 in the 69th
year of his age.

(Headstone)
In affectionate remembrance of
Richard Howells
late of Blackwood
who departed this life
January 14th 1871 Aged 74 years

(Headstone)
In affectionate memory of
Richard Rogers
(of Soudley)
who died January 23rd 1885
aged 65 years
Watch for ye know not what hour your
Lord doth come Mathew XX1V.24
also Sarah
Wife of the above
who died February 25th 1900
aged 73 years
"Thy will be done"

(headstone)
Sacred to the memory of
Mary Ann the Wife of
William Yapp
of Middlehope She died
December 23rd 1856
aged 52 years

(Headstone)
In memory of Jane
the Beloved Wife of
Charles Roberts of Birtley
who died May 16 1888 aged 31 years
"Safe in the Arms of Jesus"
also of Margaret
Wife of Thomas Roberts
who died October 20 1889
aged 65 years God is love

(Ledger)
In memory of Augusta Sophia fifth
daughter of Thomas and Mary Hince
of New Hall in the Parish She died
of Diptheria Aug 21st 1859 aged 4 years
and 3 months. Suffer the little
children to come unto me and forbid
them not, for such is the Kingdom of
God Mark X 1V

(Headstone
In remembrance of
Jane the Beloved Wife of
John Elson (of Haywood)
who departed this life Feb 11 1872
aged 64
Blessed are the dead that die in the
Lord
also of John Elson

Husband of the above
who died June 13 1883 aged 71 years
His end was Peace

(Headstone)
In memory of
Martha Carter
the Beloved Wife of
Thomas Carter
late of Cuckoo's Nest who died
Augst 12th 1861 aged 76 years
also the following children of
Thomas and Martha Carter
William died Jany 1st 1861 aged 1
Priscilla died Sept 6th 1861 aged
14 weeks
George died May 29th 1880 aged 18
years. Be ye also ready Matt XX1V
Herbert Carter born March 1 1857
died November 1st 1875 aged 18
years

(headstone)
In memory of Richard ye
son of Richard Sprag
and Mary who died June
the 25th 1767 aged 17
My time was short
the longer is my best
God oft takes first
Those whom he loveth best

(Headstone)
In loving memory of
Thomas Roberts of Birtley
who died February 1 1895
aged 81 years
"Looking for the Mercy of our
Lord Jesus Christ into eternal
Life"

(Ledger)
In memory of Ellen Carter
who died Dec 19th 1859 aged
6 weeks
Hark they whisper, angels say
sister spirit come away

(Headstone)
In memory of
Thomas Hamer
late of East Wall
who departed this life
Sept 9th 1843
aged 81 years
Death call'd for me today
'tis time

Tomorrow he may call for you

(Ledger)
In memory of John Hamer
who died May 27th 1881
aged 83 years

(Headstone)
Sacred to the memory of
Richard Smart of Westhope
son of Francis and Ann Smart
late of Upper Millichope
who departed this life April 16 1868
aged 67 years

(small headstone, face almost
entirely chipped off - the name
'Smart' being the only word
that remains)

(Headstone)
In memory of
Thomas Goodman (of Heywood)
who departed this life
April 26th 1884
aged 84 years
Gone but not forgotten

(Headstone)
Here lie the remains of
John Harris of Haywood
in the Parish he died August --
aged 68 years
Elizabeth Harris Wife of the above
who died Feb 24 1854 aged 84 years
also of Elizabeth Dolphin their
daughter who died July 17th 1848
aged 33 years
Blessed are the dead who die in the
Lord

(new Headstone)
In memory of John Hamer
of East Wall
died January 4th 1913

(Headstone)
To the memory of
Frances daughter of John
and Elizabeth Harris
She died April 21 1830
aged 48(?)years
also Richard Harris son of the
above He died Dec 29th 1836
aged 31 years

How lov'd, how valu'd, only
avail thee not
To whom related, or to whom begot
avail thee not,
a heap of dust alone remains of
thee, Tis all THOU art and all
PROUD shall be

(Headstone)
To the memory of
John Williams (of Soudley)
who died March 3rd 1837
aged 29 years
also of Ann daughter of
John and Mary Williams
Who died February 28th 1837
Why do we morn departed friends
or shake at death's alarms
Tis but the voice that Jesus sends
To call them to his arms
also of Mary widow of the above
and wife of Thomas Goodman
who died Dec 13 1873

(Headstone)
In memory of
George Harris late of Haywood
who died Aug 2nd 1869 aged 71
years also Ann the beloved wife of
the above who died Dec 29th 1867
aged 67 years
also the children of the above
George died Sept 12th 1833 aged
17 years
John died Oct 4th 1839 aged 17
years
Isiah died March 20th 1840 aged
15 years
Rosamond died Dept 9th 1841 aged
18 years
Thomas died March 21st 184- aged
3 years
Mary died Sept 25th 1846 aged
17 years

(Double headstone, slate)

To the Sacred memory of
Mary the daughter of George Duckett
and Ann his Wife of Haywood
who died Ap 24 1834 aged 6
Forbear my friends forbear this
mournful strain
Your grief how useless and tears
how vain,
Your child escap'd from pain and woe
Which those who stay behind must
undergo

Sacred to the memory of
George Duckett He died
Dec 24th 1838 aged 46 years
Here to our grief doth lie our
friend, left us behind some
tears to spend, Tho loss to us
Death was his gain, in Heaven
we trust, his Soul remains
also of Ann wife of
George Duckett who died Jan 25
1871 aged 78 years Behold I come
quickly

(Flat slabs behind marked)
 M D - G D - A D

(Headstone)
In memory of Ann daughter of
George & Ann Duckett (of Haywood)
who died May 17 1880 aged 52 years
"Thy will be done"

Outside vestry door
(flat slab furthest from door)
Here lyeth the Body of
John Oxenbold who departed
this Life May the 23rd a Dom 1725
in the 48 year of his age
also on the north side this stone
is interred the Body of Mary wife of
John Oxenbold late of Ticklerton
she died June 24th 1769 aged 87 years

(flat slab nearest door)
In memory of Ann
the Wife of Francis Wainwright
who departed this Life
January 4 1788 aged 82 years

(Raised tomb, table shape)
Here lyeth the Body of
John Corfield Jun of Ticklerton
who Departed this Life the 10th
Day of January 1735 in the 27th year
of his age
also on the south side lyeth the Body
of John Corfield Senior who departed
this life ye 14th June 1741 aged 65

(Headstone behind tomb)
"Corfield Arms"
In memory of
Margaret Corfield
who died January ????
 ? ? 1819   years

    Prepare....(verse etc worn away)

    (Coat of arms)
also interred under this stone
the Body of Thomas Corfield of
Ticklerton (late of Church Stretton
Ironmonger) he departed this life the
18th day of March 1793 aged 87 years

(reverse side of above stone)
North side this stone
lyeth Hannah wife of Thomas
Corfield of Ticklerton (late of
Church Stretton, Ironmonger)
He is the author and sole cause
of the mending of the roads
in his (bad) very very bad)
neighbourhood) She died the 23rd
April 1781 aged 76 years

(Row of 5 headstones, the 'bad roads' (above) is the first)
No2
In memory of
Elizabeth the daughter of Joseph and
Sarah Jones She died the 14th of
February in the year 1826 aged 14 days
When I was an infant dear
and sucking yet my mother's breast
The Lord one night for me did call
and took me to a place of rest

No3
In memory of
William son of Joseph and Sarah
Jones He died July 23rd 1829
aged 1 year and 10 months
Short was his day of life and just
his fate Short was his suffering
yet his life transgrest
Oh could you look within the vail
and see your William clothed with
immortality and hear him join the
blessed s..To shout the wonders of

No4
Sacred to the memory of
Martha daughter of Joseph and Sarah
died Ap 19 1832 aged 11 months
For what is your life! it is even a
vapour that appeareth for a little
time and then vanisheth away

(small flat stone near above row)
Here lieth the Body of
Mary Ward
who died 25th of December 1760
aged 72

(Marble cross)
In loving memory of
Richard Davies late of Middlehope
who died Nov 30th 1914 aged 71 years
Thy Will be done

(Double flat stone opposite porch)
In memory of Theodosia Evans
who died Jan -- 1814 aged 84 years
    Kind reader mark perhaps man in thy prime
    The stealing steps of never fading time
    Thou!! We what we are catch the present hour
    Employ that well for that's within thy power

(adjoining double flat slab,top ornament worn away)
Near this place lyeth the Body of
Francis Smout Died November 15 1754
aged 53

No5
In memory of Ann daughter of
Joseph and Sarah Jones
died Mar 8th 1837 aged 4 years
She's safely landed in your World
of Light
She's crown'd with glory rob' in
spotless white
Could you but hear her happy
spirit tell How Jesus died to
ransom her from hell

(small headstone)
Here lyeth ye Body of
Roger Green
who died August ye 8th.....
aged....

(marble headstone)
In loving memory of
Edward the beloved son of
Mary & the late William Kirkham
Claybrook who died March 14 1908
aged 21 years
also of John their infant son
who died May 25th 1893
aged 8 months
"We cannot Lord thy purpose see
but all is well tht's done by thee

also Willm Evans
He died Jan 31 1823 aged 90 years

also
Elizabeth Wife of Francis Smout
Died November 10th 1790
aged 85 years

    Elizabeth Daughter of Francis and Elizabeth
    Smout died May the 9th 1768 aged 33 years

Right of path leading up from the Gate
(Headstone)
In loving memory of
Edward beloved husband of Mary Jones
of Eaton
who died April 26th 1915
aged 68 years
A Light is from an household gone
A man we loved is still
A place is vacant in our Home
which never can be filled

(Headstone)
In loving memory of
Cornelius Jones
late of Lily Wood
who died August 4th 1889
aged 75 years
This Languishing head is at rest
His thinking and asking are o'er
This quiet immovable breast
Is hea...ed by affliction no more
also Esther his Wife
who died October 28th 1889
aged 71 years
This heart is no longer the seat
of Trouble and torturing pain
It ceased to flutter and beat
It never shall flutter again

(headstone)
Sacred to the memory of
William son of Francis Smout
late of Westhope
who departed this life May 22nd 1885
aged 77 years

(Small ledger)
Underneath lyeth the Body of
Eliza Daughter of Edward and Margt
Bird who died Dec 5 1840 aged 7 mons

Reverse side
Like a Bird of Prey Death stole a way
This young and tender dove
Her heart so pure is now secure
With Christ in Heaven above

(Headstone)
In affectionate remembrance of
Samuel Marsie of Bradeley
who departed this life
Dec 1st 1883 in the 9th year of
his age
also
Anne Marsie Wife of the above
who departed this life Oct 3rd 1883
In the 76 year of her age
"Come unto me & I will give you rest"

(large headstone)
Sacred to the memory of
Frances the Wife of William
Davies of Upper Millichope
She departed this life May 23rd
1833 aged 49 years
Frances Daughter of the above
who died July 28th 1833
aged 18 years

(ledger)
To the memory of
William Davies late of Upper
Millichope who died November 26th
1857 aged 85 years
Reverse side
Sacred to the memory of Frances
Wife of William Davies of Upper
Millichope who died May 23rd
1833 aged 49 years

(Headstone)
In affectionate remembrance of
Ann the Beloved daughter of
Walter and Elizabeth Lewis
of Soudley who died March 29th
1882 aged 25 years
Looking unto Jesus
also of Elizabeth the beloved
Wife of Walter Lewis who died
July 8th 1896 aged 74 years
also of Walter Lewis who died
April 13th 1911 aged 80 years

Part of Church yard to left of path from gate
(Marble cross)
In loving memory of
Mary Jane wife of
Thomas Haywood (school)
who died Feb 1st 1915
aged 59 years
In my Father's house are many mansions

(Headstone)
In loving memory of
Edwin Evans Ticklerton
died December 24th 1896
aged 56 years
In the midst of Life we are in
Death
also Eliza wife of the above
died Oct 21st 1906 aged 63 years
Her end was Peace

(Headstone)
In loving memory of
Elizabeth wife of John Venables
(of Eaton Manor)
who died September 13th 1913
aged 39
"He giveth his beloved sleep"
also of John son of the above
who died June 14th 1910 aged 42
Thy will be done
also John Venables who died
January 16th 1915 aged 74
Rest in the Lord

Some old flat stones between the buttresses on the North side of the
Church - many worn away
(First set - left to right)

No.1 worn away entirely

No.3 top part & most of rest worn
away - probably a Pinches monument
Rich......   ...ohn
16...   ..:vile
        1757

No.2.
Here lyeth ye Body of Ann Pinches
late of Ticklerton who departed
this life ye 7..... aged...
(verse illegible)

No.4 quite worn away
(Second set - left to right)

No.1
In memory of
Richard Matthews
he departed this life
June 2nd 178- aged 56
Blessed are the dead that die in the Lord

No.2
Here lyeth the Body of
Mary wife of Richard Matthews
of Strefford who departed this
life December ye ? 1750 aged ?

...lieth the body of Mary wife of
the said(?) Richard Matthews She died
Dec 1818 aged 84 years
A loving wife, a tender Mother,
a Sincere friend, and a good neighbour

No.3
In memory of
Thos Matthews of Eaton
He died March ye 29 1819

also here lieth ye Body of
Henry Matthews of Eaton
He died Sept 25 1812 aged 45 years

No.4. entirely worn away

A gravestone in Eaton Churchyard, but disappeared long ago, is described
as follows:

"Here lieth the remains of 6 children, the offsprings of George and Ann
Harris
     Six lovely children
     In their bloom
     Where hurried swiftly to the tomb
     Their soles do rest in heaven ABOVE
     A long with Jesus whom they loved

(recorded by J P Walker Esq.1864, accompanied by drawings of Eaton Church)

R side of gate

In loving memory of
Cornelius Jones
who died January 9th 1939
Aged 54 years
Also, in loving memory of
Robert Jones
who died May 25th 1916
Aged 25 years
Also Harry and Esther
who died July 12th 1806
aged 14 days
Also Henry who died
years
September 26th 1898
aged 13 months

In loving memory of
Arthur Jones
late of Crow Leasow, Ludlow
Died January 7th 1921
Aged 40 years
Also Mary Ann, wife of the above
died April 16th 1966
aged 74 years

R of porch
In memory of
John Hamer
of East Wall
died January 4th 1913 aged 68

N wall of chancel

In loving memory of
Mabel Constance Gatehouse
Who died 22 April 1945
aged 76

Between SE end of the Church and boundary wall

In loving memory of
Alan Bertram Hanbury Sparrow
of Hillside, Church Stretton
youngest son of Arthur Sparrow
of Preen Manor, Shrewsbury
died September 28th 1936
aged 73 years

R side of gate

Jasper Jones
Called to rest
March 9th 1957
Aged 69 years

In loving memory of Emma Davies
(late of Whitefields)
who died August 20th 1908
aged 54 years
also Francis Davies of Stone House
Wall brother of above who died
November 17th 1924 aged 79 years
also Lucie Annie Davies
who died March 2nd 1955
aged 81 years

R hand corner, to the right of E end of Church

In loving memory of
Margaret Roberts of Ticklerton
who died Sept 5th 1955
aged 56 years

In loving memory of
Alfred Roberts
who died March 7th 1967
aged 76 years

In loving memory of
Charles Henry Roberts
who died January 1st 1968
aged 63 years

(small wooden cross)

Adam B Morse

In loving memory of
Ruth Helena Beasley
1919 - 1987

In loving memory of
John Francis Roberts
died December 12th 1975
aged 66 years

Richard Hurle Treasure
1912 - 1986

In loving memory of
Charles beloved husband of
Mary Roberts of Ticklerton
           who died May 7th 1923
aged 65 years
also Mary his beloved wife
who died January 4th 1954
aged 81 years

In loving memory of
Mary Annie Roberts
who died April 27th 1967
aged 66 years
and in loving memory of
Enoch Ernest Robert
who died 12th July 1971
aged 66 years

Alexander Brindley
1905 - 1984

In loving memory of
Herbert Roberts
died January 19th 1973
aged 78 years

near E boundary

In loving memory of
Annie Hall of Walls Bank
who died 6th January 1951
the daughter of Sarah
also John Hall of Lichfield
beloved grandson of Sarah

In loving memory of Sarah
beloved wife of the late
Joe Hall of Cressage
died January 5th 1925
aged 82 years

E end - Buddicom plot

In memory of
William Squire Buddicom
of Ticklerton Court
who died February 26th 1922
aged 82 years

In memory of
John Alfred LeMesurier Hayward
of Quorn Place, Leicestershire
died January 14th 1922 aged 63
also of Lilian Holland Hayward
his wife Daughter of William
Squire Buddicom and Elizabeth
Haughton Buddicom born Dec 8th
1878 died 15th June 1964

NE corner

In loving memory of
Thomas Cleeton who died
October 26th 1920
aged 86 years
also of Mary wife of the above
who died December 19th 1930

In loving memory of
William Downes died
November 12th 1924
aged 77 (?) years

Parallel with E end of the Church

In loving memory of
Beatrice Isabel Cox
died August 3rd 1986
aged 89 years
also John Henry Cox
of Ticklerton died May29th
1923 aged 5 days
also Frances Mary Cox
died October 18th 1928
aged 2 years and 11 months

In loving memory of
Edith wife of Edward Cox
of Claybrook who died
February 24th 1939
aged 52 years
also Annie Louisa
daughter of the above who
died August 13th 1935
aged 16 years
also Edward Cox who died
April 26th 1947 aged 69 years

In loving memory of
John Cox of Ticklerton
who died June 13th 1937
aged 86 years
also of Louisa Cox who
died December 27th 1946
aged 93 years

To the beloved memory of
Mary Jane Hall of Birtley
who passed away February 8th
1939 aged 57 years
also of Edward beloved husband
of the above who passed away
October 21st 1949 aged 70 years

11256584 Gunner J R Teece
Royal Artillery who died
6th August 1942 aged 40

In memory of
Hugh Gerard Gibson Herklots
M.A. Cantab. D.D. Manitoba
Canon of Peterborough Cathedral
Born 5th September 1903 in
Sikandra, India died 17th May
1971 Lambeth A writer in the
Church and of his wife Helen
Beveridge Herklots nee Murgoci
born 1905 Bucuresti died 1980
in Hitchin

In memory of
Sylvia Agnes Wright
daughter of Canon Hugh and
Helen Herklots 3rd June 1934
to 20th February 1988

Between N side of Church and Vicarage wall

Sacred to the memory of our
dear sister Catherine McMichael
who passed away on July 19th 1959
at the Forge Ticklerton aged 55

In loving memory of
Florence Edith Edwards
died March 14th 1977
aged 91 also husband
Archer George died September
8th 1971 aged 87

In loving memory of
Mabel Constance Gatehouse
who died 26th April 1945

In memory of
Richard Jones of
Little Stretton died
September 18th 1920
also Elizabeth wife of the above who died June 26th 1938 aged 96 years

In loving memory of my dear
husband William Henry Pugh
who died October 12th 1962
aged 82 years
also his beloved wife Emma
Pugh who died December 23rd
1971 aged 90 years

In loving memory of
James Venables died
October 21st 1950
aged 78 years

To the left of the path

In loving memory of
Thomas Anson late of
New Hall Mill who departed
this life October 17th 1917
aged 69 years also Emma
beloved wife of the above
who departed this life
1927 December 3rd(?)
aged 79 years

In loving memory of
Reginald Frank Marpole
aged 85 and his wife Edith
Lydia died 21st June 1985
aged 84

In loving memory of
Elizabeth Griffith who
died January 26th 1984
aged 85 years
also her beloved husband
George who died November 19th
1971 aged 98 years

In loving memory of
Gordon Graham Unwin
died January 7th 1946
aged 10 months

In loving memory of
Fanny Downes of
Upper Millichope who
died March 26th 1939
aged 84 years

In loving memory of
Clement William Venables
died August 21st 1954
aged 76 years also his
wife Elizabeth Frances
died March 7th 1968
aged 87 years

In memory of
Samuel Venables of Eaton
who died May 25th 1933
in his 63rd year

In loving memory of
Joseph Henry Madeley
died 10th August 1957
aged 91 years
also of his wife
Mary Elizabeth who died
21st November 1961
aged 86 years

In loving memory of
Lydia Thomas of Birtley
died July 20th 1947
aged 72 also her husband
Benjamin Thomas died
February 15th 1953 aged 82

INDEX OF PEOPLE AND PLACE NAMES

The following abbreviations are used in the index, Albert-Alb,Alfred-Alf,Ambrose-Amb,
Andrew-And,Arthur-Art,Bartholomew-Bart,Benjamin-Ben,Bernard-Bern,Bertram-Bert,
Bessie-Bess,Betsy-Bet,Bridget-Brg,Caroline-Car,Batherine-Cat,Cecilia-Cec,Charles-Ch,
Charlotte-Char,Christiana-Chrs,Cicely-Cic,Cornelius-Corn,Daniel-Dan,David-Dav,
Dinah-Din,Dorothy-Dor,Edmund-Edm,Edward-Edw,Edwin-Edn,Eleanor-Ele,Elizabeth-Eliz,
Elisha-Eli,Ellen-Ell,Emanuel-Eman,Emily-Emy,Ernest-Ern,Esther-Est,Evelyn-Eve,
Fanny-Fan,Frederick-Fred,Geoffrey-Geof,George-Geo,Gilbert-Gil,Gladys-Gla,
Gregory-Greg,Hannah-Han,Harriet-Har,Harry-Hry,Henry-Hny,Herbert-Herb,Hubert-Hub,
Humphrey-Hum,Isabella-Isa,Jacob-Jac,James-Jam,Jasper-Jas,Jenks-Jen,John-Jhn,
Joseph-Jos,Joyce-Joy,Katherine-Kath,Leonard-Lnd,Lilian-Lil,Lizzie-Liz,Louisa-Lsa,
Lucretia-Luc,Margaret-Mgt,Margery-Mgy,Martha-Mar,Martin-Mrt,Mary-My,Mathew-Math,
Matilda-Mat,Michael-Mich,Mildred-Mil,Minnie-Min,Monica-Mon,Nevil-Nev,Norman-Nor,
Patrick-Pat,Penelope-Pen,Percy-Per,Peter-Pet,Philip-Phil,Rebecca-Reb,Reginald-Reg,
Richard-Rch,Robert-Rob,Roger-Rog,Roland-Rol,Rowland-Row,Samuel-Sam,Sarah-Sar,Selina-
Sel,Sidney-Sid,Sophia-Sop,Susan-Sus,Thomas-Th,Vincent-Vin,Walter-Wal,William-Wm,

BOTFIELD,Jhn 27,
BOUCHIER,CLJ 155,
BOULIE de,99,
BOUNDS,Edm 190,Edn 190,Sar 190,
BOWDLER,Alice 28,Cic 28,Sir Stephen 18,28,
BOWEN,Ann 187,Edn 187,193,Jam 187,My 187,
Nellie 187,Rob 187,
BOWNES,133
BOWYER,Eliz 199,Rch 199,
BOYER,Rev 141,
BRADBURNE,Jhn 29,
BRADLEY,Ch 207,E 150,Eliz 207,Jane 207,
Sar 207,Wm 207,
BRAY,Ann 187,Harvey 187,Hny 187,Jhn 187,
My 187,208,Rch 187,Sar 187, 208,Th 71,187,
Wm 187,208,
BREEZE,155,175 Emy 175,
Brest,99,
BRETHERTON,L 205,
Bridgnorth 2,27,
BRIDGWATER,Jhn 211,
BRIGGS,Wm 214,
BRIGHT,Ann 194,202,Edw 192,Eliz 194,
Rch 191,Sam 190,Th 191,Wm 190,
BRINDLEY,Alex 236,
Brockhampton 25,
BROMFIELD,Mch 36,
BROMLEY,Ben 215,Eliza 215,Jos 215,
My 215,Th 215,Wm 215,
BROOM,Wm 188,
Broome 26,
BROWN,Jen 101,Jhn 98,N 204,Simon 101,
BRUNT,Han 194,
BRYANT,Rev Ch 147,
BUCKLES,128,
BUDDICOM,93,Family Tree 101,Ann 159,
Ell 102,106,Eliz 67,85,96/7,103/4/6,121-
149,195,224,237,Geo 97,Guinever 110,
113/5/6,Jacintha 110,113/4/5,Kate 141,
Lil 93,107/9,110,121-149,161/4,190,216,
R A(Rab) 66,108/9,110,117,122/5/7,195,
Dr RJ 99,Rev RJ 26,64/7,85,95/6/7,
103/4/5/6/7,113,159,194/5,223/4,Robert
102,Robert Prosper 100,114/5/6/7,192/3,
Wm 42,Wm Barber 99,100,159,Wm Squire 52,
67,97/8,1022/6/7/8,113/7,121-149,152/5,
174,195,224,237,
BULLOCK,Ch 185,Jhn 227,My 185,227,
Th 185,Wm 185,227
BUNGER,Eliz 214,
BURD,Th 211,
BURDEN,145
BURD & EVANS,117
BURGESS,Eliz 211,Jane 214,Jhn 211,
Mar 211/4,My 214,Phil 199,Wm 211/4,
BURROWS,Jhn 98,
Burwood 134
BUTLER,Dr Sam 102,

CADWALLADER,Mar 188,191,Rch 201/8,
Caen 100,
CALIKN,My 200,
Camarthen 4,
CAMBRAY,Jenkyn 28,
CAMPERDOWN,Marquess 126,
CANTRELL,Har 196,
Cardington,93,161,

CARNFIELD,Frances 194,
CARNSEW J C 144,
CARTER,195,Ann 211,Art 145,Bet 195,
Car 189,Eliza 195/7,206,Ell 230,
Geo 185,195,230,Han 193,Har 185,
Her 185,230,Jam 127,206,213,
Jhn 200,208,Mar 185,211,230,Mgt 194,
My 160,195/7,206,213,226,Priscilla 230,
Rch 197,206/8,Th 159,185,194/5/7/9,
206/8,230,Titty 174,Wm 33,192/5,206,
213,226,
CARTWRIGHT,Wm 189,
CARVER,HP 66,197,
CHALLONER,Rog 61,
CHANDLER,Ann 189,
CHARLES 11,55,
CHEETHAM,133
Chelmick 16,34,116,125,173,
Cheltenham 107,110,
Cherbourg 100,
Chester 2,11,156,
CHILD,Edw 37,Mar 187,Mgt 37,R 187,
CHILDE,E S 150,
CHILDS,Elsie 146,WJ 150,
CHINEY,My 198,
CHISHOLM,Edw 199,
CHURCHILL,Winston 108,
Church Stretton 24,49,73,105,117,120/3/5,
132/3/5/8/9,141/3/6/7,152/6,161/7/9,176,
181/2,
CLARKE,John 23,Kate 107,
CLEARKE,Rch 35,
CLEETON,47, 125/9,162,Bess 160,Ch 203,
E 189,Edw 157,160,202/3,Eliz 203,HR 150,
Hny 203,Jane 189,Mrs M 189,Maria 186,
Mgt 121,My 126,160/1,237,R 150,Rch 126,
160/1,186,203,Ruth 126,145,Sar 186,203,
Th 160,189,203,237
CLEMENT,Mr 106,
Cleobury North 27,
CLIBURY,Wm 35,
Clunbury 19
CLUTTERBUCK,Step 210,
COK,John 17,
COLLEY,Cic 205,Ben 204/5,Rch 188,T 141/6,
175,Wm 205,
COLLINS,Rch 209,
COLLYNG,Dor 28,Sir Walter 28,
CONNOP,146
COOK,Eliz 195,
COOKE,Jos 222,My 222,Randle 106,
COPLAND,Jhn 98,
CORBETT,Pet 4,
CORBETT-WINDER,Rev E 141,Wm 111,
CORFIELD,128,C 121,150,Clara 126,142,198,
Edith 211,Edw 198,Edn 211,Hub 211,Geo 45,
Han 232,Har 191,Jhn 232,Maria 198,Mgt 232,
My 198,211,RC 150,Rch 191,Rob 211,Sar 198,
Th 75,186,211,Wm 169,211,
COX,33,63,127/8/9,Alf 166,Ann 206,227,237,
Beatrice 237,Lsa 237,Edith 237,Edw 206/9,
215,227,237,Eliz 134,145,206,Emma 123,
Fanny 206/9,Frances 206,227,237,H 150,
Har 193,Jhn 63, 113,126,140/7,193,206/9,
215,237,Leonora 215,M 145,Mgt 206/7,222,
Maria 206,My 206/9,227,Ron 166,212,
Sar 206,227,Wm 206,214,227,
Cotes & Radnor 29,

241